PRAISE FOR
LIFE ON THE SILENT PLANET

"For years, careful readers have come to rely on the thoughtful excellence of anything under the Davenant imprint; *Life on the Silent Planet* only adds to that well-deserved reputation. As editor and contributor Rhys Laverty intriguingly suggests, Lewis's foray into science fiction offers more than a flight of fantasy; the contributions to this critical collection of essays make clear in many ways that C. S. Lewis's prescient and prophetic voice still speaks, all the more in our age. Its compelling combination of established experts such as Michael Ward and Holly Ordway alongside wise and emerging voices commends the deeply engaging *Life on the Silent Planet* to anyone who would think more clearly about the Ransom Trilogy and about Lewis himself."

—ANDREW LAZO
Co-editor, Mere Christians: Inspiring Encounters with C.S. Lewis

"This book opened up the Ransom Trilogy to me like no other. With a section of essays on each book in the trilogy, the authors provide new insights on almost every page, especially Lewis's ideas on masculinity, femininity, and marriage, which our world desperately needs to heed, but also Lewis on pleasure, the Un-Man, Merlin, Bragdon Wood, the Law of Nature, the Pendragon, and many others. If you read only one book on Lewis this year, read this one."

—JOEL HECK
Concordia Lutheran Seminary

"If there remains an undiscovered country of Lewis's writings, for many it is the world of his Ransom Trilogy. *Life on the Silent Planet* provides readers with a collection of helpful roadmaps and knowledgeable traveling companions. Lewis fans—both novice and experienced—will find valuable insights, useful background information, and clear applications to their own lives and times."

—DEVIN BROWN

Professor of English, Asbury University and author of A Life Observed: A Spiritual Biography of C. S. Lewis

"What sets this book apart is the way it provides thoughtful application of Lewis's ideas to the Christian life while at the same time accessing the very best of Lewis scholarship. This is no mean achievement, and the result is a book I've been longing for: substantial insight into the Christian life grounded in a serious and nuanced understanding of Lewis's work. I devoured it, and I will return to it again and again. This book is a gift to thoughtful Christians. "

—DIANA PAVLAC GLYER

Azusa Pacific University and co-editor of A Compass for Deep Heaven: Navigating the C.S. Lewis Ransom Trilogy

"I get to speak to lots of Christian audiences about C. S. Lewis. If I ask how many of the attendees have read at least one of the Chronicles of Narnia, practically every hand in the room will go up. If I ask who has read at least one volume of the Ransom trilogy, I get only a bare scattering of hands, if any at all. Only the most diehard Lewisians are still reading the planetary series. The editor and contributors to *Life on the Silent Planet* think this is a tragedy, and they want to change it by convincing us that the books are both good fiction and piercingly relevant, indeed, a more "retroactively prophetic set of novels for our day" than anyone could have written if they had tried.

They face a challenge in doing so. How do you get someone to read a whole book whose purpose is to convince him to read three other books? Well, you can entice him with the name of Lewis and the promise of relevance to Christian living. The initial essays, on *Out of the Silent Planet*, are heavy on summary and paraphrase, not assuming familiarity, but with enough insight to serve as an appetizer. Then, assuming that the reader is hooked, the later essays on *Perelandra* and *That Hideous Strength* focus more on analysis. They have some good analysis too, e.g. on what it means to be human (Bethel McGrew) or on what makes a paradise a paradise (Rhys Laverty). Michael Ward does one of his typical schemas that just keeps on generating insight despite its seeming simplicity: Book one (Mars) is about the masculine, book two (Venus) the feminine, which leads to book three combining them and being about matrimony. That one essay justifies the "retroactively prophetic" claim all by itself.

In short, these folks have made as good a case for renewed interest in the Ransom books as could have been made. The world will be a better place to the extent that they succeed."

—DONALD T. WILLIAMS
Professor Emeritus, Toccoa Falls College

"With the passing of the years Lewis's Ransom Trilogy proves itself to be more profound and prescient than even his most devoted readers had guessed. Perhaps, in time, it will be prized even more than the Chronicles of Narnia, or his apologetics. This is a marvelous collection of essays on the trilogy, several of them written by friends. I'll return to this book many times in the coming years. Read it and you will too."

—C.R. WILEY

Author of In the House of Tom Bombadil *and* The Household and the War for the Cosmos

"As our world is ever more confused about gender and drinks more deeply from the well of AI and transhumanism, C.S. Lewis's Ransom Trilogy become more and more prescient. This is a fascinating collection of insightful, readable essays from experts who have thought long and hard about what a silent planet needs to hear loud and clear."

—JAMES CARY

Sitcom writer, co-host of Cooper & Cary Have Words, *author of* The Sacred Art of Joking *and* The Gospel According to a Sitcom Writer

"Joe Rigney says that the book club, in which an invested community reads sections aloud and shares comments along the way, is the best method for teaching C.S. Lewis. This collection of essays comes as close as it can to providing the book club experience in text as an array of Lewis enthusiasts come together to provide different angles of insight into Lewis's underappreciated Ransom series. Each of the contributors plays a significant role in calling us out of the "space" of the modern age and into the substance of the heavens. With this substance, we too are called to be substantial in our engagement with the present and with our aims for the future."

—ANDREW SNYDER
Host of the Mythic Mind Podcast

"It is a joy to see Lewis's prophetic Ransom Trilogy receiving the heightened attention and reflection it has always deserved in such an excellent volume. If Lewis's books open up the beauties of creation and the heavens for readers with eyes to see, the authors' insights here open up the trilogy itself for the deeper appreciation and understanding of fresh readers and longstanding admirers alike."

—PHILIP BUNN
Assistant Professor of Political Science, Covenant College

LIFE ON THE SILENT PLANET

LIFE ON THE SILENT PLANET

Essays on Christian Living from C.S. Lewis's Ransom Trilogy

EDITED BY RHYS LAVERTY

DAVENANT PRESS 2024

Copyright © 2024 The Davenant Press

All rights reserved.
All Scripture quotations, unless otherwise indicated, are taken from the following Bible translations:

ESV – The Holy Bible, English Standard Version® (ESV®), copyright © 2001 by Crossway, a publishing ministry of Good News Publishers. Used by permission. All rights reserved.

NIV – The Holy Bible, New International Version® (NIV®), copyright © 1973, 1978, 1984, 2011 by Biblica, Inc.™ Used by permission. All rights reserved worldwide.

NKJV – Scripture taken from the New King James Version®. Copyright © 1982 by Thomas Nelson. Used by permission. All rights reserved.

All extracts by C.S. Lewis copyright © C.S. Lewis Pte. Ltd. Reprinted by permission.

All rights to the content of this book are reserved by the respective copyright holders of the translations.

ISBN: 1-949716-25-2
ISBN-13: 978-1-949716-25-2

Cover design and typesetting by
Rachel Rosales, Orange Peel Design

Proofread and indexed by John Barach

LIST OF CONTRIBUTORS

Susannah Black-Roberts is a senior editor of *Plough Quarterly* and has written for publications including *First Things*, *Fare Forward*, *Front Porch Republic*, *Mere Orthodoxy*, and *The American Conservative*. She is the editor, with Anne Snyder, of *Breaking Ground: Charting Our Future in a Pandemic Year*.

Christiana Hale teaches English and Latin at Logos School in Moscow, Idaho. She is the author of *Deeper Heaven: A Reader's Guide to C. S. Lewis's Ransom Trilogy*.

Rhys Laverty is the Senior Managing Editor of the Davenant Press, Senior Editor of *Ad Fontes*, and Communications Director for the Davenant Institute. His writing has been published in *The Spectator*, *The Critic*, *Plough Quarterly*, *Ad Fontes*, *Mere Orthodoxy*, *Theopolis*, and *WORLD*, as well as on his Substack, The New Albion.

Louis Markos (PhD, University of Michigan) is a professor of English and humanities at Houston Christian University. He is an authority on C. S. Lewis, apologetics, and ancient Greece and Rome, and lectures widely for classical Christian and classical charter schools and conferences. He is the author of twenty-five books, including *On the Shoulders of Hobbits: The Road to Virtue with Tolkien and Lewis*, *C. S. Lewis for Beginners*, *Restoring Beauty: The Good, the True, and the Beautiful in the Writings of C. S.

Lewis, and *Lewis Agonistes: How C. S. Lewis Can Train Us to Wrestle with the Modern and Postmodern World*.

Bethel McGrew (Ph.D, Western Michigan University) is a freelance writer. Her work has appeared in *First Things, National Review, The Spectator, WORLD*, and many other outlets, covering social criticism, literature, film, music, and history. Her Substack, Further Up, is one of the top paid newsletters in "Faith & Spirituality" on the platform. She has also contributed to two essay anthologies on Jordan Peterson.

Jake Meador is the Editor-in-Chief of *Mere Orthodoxy*. He is the author of *In Search of the Common Good: Christian Fidelity in a Fractured World* and *What Are Christians For? Life Together at the End of the World.* His writing has appeared in *The Atlantic, Commonweal, Christianity Today, Fare Forward, The University Bookman, Books & Culture, First Things, National Review, Front Porch Republic*, and *The Run of Play*

Joseph Minich (PhD, The University of Texas at Dallas) is a Residential Teaching Fellow at the Davenant Institute in Landrum, South Carolina. He is the author of *Enduring Divine Absence: The Challenge of Modern Atheism* and *Bulwarks of Unbelief: Atheism and Divine Absence in a Secular Age*, the editor of several works with the Davenant Press, as well as the founding editor of *Ad Fontes*. He is also a host of The Pilgrim Faith Podcast.

Holly Ordway (PhD, University of Massachusetts Amherst) is the Cardinal Francis George Professor of Faith and Culture at the Word on Fire Institute, Visiting Professor of Apologetics at Houston Christian University, and a Subject Editor for the *Journal of Inklings Studies*. She is the author of *Tolkien's Modern Reading: Middle-Earth Beyond the Middle Ages* and *Tolkien's Faith: A Spiritual Biography*.

Colin Redemer (PhD candidate, University of Aberdeen) is an Adjunct Associate Professor at Saint Mary's College of California, Managing Director at Beck & Stone, and Director of Education at American Reformer. He previously served as Vice President of the Davenant Institute. He has edited and modernized two volumes of Thomas Traherne's *Christian Ethics* and his writing has been widely published in various outlets.

Joe Rigney (PhD, University of Chester) serves as Fellow of Theology at New Saint Andrews College in Moscow, Idaho. He is the author of seven books including *Live Like a Narnian: Christian Discipleship in Lewis's Chronicles* and *Lewis on the Christian Life: Becoming Truly Human in the Presence of God*. Previously, Joe served as a professor and president of Bethlehem College & Seminary in Minneapolis, a pastor at Cities Church in St. Paul, and a teacher at Desiring God.

Colin Smothers (PhD, Southern Baptist Seminary) serves as Executive Director of the Council on Biblical Manhood and Womanhood. He is the author of *In Your Mouth and Your Heart: A Study of Deuteronomy 30:12-14* *in Paul's Letters to the Romans in Canonical Context* and *Male and Female He Created Them: A Study on Gender, Sexuality, and Marriage* (with Denny Burk and David Closson).

Michael Ward (PhD, University of St. Andrews) is an Associate Member of the Faculty of Theology and Religion at the University of Oxford. He is the author of the award-winning and best-selling *Planet Narnia: The Seven Heavens in the Imagination of C. S. Lewis* and of *After Humanity: A Guide to C. S. Lewis's The Abolition of Man*. He is the co-editor of *The Cambridge Companion to C. S. Lewis*.

TABLE OF CONTENTS

Introduction: The Discarded Lewis — i
Rhys Laverty

A Note on the Text — xxv

OUT OF THE SILENT PLANET

I **Which Way, Weston Man?** — 1
Good, Evil and Cosmological Models
in *Out of the Silent Planet*
Louis Markos

II **The Education of Dr. Ransom:** — 23
First Steps from Pedestrian to Pendragon
Joe Rigney

III **Men Are From Mars:** — 49
Masculinity in *Out of the Silent Planet*
Colin Smothers

PERELANDRA

IV **Enjoyment and Contemplation:** — 75
The Green Lady, Self-Knowledge,
and Growth in Maturity
Christiana Hale

V **The Devil Went Down to Venus:** — 99
Lessons from the Un-man
Bethel McGrew

VI **A Taste of Paradise:** — 123
Naming, Restraining, and Embracing
Pleasure on Perelandra
Rhys Laverty

THAT HIDEOUS STRENGTH

VII	Selling the Well and the Wood: *That Hideous Strength* and the Abolition of Matrimony Michael Ward	149
VIII	Lewis's Apocalypse and Ours Joseph Minich	185
IX	The Untabled Law of Nature Colin Redemer	213
X	Athur in Edgestow Holly Ordway	241
XI	The Problem of Jane Susannah Black-Roberts	271
XII	Bureaucratic Speech in *That Hideous Strength* Jake Meador	293
	Scripture Index	319
	Author and Subject Index	323

INTRODUCTION:
THE DISCARDED LEWIS

Rhys Laverty

Growing up, I encountered three different C. S. Lewises. First, there was Lewis the Children's Author. I inherited a box set of *The Chronicles of Narnia* from my brother, which I still have, and enjoyed them as much as the next child. Second, once I had been converted into the world of British evangelicalism, I encountered Lewis the Apologist. After coming to faith at the age of 12, I swiftly read *Mere Christianity*, and it soon became obvious that Lewis was ubiquitous in evangelical preaching via a few oft-repeated quotations, sermon illustrations, and book recommendations. Third, once I reached university to study English, I encountered Lewis the Literary Scholar. In all honesty, it was odd to realize that Lewis had a day job and wasn't a full-time Christian apologist, but I supposed that a man had to earn a living—and I was soon glad to have him on my side in the critical theory maelstrom that my English degree turned out to be.

It took me, however, the best part of a decade to realize that there was, in fact, a fourth Lewis—one conspicuously absent from the writing and preaching to which I was accustomed. Evangelical Christians have heard countless preachers say that Jesus is "not safe, but he's good"; we are used to (justified) rebukes for being "far too easily pleased." My life was awash with *The Screwtape Letters*, *The Problem of Pain*, and *Surprised by Joy*, and even the occasional nod to something like *Letters to Malcolm* or *A Grief Observed*. Pretentious young humanities student that I was, I was confident during early adulthood that heaping praise on *The Horse and His Boy* and having *The Great Divorce* as my favorite was enough to mark me out as a Lewis aficionado among the hoi polloi.

And then I entered a different orbit, a different sphere of influence. I fell in with a different crowd—many of whom, I am glad and humbled to say, have contributed to the volume you hold now in your hands. As I drifted into the circles of the Davenant Institute—from purchaser of its books, to volunteer editor, to student, and eventually to staff member—I heard Lewis everywhere, yet in a different key. The go-to references here were not to Narnia or Screwtape or mud pies. The talk was all of men without chests, of *eldila*, of the medieval cosmos. I was able to dimly connect some of this to memories of watching Michael Ward's documentary *The Narnia Code* when it was broadcast on the BBC in 2009, but I felt like an Englishman listening to the Dutch, picking out isolated familiar words but all the more disoriented for it. This was a whole dialect of Lewis-talk hitherto unknown.

Here emerged the fourth Lewis—what I have elsewhere called "Lewis the Prophet."[1] Principally, this is the

---

1. See my article "Lewis the Prophet," *The Critic*, November 2023, https://thecritic.co.uk/issues/november-2023/lewis-the-prophet/.

Introduction

Lewis of *The Abolition of Man* and the Ransom Trilogy (or, if you prefer, the Cosmic Trilogy, but never, no never, the Space Trilogy). In these texts, with greater depth and in a more explicit fashion than anywhere else, Lewis locks horns with the challenges and evils of modernity, both identifying their influence in his own day and predicting how they would develop in the future.

In reality, there are not hard lines to be drawn between these various personae. Lewis shifts between them within the same work, even within the same paragraph, and sometimes they are indistinguishable. I am not wed to this fourfold office of Lewis. It is by no means perfect.[2] As the Apologist, he necessarily engages modernity and its apparent challenges to religious belief, and this work is something he does as a self-consciously modern man.[3] Elsewhere, in his children's fiction, Lewis clearly has modernity in the crosshairs: any mention of schools in the Narnia books is as much an evisceration of modern education as anything in *The Abolition of Man*. The fact is that those first three strands of Lewis's identity—Children's

---

It was only after writing this piece that I found that I am in good company in referring to Lewis as a prophet, with Lewis scholars such as Michael Ward and Malcolm Guite describing *The Abolition of Man* as displaying Lewis's "prophetic mode."

2. *Till We Have Faces*, for instance, as Lewis's latest and perhaps greatest achievement (during his lifetime anyway), arguably does not fit entirely well within the framework.

3. For an exploration of Lewis's self-conscious status as a modern man evangelizing other modern men, see my colleague and fellow contributor Joseph Minich's lecture "C. S. Lewis as Sage of Modernity," *YouTube*, January 21, 2021, https://www.youtube.com/watch?v=Mh-G0I-EwAso.

Author, Apologist, Literary Scholar—are almost always entwined with one another at any given moment and were, I suspect, largely indistinguishable to Lewis himself. To weave tales that connected the truths of Spenser to Greek myth to the gospel and served to fortify a believer's mind against the alluring sophistry of materialism—such a thing was for Lewis an almost reflexive act with a singular integrity, even if we could later logically distinguish the various elements.

It may in fact be that, rather than simply being a fourth strand among many, Lewis's status as a "Prophet" is either the sum greater than all the parts, or simply what he is at a more basic level. Certainly, part of the reason that his legacy has endured since his death over sixty years ago is that he was a man peculiarly gifted and providentially placed in the pivotal moment of the first half of the twentieth century. His intellect was truly brilliant—a fact insufficiently appreciated by his popular audience, and willfully overlooked by scholars precisely *because* he has a popular audience. Further, he was born long enough ago that it was still possible for a solidly middle class boy from Ulster to receive a thorough education that incorporated enforced study of classical languages alongside vast swathes of unsupervised free time in which to read mountains of classical literature, and yet born recently enough to be, as we have noted, a native modern in his patterns of thought.

A PROPHET OBSCURED?

Why, then, was Lewis the Prophet seemingly hidden from view during my younger years? Why was it a matter of course to take me through the wardrobe and caution me about Screwtape but not to tell me how to spot a man without a chest?

Selective Memory?

Perhaps, like so many evangelicals who gripe about aspects of their upbringing, my memory has become selective. Maybe *The Abolition of Man* was being quoted regularly and I just did not have ears to hear. Certainly, I have been surprised to find out that certain older saints from my past are fans of the Ransom Trilogy. One former church elder told me that, years ago, he had read one morning the passage in *Perelandra* in which Ransom discovers that the Un-man has been eviscerating frogs; that afternoon, he paid a visit to a mentally troubled church member who confessed she had been having visions of killing her dog. If you've ever been skeptical of the idea that reading fiction can have a payoff in pastoral ministry, perhaps this anecdote has disabused you.

Adult Content

It is also possible that the Ransom Trilogy appears somewhat neglected, at least compared to Narnia, because it is not a children's book. Pastors and writers can often assume with an evangelical audience that most people will have some familiarity with Narnia from their childhood and so are likely quicker to draw on it for sermon illustrations and suchlike. This is not the case with the Ransom Trilogy however, since it was written for adults, and so is perhaps assumed to be less useful for teaching and discussion.[4]

---

4. I am grateful to John Barach for making this point.

A Question of Genre

Another reason for the neglect of the Ransom Trilogy specifically is simply the matter of genre. While science fiction is more popular than ever, it has moved on a great deal from the days of the genre's father, H. G. Wells. Wells's style can seem quaint, pulpy, and a little dull today—unsurprising, since his two most famous works, *The Time Machine* and *The War of the Worlds*, were published in the late 1800s. Wells's name conjures images of inelegant spacecraft made of pig iron, clean-shaven white male protagonists in Edwardian suits, and prose that could be read aloud in the tones of an over-earnest newsreader from the earliest days of broadcasting. By contrast, science fiction today is an ever sprawling playground for high concept storytelling, moral gray areas, and queer sexuality.

Despite being engaged in what has been called a "war of the worldviews" with Wells,[5] Lewis became an unashamed lover of "scientifiction" and a lifelong fan of Wells after first encountering his books at school.[6] Indeed, he regarded himself as an early enthusiast, long before "a bulge in production of such stories" began,[7] and *Out of the Silent Planet* contains a prefatory note refuting any suggestions that Lewis was "too stupid to have enjoyed Mr. H. G. Wells's fantasies or too ungrateful to acknowledge

---

5. See Brenton Dickieson, "The War of the Worldviews: H. G. Wells vs. C. S. Lewis (Part 1)," A Pilgrim in Narnia, August 28 2012, https://apilgriminnarnia.com/2012/08/28/warofworldviews1/.

6. C. S. Lewis, *Surprised by Joy* (London: Collins, 2012), 38.

7. C. S. Lewis, "On Science Fiction," in *Of Other Worlds* (London: HarperOne, London, 2017), 93.

Introduction

his debt to them."[8] The novel came out of an agreement Lewis made with J. R. R. Tolkien that they would each try to write the kind of stories they both enjoyed reading—time-travel for Tolkien, science fiction for Lewis.[9] Tolkien's effort never saw the light of day during his lifetime, but Lewis produced what became the first novel in the Ransom Trilogy. The book has a self-consciously Wellsian feel, and it is precisely this Wellsian feel that I think leads many today to avoid picking the novel up in the first place. Whereas works of fantasy (a genre which, like science fiction, is more popular now than it has ever been) remain relatively timeless, any science fiction produced prior to the Golden Age of Science Fiction in the 1930s and 40s (and, increasingly it seems to be, anything produced prior to the 1980s) is effectively regarded these days as "proto-science fiction" and so as less amenable to our twenty-first century sensibilities. As you will imagine, since I am editing a book of essays on the trilogy, I regard this as a great shame in its own right, but doubly so given that *Perelandra* and *That Hideous Strength* are each of a totally different genre from their predecessor.[10]

---

8. C. S. Lewis, *Out of the Silent Planet* (London: HarperCollins, 2005), vii.

9. Tolkien recounts this story in his letter to Christopher Bretherton, dated July 16, 1964, in *The Letters of J.R.R. Tolkien*, rev. ed., ed. Humphrey Carpenter with Christopher Tolkien (London: Harper Collins, 2023), 487.

10. I am of the opinion that *Out of the Silent Planet* is one of two or three (maybe four) novels Lewis ever wrote. Most of his fictional works are other things disguised as novels.

Needless Obscurity?

Lewis the Prophet has also surely been given short shrift because his most "prophetic" texts (that is, the Ransom Trilogy and *Abolition*) are by no means his most accessible. Despite its brevity, *Abolition* is a work so dense that it has entered the elite circle of books that have spawned their own commentaries.[11] As Michael Ward notes, Lewis himself believed that the book had sold poorly, and his friend and biographer George Sayer attributed this in part to its inaccessibility.[12] Yet Ward points out that *Abolition* actually sold well for a volume of academic philosophy, was reviewed well upon release, and

> has gone on to establish a reputation as a genuine and seminal classic. It has proved to be influential with a large and diverse readership—philosophers, educators, literary critics, intellectual historians, jurists, atheists, agnostics, people of faith—and is now generously (though of course not unanimously) considered among his most perceptive, penetrating, and important pieces of writing.[13]

Plenty, then, honored Lewis the Prophet in his hometown upon publication and have continued to pay heed to

---

11. I am referring to Michael Ward's *After Humanity: A Guide to C. S. Lewis's* The Abolition of Man (Park Ridge: Word on Fire Academic, 2021).

12. Ward, *After Humanity*, 1.

13. Ward, *After Humanity*, 2.

him since. Yet it seems reasonable to assume that whatever audience helped to make *Abolition* a solid seller in its day were still the beneficiaries of a general education—or at least a cultural *milieu*—that allowed them to keep up with Lewis (and even back then, such educations were on the decline, this being the whole point of *Abolition*). In the decades since, such an education has become almost solely the reserve of the highest elite—the philosophers and such who, Ward notes, acknowledge their debt to *Abolition*. And even today's elites are lucky if they get schooled in the most basic classical and medieval references.[14] Ward references John Lucas, Alan Jacobs, A. N. Wilson, Tony Nuttall, Mary Midgley, Mark Souder, Leon Kass, Joseph Ratzinger, Hans Urs von Balthasar, Francis Fukuyama, and Wendell Berry as among those who have praised *Abolition*. The youngest of these was born in 1958. Anyone born and educated since then, elite or not, has faced an uphill struggle to be able to enter Lewis's thought-world.

Much the same can be said of the Ransom Trilogy. Lewis's semi-fictional world draws on, alludes to, and even outright incorporates elements from an innumerable array of philosophical and literary sources ranging from Plato to Arthuriana to H. G. Wells. As such, there has arguably been an ever-growing barrier to entry if readers are

---

14. As mentioned, I spent my undergraduate years at the University of Exeter (2011–2014), a member of the Russell Group (the British equivalent of the Ivy League) being schooled in critical theory, and it took me a few years into graduate life to realize I had not actually been taught anything about literature. And this was a decade ago, before we reached the critical theory inflection point of more recent years, when the ideas swirling around my undergrad lecture halls spilled out into the mainstream.

to appreciate and enjoy the series. Certainly, many have enjoyed the books over the years knowing little to nothing about Lewis's sources. Lewis, with his penchant for atmosphere, or "Donegality," possesses a marked ability to write books that are in incredibly close dialogue with other texts and yet stand entirely on their own two feet.[15] *The Great Divorce* was my favorite Lewis work long before I knew anything about Dante, and the general public enjoyed the Chronicles of Narnia for decades before Michael Ward cracked the Narnia Code.[16] Yet the Ransom Trilogy places its allusions and references somewhat closer to the surface than either of these, and so perhaps requires something more of a "working knowledge" to be entered into. The series may still have been relatively accessible in its day, but ironically it has become less so in ours precisely due to the modern ills about which it warns us.[17] It is

---

15. Lewis refers to the "Donegality" of Donegal in *Spenser's Images of Life* (Cambridge: Cambridge University Press, 1967), 115. Michael Ward effectively coined it as a phrase in Lewis studies in his *Planet Narnia*.

16. See Michael Ward, *Planet Narnia: The Seven Heavens in the Imagination of C. S. Lewis* (Oxford: Oxford University Press, 2010). I am aware that some still question the overall thesis of Ward's book, but quite frankly I find opposition to it baffling and have yet to read an attempted refutation of it, scholarly or otherwise, which is anything approaching convincing.

17. It might be suggested that Lewis had simply not yet honed his craft as well as he would later on with Narnia, or that he had not learned the kind of restraint needed to write things that were richly allusive and yet still accessible. I am unconvinced by this however. By 1943, the same year that *Abolition* was published and *That Hideous Strength* was drafted, Lewis had acknowledged that his first work of fiction, *The Pilgrim's Regress*, suffered from "needless obscurity" ("Preface to

not so much that the barrier to entry has become higher over time; rather we, having received educations that were neither scientific nor classical but simply "modern," have sunk lower and lower.

Pietism

The final—and I suspect, major—reason that evangelicals have overlooked *Abolition* and the Ransom Trilogy is because of our tendency toward pietism. David Bebbington famously listed evangelicalism's four defining features as biblicism, crucicentrism, conversionism, and activism.[18] Together, the combination of all four tends toward a form of pietism, by which I mean a fairly narrow focus on individual salvation and godliness.

With this in mind it is easy to see why Lewis the Children's Author and Lewis the Apologist have been so popular with evangelicals, despite Lewis being no evangelical himself and being first regarded by the constituency as "a smoker, a drinker, and a liberal"[19] (and even acciden-

---

the Third Edition" in *The Pilgrim's Regress* [London: Fount, 1977], 9). He also began writing the elegant *The Great Divorce* in 1944, while finishing off *That Hideous Strength*. So it seems that, by the time Lewis was writing both the Ransom Trilogy (certainly the third novel, at any rate) and his *Abolition* lectures, he was well aware of the dangers of needless obscurity and was more than capable of hiding his influences in plain sight if he wanted to. Perhaps he chose at times to engage in some "needful obscurity" as he felt led, but it seems unjustified to view obscurity as a major vice for him by the time he hit his literary stride during the war years.

18. David W. Bebbington, *Evangelicalism in Modern Britain: A History from the 1730s to the 1980s* (London: Routledge, 1989), 2–3.

19. Quoted in Stewart Goetz, *A Philosophical Walking Tour with C. S.*

tally as a Roman Catholic!)[20] when his works arrived in the USA. His straightforwardly apologetical works, aimed principally at non-believers, such as *The Problem of Pain*, *Mere Christianity*, and *Miracles*, push readers, to varying degrees, toward conversion to the crucicentric Christian faith, or at the very least toward the same preliminary "mere theism" to which Lewis famously became the most reluctant convert before fully embracing Christianity. The Narnia books can do much the same, smuggling in apologetics under the guise of narrative. Absorbing quotations and arguments from these works, or even just giving the works to unbelievers as gifts, has long been part of evangelical activism.

Furthermore, works such as *The Screwtape Letters*, *The Great Divorce*, *A Grief Observed*, and *Letters to Malcolm*, along with the Chronicles of Narnia, have fairly obvious and immediate applications to personal devotion to Christ. In particular, the character of Aslan has always played well to evangelical emphases: his trustworthy signs for Jill Pole resonate with biblicism; his death at the Stone Table with crucicentrism; his undragoning of Eustace Scrubb with conversionism; his ability to inspire the embattled Old Narnians with activism. *Screwtape* remains an immensely practical work of spirituality, and it is perhaps telling that it is this work more than any others that opened a door for Lewis with evangelical readers.

Lewis: Why It Did Not Include Rome (New York: Bloomsbury, 2015), 6.

20. Mark Noll, *C. S. Lewis in America* (Downers Grove: InterVarsity Press, 2023), 106.

Introduction

By contrast, *Abolition* and the Ransom Trilogy do not seem as directly concerned with questions of apologetics or personal piety (note, I do emphasize the "seem" here). Certainly, parts of the trilogy are quite obviously applicable to conversionism and activism.[21] But for the most part, tracing lines from the Ransom books to contemporary Christian living requires more effort and reflection than doing so from Narnia. One way to illustrate this point is simply to note that Maleldil is simply not as present in the Ransom Trilogy in the same way that Aslan is in the Chronicles of Narnia. If Lewis shows something of his hand regarding the motivation behind the Narnia Chronicles when Aslan says he drew Eustace and the Pevensies into Narnia that they might "know him better" by "a different name" in their own world, he does not seem to be holding similar cards when penning the Ransom books.

Similarly, the Ransom books are undoubtedly an apologetical project in the same vein as Narnia, stealing past watchful dragons with fictionalized Christian truth.[22] Yet the form and structure of the trilogy does not lend itself to quotable references or images fit for sermons or quickfire apologetic debates in the same way that other Lewis works do. Lewis is undoubtedly aiming at what we

---

21. See Gavin Ortlund, "Conversion in C. S. Lewis's *That Hideous Strength*," *Themelios* 41, no. 1 (April 2016), https://www.thegospel-coalition.org/themelios/article/conversion-in-c-s-lewis-that-hideous-strength/.

22. The image of "stealing past watchful dragons" is used by Lewis to describe precisely this in his essay "Sometimes Fairy Stories May Say Best What's to Be Said," in *On Stories: And Other Essays on Literature* (London: HarperOne, 2017), 70.

would today call a "reenchantment" for modern readers in the Ransom Trilogy, but it is as if it comes about by way of a very long incantation that cannot be interrupted without having to start again.

THE RANSOM MOMENT

This latter point on pietism brings us squarely to the purpose of this essay collection. The shared conviction of this volume's contributors is that it has been a profound mistake to think that the Ransom Trilogy lacks immediate relevance to the Christian life, and that it is time for this to change.

For one thing, the trilogy overlaps far more than is often thought with some of Lewis's most practical works. Take *Perelandra* for instance: the novel is largely taken up with Ransom being face to face with the Devil himself while trying to prevent the Green Lady, the Eve of Venus, from falling into sin. As such, it has more than one or two things in common with *The Screwtape Letters*.[23]

For another (and this is the more substantial point), while the trilogy's principle concerns may *seem* quite removed from the Christian life, as we move further into the twenty-first century, it is becoming increasingly clear that they are in fact matters of utmost urgency and practical import for orthodox Christian believers. Christians of all stripes do not see this because, all too often, we have made

---

23. Indeed, as Brenton Dickieson discovered in 2015, Lewis's original prologue to *The Screwtape Letters* presented them as a set of fictional correspondence that had fallen into the hands not of an unnamed editor, but of Dr. Ransom himself. See Brenton Dickieson, "A Cosmic Find in The Screwtape Letters," October 28, 2015, https://apilgrim-innarnia.com/2015/10/28/a-cosmic-find/.

Introduction

our peace with the modern ills that Lewis is trying to highlight—and evangelicals do so to the detriment of the personal piety with which they are supposedly so concerned.

By way of example, consider two of the Ransom Trilogy's most prominent (and strongly related) themes: technology and gender. At the macro-level, our politics today is increasingly dominated by both a technocracy that sees technological innovation (including transhumanism) as the solution to all civilizational ills, and by an ideological rejection of the natural givenness of sex and gender that has reached its most extreme manifestation in an embrace of transgenderism but that was at work long before then. At the micro-level, our daily lives are increasingly frayed at the edges by the addictive yet alienating tug of screens and haunted by the directionlessness of men and women who struggle to know what on earth being either of those things actually means.

The damage wrought by this current *zeitgeist* around technology and gender is becoming more and more evident. And it is for this reason that we find ourselves in a "moment" in which the Ransom Trilogy has truly come into its own. Upon first discovering the trilogy a few years ago, I was simply floored on page after page after page by its prescience and scandalized that no one had thrust it into my hands with urgency sooner. One could scarcely have designed a more retroactively prophetic set of novels for our day if they had tried. The unashamed aim of *Life on the Silent Planet* is to bring Lewis's Ransom Trilogy into popular discussion about Christian living such that it gains its rightful place as the equal of the Chronicles of Narnia and Lewis's most famous Christian nonfiction.

It is worth saying at the outset that the relevance of the essays for Christian living is not to simply argue that for Christians to survive and thrive in modernity, they must turn back the clock. Lewis himself knew that we can never "go back" and "unmodernize" ourselves. Some kind of massive future technological collapse aside (a possibility not to be discounted), *modernity happened*, and there's nothing we can do about it. We're all Moderns now. Our *felt* experience of the world is a million miles away from that of the Medievals who so fascinated Lewis. We noted technology and gender as two particular challenges above, but of these two, technology is the more fundamental. It profoundly warps the way in which we inhabit the world. When it comes to the existence of God, for instance, my colleague and fellow contributor Joseph Minich explains that, in the modern world, "whatever one believes propositionally about the question of God, God's existence is not *felt* to be obvious in the same way that, for instance, the fact that you are reading this right now feels obvious."[24] Minich roots much of this sense of divine absence in the alienation caused by what he calls "modern technoculture."[25] A creation in which technology dominates so much, especially our daily labor, cannot help but feel radically different from what came before—to the extent that even the Creator himself grows strangely dim to us.

Much the same can be said of the reality of sex and gender difference. When embroiled in gender debates,

---

24. Joseph Minich, *Bulwarks of Unbelief: Atheism and Divine Absence in a Secular Age* (Bellingham: Lexham Academic, 2023), 5.

25. Minich, *Bulwarks of Unbelief*, 6.

Introduction

Christians far too often begin the discussion with the explosion of feminism in the 1950s and '60s and assume that modern gender confusion simply arises from ideology. But Lewis wrote Jane Studdock in the early '40s, and he died in 1963, the year that, according to Philip Larkin, sexual intercourse began. The great gender crack-up, then, clearly goes back further than the middle year of the twentieth century and arises from more than mere ideology. Increasingly, Christian thinkers are casting their minds further back to the technological innovations of the Industrial Revolution as the true starting point for our modern gender wars. Our ideological ructions have largely been downstream of this and are unimaginable without certain technologies underpinning them.[26]

Although reconceiving our modern problems this way is more accurate, it can at first be a great deal more depressing. If the reality of technological innovation means that we cannot reverse the clock, that we cannot make things such as God's existence or the goodness of gender difference intuitive in the way that they once were, then why bother? We can see immediately why it is so tempting to believe this is all a matter of ideology, since we can always either tantalize ourselves with the possibility that we will win the battle of ideas, or savor the self-righteousness in the long defeat of martyrdom when we don't. Most contemporary Christians, however, *do* simply admit de-

---

26. A seminal text in this regard is Ivan Illich's 1982 book *Gender*, which has been gaining currency among Christian thinkers in recent years. I am particularly indebted to the labors of my friend and colleague Alastair Roberts in this area (he is also the husband of one of our contributors).

feat, absorbing to varying degrees the prevailing modern consensus on technocracy and gender and finding ways to whitewash it with respectable religious language. Evangelicals in particular do this with one well-intentioned but profoundly misguided eye on evangelism: to the men without chests, we become men without chests.

The fruitful path for modern Christians that Lewis imagines, however, is different. It is neither tilting at windmills in some endless ideological conflict between "liberalism" and "conservatism," nor is it a weak-kneed embrace of the modern status quo. To put it crudely, when confronting the ills of modernity, the Ransom Trilogy suggests something like "the only way out is through." This does not mean a teeth-gritting charge through with our heads down, as if modernity isn't happening and as if it doesn't have some genuine benefits. No; we will all be—and have already been—changed. Joseph Minich has described modernity as "the simultaneous global renegotiation of all human custom"—a remarkably accurate definition I think, but it can be one that causes us to throw up our hands again.[27] What hope have we of coming back from a point where all human existence has become negotiable? But the *Tao*, which Lewis defines and defends so expertly in *The Abolition of Man*, is such that *it will out* in the end, and it is possible to have passed through the gauntlet of modernity—indeed, to still be living within it—and to sincerely reembrace, in our own way, those things that our ancestors did not have to think twice about. Indeed, if

---

27. Joseph Minich, "A Very Nuanced Take on Everything," *Ad Fontes*, June 11, 2022, https://adfontesjournal.com/pilgrim-faith/a-very-nuanced-take-on-everything/.

the *Tao* is real, this simply *must* be the case. It is particularly helpful here to remember that one of Lewis's other names for the *Tao* is "The Way": "It is *the Way in which the universe goes on*, the Way in which things everlastingly emerge, stilly and tranquilly into space and time. It is also the Way which every man should tread in imitation of that supercosmic progression, conforming all activities to that great exemplar."[28] Without doubt, hard-nosed opposition to and rejection of much of the modern project is called for, and Lewis knew this. "Ethics, theology, and politics" are all at stake when the *Tao* is forgotten, and so political solutions can and should be sought.[29] And yet Lewis seems resolutely, insouciantly convinced that it is possible for us to be, in some sense, modern men, women, and Christians who are nevertheless in step with the *Tao*—and indeed, we could perhaps even read him in places as seeing a kind of *felix culpa* in modernity, as something intended ultimately for man's good by divine providence. We may live on Thulcandra, the silent planet—our fallen home, out of tune with the intended music of creation—and perhaps, in the modern era, with its rejection of the very idea of such a thing as the *Tao*, the silence has become particularly deafening. And yet we know that Maleldil has "taken strange counsel and dared terrible things, wrestling with the Bent One in Thulcandra," and so life on the silent planet is always, for the Christian, possible.[30]

---

28. Lewis, *The Abolition of Man*, 28. Emphasis added.

29. Lewis, *The Abolition of Man*, 16.

30. Lewis, *Out of the Silent Planet*, 154.

SUMMARY OF CHAPTERS

Our volume dedicates three chapters each to *Out of the Silent Planet* and *Perelandra*, and six to *That Hideous Strength*. This disparity is a proportionate one, since the third novel is longer than the previous two put together.[31] We begin with renowned Lewis scholar Dr. Louis Markos's chapter "Which Way, Weston Man? Good, Evil, and Cosmological Models in *Out of the Silent Planet*." From the outset, I wanted this book to begin with a chapter that made clear the importance of Lewis's reappropriation of the medieval cosmos for the trilogy, since this is the backdrop against which the drama of the whole series is staged. It is the *sine qua non*, and Dr. Markos provides a stellar account of why this is the case. In the second chapter, "The Education of Dr. Ransom: First Steps from Pedestrian to Pendragon," Joe Rigney considers the transformation we begin to see in the trilogy's titular protagonist as he finds himself transported to Malacandra. Ransom's chief vice at the outset, Dr. Rigney argues convincingly, is the passion of fear—something that he begins to overcome only as he uncovers the true order of the cosmos. Colin Smothers then surveys the vital theme of masculinity in our third chapter, "Men Are From Mars: Masculinity in *Out of the Silent Planet*," zeroing in particularly on how Lewis shows us masculinity in courage, responsible fatherhood, and self-sacrifice.

In our first *Perelandra* chapter, "Enjoyment and Contemplation: The Green Lady, Self-Knowledge, and Growth in Maturity," Christiana Hale pairs the novel with Lewis's essay "Meditation in a Toolshed," beautifully applying

---

31. I am grateful to fellow contributor Joe Rigney for making this suggestion at the outset of the project.

Introduction

Lewis's categories of "enjoyment" and "contemplation" to the Christian life in service of true humility and true obedience. In the next chapter, Bethel McGrew grapples with the Screwtapery of *Perelandra* in "The Devil Went Down to Venus: Lessons from the Un-man," considering in particular the thorny question of how we can possibly love enemies who are so deeply in thrall to the Bent One. In the final chapter of this section, "A Taste of Paradise: Naming, Restraining, and Embracing Pleasure on Perelandra," my own contribution, I take a close look at how Lewis portrays unfallen sensual pleasure on Perelandra and what it can teach us about the highs and lows of pleasure here and now.

Our third section begins with Dr. Michael Ward's chapter "Selling the Well and the Wood: *That Hideous Strength* and the Abolition of Matrimony." This chapter expands on a 2022 *First Things* article by Dr. Ward entitled "C. S. Lewis and Contraception," making a provocative but thoroughly convincing case for *That Hideous Strength* being a sustained critique of the use of contraceptive technology.[32] Then, in "Lewis's Apocalypse and Ours," Dr. Joseph Minich considers how Lewis's "apocalyptic" vision of modernity compares to recent attitudes toward the End Times among some evangelicals, and how it can help to reorient us within the culture wars, particularly when it comes to gender. Next, in his chapter "The Untabled Law of Nature," Colin Redemer makes a compelling argument that *That Hideous Strength* portrays modern men not

---

32. Michael Ward, "C. S. Lewis and Contraception," *First Things*, November 3, 2022, https://www.firstthings.com/web-exclusives/2022/11/c-s-lewis-and-contraception.

xxi

simply as lacking chests but as lacking another important, and distinctly male, body part—one that we sorely need to regrow if we are to compete for the *Tao*. In "Arthur in Edgestow," Dr. Holly Ordway takes on the daunting task not only of making sense of what on earth Lewis is doing with the Arthurian elements of his novel, but what their relevance could possibly be for the Christian life (and she succeeds with characteristic aplomb). In the penultimate chapter, "The Problem of Jane," Susannah Black-Roberts tackles the supposed boogeyman (or perhaps, boogeywoman) of Lewis's attitude to women's sexuality, skewering misplaced feminist critiques and revealing that the so-called problem of Jane ultimately has nothing to do with sex, or women, at all. Finally, Jake Meador concludes our collection with "Bureaucratic Speech in *That Hideous Strength*," attempting the impossible task of making sense of the NICE's internal conversations and ably pointing out how Lewis's satirical diagnosis of obfuscatory modern speech is as relevant now as it was then.

It has been a true privilege to have worked with the contributors for this volume, and I am grateful to them all for their hard work, research, and willing collaboration during the editorial process. These chapters have, I believe, broken genuinely new ground, either by unearthing insights and connections hitherto unseen or by finally providing long overdue go-to surveys of particular themes or topics in the Ransom Trilogy. All of them, even those more scholarly ones, have remained firmly on-task in applying Lewis's work to the topic of Christian living.

I am especially glad to have brought together established Lewis scholars with friends and colleagues from the Davenant Institute and its network. I myself am entirely

Introduction

indebted to this latter group for plunging me head first into the world of the Ransom Trilogy, and made it my mission in part to bring their appreciation for these novels—as practical as it is scholarly—to a wider audience. In part, I hope for that wider audience to consist of Lewis scholars; mostly, however, I hope that it will consist of Christian laypeople and pastors who are willing to let these books work their way into areas of their Christian lives that may otherwise have gone unexamined. That, certainly, is what these books have done for me.

Here on the silent planet, we are out of tune with the music of the spheres, out of step with what *Perelandra* calls the Great Dance. But, in Maleldil's grace, the music plays on, and we are invited out of the silence and into the dance. He who has ears to hear, let him hear.

Rhys Laverty
Editor
July 2024

A NOTE ON THE TEXT

There are many different editions of the novels in Lewis's Ransom Trilogy, and doubtless new editions will be published in the future. In this collection, we have opted for the 2005 HarperCollins UK paperbacks of *Out of the Silent Planet* and *Perelandra*, and the accompanying 2003 HarperCollins edition of *That Hideous Strength* as our editions of choice since, at the time of publication, these editions are some of the most recent and widely read and retain Lewis's native British English spelling. For ease of reference, however, we have given the chapter numbers for all citations along with the page numbers. This should allow readers reading along with other editions to look up quotations with relative ease and minimal page turning.

OUT OF
THE SILENT
PLANET

I

WHICH WAY, WESTON MAN?
GOOD, EVIL, AND COSMOLOGICAL MODELS IN *OUT OF THE SILENT PLANET*

Louis Markos

The world of Narnia studies was changed forever by the publication of Michael Ward's *Planet Narnia* in 2008.[1] How could readers of the Chronicles of Narnia and lovers of C. S. Lewis not have seen it all along? Lewis was a great explicators of the medieval cosmological model, and Ward masterfully revealed that the Narnia books clearly take place in a world inspired by it. Prior to publishing *The Lion, the Witch, and the Wardrobe* in 1950, Lewis had even written his science fiction Ransom Trilogy of novels, explicitly engaging the medieval cosmological mode as he

---

1. Portions of this essay have appeared previously in "Apologist for the Past: The Medieval Vision of C. S. Lewis's 'Space Trilogy' and Chronicles of Narnia," *Mythlore* 23, no. 2 (Spring 2001): 24–35, and in Chapter 3 of *Lewis Agonistes* (Brentwood: Broadman & Holman, 2003).

transported readers to Mars (*Out of the Silent Planet*) and Venus (*Perelandra*), before bringing the influences of those two planets, and others, down to Earth to help good triumph over evil (*That Hideous Strength*).

Ward connected the dots between Lewis's love of the medieval cosmos and his fiction, arguing that both Narnia and the Ransom Trilogy allow modern readers to experience on a deep, intuitive level the ethos and ambiance of the Middle Ages—or, to put it more sharply, the ethos and ambiance of reality. Lewis once off-handedly referred to the atmosphere of Donegal as "Donegality," and in *Planet Narnia*, Ward adopted this word to refer to Lewis's approach to "atmosphere" in general.[2] Ward defines it as

> the spiritual essence or quiddity ["thingness"] of a work of art as intended by the artist and inhabited unconsciously by the reader. The donegality of a story is its peculiar and deliberated atmosphere or quality; its pervasive and purposed integral tone or flavour; its tutelary but tacit spirit, a spirit that the author consciously sought to conjure but which was designed to remain implicit in the matter of the text.[3]

To read Lewis's fiction is to absorb the donegality of the medieval cosmos. In what follows, I shall first map

---

2. C. S. Lewis, *Spenser's Images of Life*, ed. Alastair Fowler (Cambridge: Cambridge University Press, 1967), 115. It is now often said that Ward coined "donegality," but this is obviously not the case.

3. Michael Ward, *Planet Narnia: The Seven Heavens in the Imagination of C. S. Lewis* (Oxford: Oxford University Press, 2008), 75.

out, physically and spiritually, the medieval cosmological model as Lewis describes it in *The Discarded Image*, a work completed shortly before his death in 1963 but not published until the following year. I shall then show how, in *Out of the Silent Planet*, the responses that the characters Ransom and Weston have to this model push them toward opposing poles of good and evil. Finally, I shall discuss what Christians today can learn from that polarization.

• • •

Arriving at Oxford in the years following the First World War, Lewis accepted with little question the post-Enlightenment belief that the medieval world was a Dark Age of ignorance, superstition, and obscurantism. Luckily, with the help of such friends as Owen Barfield and J. R. R. Tolkien, he overcame his chronological snobbery, eventually becoming both a Christian and an apologist of the age he had once derided.

Though scholarly assessments are changing, many still dismiss the Middle Ages, derisively assuming, among other things, that the Medievals thought the earth was flat. Lewis debunks this decisively. "Physically considered," writes Lewis in *The Discarded Image*, "the Earth is a globe; all the authors of the high Middle Ages are agreed on this."[4]

It is true that the Medievals believed that the earth was at the center of the universe, but that is only because,

---

4. C. S. Lewis, *The Discarded Image: An Introduction to Medieval and Renaissance Literature* (Cambridge: Cambridge University Press, 1964), 140.

absent modern telescopes, this made the most sense of the celestial phenomena that could be perceived with the human eye.[5] They did not center the Earth out of pride. Rather, they considered Earth the darkest, heaviest, coldest spot in the cosmos, "the 'offscourings of creation,' the cosmic dust-bin."[6] Their universe was geocentric, but it was "not in the least anthropocentric."[7] To be at the center of the universe meant being at the bottom of it.

The Medievals were also aware of the vastness of the universe and the smallness of the Earth. "Earth was, by cosmic standards, a point—it had no appreciable magnitude. The stars, as the *Somnium Scipionus* ["Dream of Scipio"] had taught, were larger than it."[8] Still, they did not make the mistake of equating size with value. For all its smallness, the Earth was nonetheless imbued with beauty, purpose, and design. "[T]he Model universe of our ancestors had a built-in significance. And that in two senses; as having 'significant form' (it is an admirable design) and as a manifestation of the wisdom and goodness that created it."[9]

---

5. Copernicus's eventual discovery of heliocentrism in the sixteenth century should not be regarded as a rejection of medieval astronomy, but rather as its natural conclusion and fruition, resolving things that had puzzled astronomers for centuries. Without the diligent efforts of countless medieval Christian monks, heliocentrism would have eluded us who knows how much longer.

6. Lewis, *Discarded Image*, 63.

7. Lewis, *Discarded Image*, 55.

8. Lewis, *Discarded Image*, 97.

9. Lewis, *Discarded Image*, 204.

Neither the Ancients nor the Medievals were fools. They had eyes that saw, and they used them well. But *what* they saw and, more importantly, *how* they saw differed greatly from us. When they gazed upward at the heavens, they saw a cosmos of perfect order, balance, and harmony, an ornament—the root meaning of the Greek word, *kosmos*—fashioned by a God who is himself a being of perfect order. Around a fixed, central Earth, a series of nine concentric, crystalline spheres rotated in perfect circular orbits. Embedded in these spheres were the seven medieval planets (in ascending order the Moon, Mercury, Venus, the Sun, Mars, Jupiter, Saturn), the fixed stars, and the *primum mobile,* or "first mover," which set all the other spheres in motion and was itself set in motion by God, the Unmoved Mover.

Rubbing against each other, the rotating spheres produced a heavenly music so refined and ethereal that our dull, earthly ears could not hear it. How different our own, post-Enlightenment perception of the universe: "The 'silence' which frightened Pascal was, according to the model, wholly illusory; and the sky looks black only because we are seeing it through the dark glass of our own shadow. You must conceive yourself looking up at a world lighted, warmed, and resonant with music."[10]

As Lewis describes it in *The Discarded Image,* the medieval model struck its contemplators with all the power and beauty of an epic poem. Their universe was not, like ours, a lifeless object to be merely studied and dissected for practical benefit, but an animated presence eliciting admiration and love. Whereas our age *reasons* that the

---

10. Lewis, *Discarded Image,* 112.

vast actions and interactions of the cosmos are best defined in terms of abstract, objective *principles* (e.g., the laws of gravity and of thermodynamics), the Medievals *saw* a more personal, subjective universe whose intricate movements, like those of a dance, were set in motion and choreographed by divine *influence*.

Medieval poets like Boethius, Dante, and Chaucer, as well as Renaissance poets like Shakespeare, Donne, and Milton, lived in a sympathetic, rather than a clockwork, universe, in which the stars have something to do with us. As the planets shed down their influence, they drew certain minerals out of the earth and certain personality types out of humans. Thus, while "Mars makes iron [and] gives men the martial temperament," the Sun "produces the noblest metal, gold [and] makes men wise and liberal."[11] In the same way, the Moon, Mercury, Venus, Jupiter, and Saturn draw silver, mercury, copper, tin, and lead out of the earth and make men fickle (or "lunatics," thanks to the *lunar* influence), mercurial, amorous, jovial (thanks to *Jove*, another name for Jupiter), and melancholy (or, perhaps, "saturnine").

That is not to say that the medieval church condoned horoscopes and fortune-telling, but she did accept the interrelatedness of the changing world below and the unchanging world above. "Celestial bodies affect terrestrial bodies, including those of men. And by affecting our bodies they can, but need not, affect our reason and our will."[12] The influence is real, but our reception of it de-

---

11. Lewis, *Discarded Image*, 106.

12. Lewis, *Discarded Image*, 103.

termines our nature and character. Thus, the influence of Saturn can make us holy contemplatives or despairing suicides; the influence of the Sun can make us generous with our riches or to hoard our gold like a dragon.

For the Medievals, everything in the universe is free to follow its instincts, yet nothing is haphazard. In all things, there is order and hierarchy. Every heavenly being—from seraphim to cherubim to archangel—every man, every animal, even every plant has its place in that Great Chain of Being that stretches from God to the lowest form of inorganic life.

The medieval cosmos was indeed a thing of beauty in which all things found their proper place. Lewis celebrated it for its ability to integrate vast amounts of speculative material— pagan and Christian, philosophical and theological, scientific and poetic—into a unified system. Out of a chaos of forms and ideas, the Medievals, like the God they worshiped, forged a unified system in which order and hierarchy were the rule. And yet, as difficult as it may seem for us inhabitants of a democratic, anti-aristocratic world to believe, that order was clear, logical, and coherent and that hierarchy just, reasonable, and, in the most exalted sense of the word, human. Like Aquinas's *Summa* and Dante's *Commedia*, their cosmos was "vast in scale, but limited and intelligible. Its sublimity is not the sort that depends on anything vague or obscure.... Its contents, however rich and various, are in harmony. We see how everything links up with everything else; at one, not in flat equality, but in a hierarchical ladder."[13]

---

13. Lewis, *Discarded Image*, 12.

LIFE ON THE SILENT PLANET

• • •

Though *Out of the Silent Planet* (1938) was written a quarter of a century before *The Discarded Image* (1964), it embodies its cosmology in narrative form. It transports its readers back to a cosmos in which hierarchy, plenitude, and influence are still the rule. Thus, though Lewis adopts the modern, "correct" ordering of the planets, he presents those planets as retaining their medieval connotations, and populated by rational creatures (*hnau*) who live in unfallen, Edenic worlds of peace and plenty. Each planet, or sphere, is watched over by a guardian spirit that he calls the *Oyarsa*, who is at once a biblical archangel and the "intelligence" of ancient astronomy, both the servant of the Creator (known as Maleldil in "Old Solar," the forgotten common language of our solar system) and the master of his sphere's inhabitants. They bring order and harmony to their world, shedding over it and even radiating out into the cosmos their benign influence.

On Mars, or "Malacandra" in Old Solar, the Oyarsa oversees three distinct species of *hnau* who live in a state of innocence: a race of Homeric warriors known as the *hrossa*, resembling giant beavers or seals; a race of froglike craftsmen known as the *pfifltriggi*; and a race of tall, thin, abstract-thinking philosophers known as the *sorns*. Sadly, the situation on Earth is quite different. The Oyarsa of Earth (Satan) rebelled against Maleldil (God) and even sought "to spoil other worlds besides his own."[14] To preserve the rest of the cosmos, God quarantined the earth,

---

14. C. S. Lewis, *Out of the Silent Planet* (London: HarperCollins, 2005), ch. 18, 153.

which is why it is now called "Thulcandra" by its neighbors: "the Silent Planet." Even worse, in imitation of their Bent (evil) Oyarsa, the inhabitants of the Earth came to be rebels also, so much so that "every one of them wants to be a little Oyarsa himself."[15]

As a result, our world has become detached from the proper order and hierarchy of the cosmos. To win back the Earth, Maleldil (Christ) was sent by his Father, the Old One, to redeem Thulcandra. Nevertheless, the events of *Out of the Silent Planet* end Thulcandra's silence, opening up a new phase of cosmic spiritual warfare, one that will take place on a spiritual level that modern man knows little about. In the wonderfully apocalyptic closing chapter, Ransom, the protagonist, begins to marshal himself, the narrator, and us readers for the battle. To resist the coming evil, we need "not so much a body of belief as a body of people familiarized with certain ideas. If we could even effect in one per cent of our readers a change-over from the conception of Space to the conception of Heaven, we should have made a beginning."[16]

That such a change is possible is dramatized in Ransom's arc. Like Lewis himself, Ransom progresses from being a modern, skeptical university professor to a man of deep faith and humility whose eyes are permanently opened to the beauty, awe, and hierarchy of the cosmos, making him a better, braver, more virtuous man. Ransom's pilgrimage begins when he is kidnapped by the scientist Weston and his old college acquaintance Devine and tak-

---

15. Lewis, *Out of the Silent Planet*, ch. 16, 129.

16. Lewis, *Out of the Silent Planet*, ch. 22, 198.

en to Malacandra. From here on, he quickly undergoes an education in the wonders of the unseen world, beginning as he looks out the window of the spaceship.

> He had read of "Space": at the back of his thinking for years had lurked the dismal fancy of the black, cold vacuity, the utter deadness, which was supposed to separate the worlds.... He had thought it barren: he saw now that it was the womb of worlds.... No: Space was the wrong name. Older thinkers had been wiser when they named it simply the heavens—the heavens which declared the glory.[17]

The cosmos is not as he imagined it. It is not a cold, dark vacuum but a field of light and warmth. Life, meaning, and purpose pervade it. Slowly, like a morning glory opening to the sun, Ransom lets go of the scientistic-existential myth in which he was raised, embracing a more mystical *and* humanistic medieval myth.

This is only the beginning. Once on Malacandra, Ransom escapes and falls in with the *hrossa*. Their simple nobility forces him to rethink his instinctual privileging of technological advances—of which the *hrossa* have none—over traditional, chivalric virtues such as honor, courage, and loyalty, all of which the *hrossa* have in abundance. When the *hrossa* invite him to join them for an epic hunt, Ransom at first seeks an excuse to bow out. But then, "in obedience to something like conscience," he chooses "to hold on to his new-found manhood; now or never—with

---

17. Lewis, *Out of the Silent Planet*, ch. 5, 35.

such companions or with none—he must leave a deed on his memory instead of one more broken dream."[18]

The courage that fills Ransom's chest is not an abstraction or a vague feeling but a concrete, rational virtue that reflects and participates in the greater cosmic order. Malacandra, corresponding to the warlike Mars, exercises a *martial* influence, which Ransom lets mold him into a medieval knight, reordering and redirecting his desires so that he embraces the hunting party: "They were all *hnau*. They had stood shoulder to shoulder in the face of an enemy, and the shapes of their heads no longer mattered. And he, even Ransom, had come through it and not been disgraced. He had grown up."[19]

Having learned proper awe and gratitude before the wonders of the created cosmos and found fortitude and friendship by fighting among the *hrossa*, Ransom must overcome one last deeply-entrenched prejudice: the modern suspicion of and distaste for authority and religious hierarchy. Having experienced and accepted "heroism and poetry at the bottom" of Malacandrian society, Ransom continues to fear what he thinks is a "cold scientific intellect above it [the *sorns*], and overtopping all some dark superstition [the Oyarsa] which scientific intellect, helpless against the revenge of the emotional depths it had ignored, had neither will nor power to remove."[20] It is only when he meets and speaks with one of the *sorns* that he realizes that they do not compete politically or economically with

---

18. Lewis, *Out of the Silent Planet*, ch. 13, 99.

19. Lewis, *Out of the Silent Planet*, ch. 13, 100.

20. Lewis, *Out of the Silent Planet*, ch. 14, 107.

the *hrossa* and *pfifltriggi*. Rather, all three races respect each other's special gifts. As for the Oyarsa, Ransom discovers that, far from a soulless tyrant, he is a warm and personal patriarch who loves the creatures he rules and seeks what is best for them.

No such realization or change occurs in the hearts of Ransom's abductors. From beginning to end, Weston and Devine remain blind to the beauties of Malacandra and deaf to the gentle entreaties of the Oyarsa. To them, the inhabitants of Mars are nothing more than savages controlled by a witch doctor. Like modernist Pharisees, they have eyes but do not see, ears but do not hear.

Of the two, Devine is the lesser villain, for he is motivated by simple greed. Gold is abundant on Mars, and the avaricious Devine seeks to profit by it. Weston, in contrast, is a serious, respected, humanitarian scientist who has devoted his life to the preservation of humanity. His devotion, however, exists in a moral vacuum, cut off from the goodness, truth, and beauty that define the medieval cosmological model. He is more than willing to kill all the indigenous *hnau* of Mars if it will allow him to further his "humanitarian" ends. Refusing to accept the Oyarsa's warning "that all worlds will die," Weston explains that he will move humans to Mars if and when Earth dies, and then to another planet if and when Mars dies (though he has nothing to say when asked what he will do when all worlds die).[21]

The difference between Devine and Weston is that, while the former is "broken," according to the Malacandrian Oyarsa, the latter, like the fallen Oyarsa of Earth, is

---

21. Lewis, *Out of the Silent Planet*, ch. 20, 179.

"bent." In fact, after learning about Maleldil and the Bent One, Weston musters enough Malacandrian language to declare on which side of the cosmic-spiritual battle he falls: "You say your Maleldil let all go dead. Other one, Bent One, he fight, jump, live—not all talkee-talkee. Me no care Maleldil. Like Bent One better: me on his side."[22] Unlike Ransom, whose reception of the martial influence of Malacandra expands him into a knight and, if need be, a martyr, Weston's reception of the same shrinks him to a megalomaniac willing to commit genocide in order to achieve his idol of species survival.

Weston is part Thrasymachus, who argues, in Plato's *Republic*, that justice is the will of the stronger; part Machiavelli, who taught that the ends justify the means; and part Nietzsche, who called for a superman, an *Übermensch*, with the charisma to rise above middle-class morality and assert his absolute will to power. Lewis brilliantly exposes and deconstructs the hollowness of his high-sounding utopian rhetoric by having Weston explain his reasons for appropriating Mars for humans in his own euphemistic language and then having Ransom translate his propaganda into the innocent, unfeigned language of the unfallen Malacandrians:

> "Your tribal life with its stone-age weapons and beehive huts, its primitive coracles and elementary social structure, has nothing to compare with our civilization—with our science, medicine and law, our armies, our architecture, our commerce, and our transport system which is

---

22. Lewis, *Out of the Silent Planet*, ch. 20, 179.

rapidly annihilating space and time. Our right to supersede you is the right of the higher over the lower..."

"He says that, among you, *hnau* of one kindred all live together and the *hrossa* have spears like those we used a very long time ago and your huts are small and round and your boats small and light and like our old ones, and you have only one ruler.... He says we build very big and strong huts of stones and other things—like the *pfifltriggi*. And he says we exchange many things among ourselves and can carry heavy weights very quickly a long way. Because of all this, he says it would not be the act of a bent *hnau* if our people killed all your people."[23]

For Weston, who has blinded himself to the beauty of hierarchy, deafened himself to the music of the spheres, and severed himself from the Great Chain of Being, progress and technology become the only markers of value. Accepting no authority above himself and his cause, Weston rejects not only the geocentric universe of the Middle Ages, but the heliocentric and anthropocentric universes of the Renaissance and Enlightenment. His universe is purely and finally egocentric. Indeed, so narcissistically confident is he of the absolute justness of his cause that, after he kidnaps Ransom, he assures himself that Ransom "cannot be so small-minded as to think that the rights or

---

23. Lewis, *Out of the Silent Planet*, ch. 20, 173-4..

the life of an individual or of a million individuals are of the slightest importance in comparison with this."[24]

• • •

What then are we to learn in the twenty-first century from a book written one year before the outbreak of the Second World War? Certainly not that modern astronomical science is mistaken on a factual level. Neither Lewis nor I would advocate a return to the medieval cosmological model in astronomy. Science *has*, Lewis freely admits, disproven such medieval assumptions as the circular movements of the spheres and geocentrism. Nevertheless, he insists, this does not validate any smug self-assurance that we now have all the truth that is worth having.

Our modern cosmological model is just that: a model—one that can, at any moment, be dramatically altered by some new scientific discovery, and that is inescapably freighted with meaning and metaphor. We laugh at the Medievals for their quaint metaphorical notion that heavenly bodies move through celestial influence, but is such a view any more metaphorical than our notion that objects "obey," like citizens, the "laws" of gravity? "Hardly any battery of new facts," Lewis explains in the Epilogue to *The Discarded Image*, "could have persuaded a Greek that the universe had an attribute so repugnant to him as infinity; hardly any such battery could persuade a modern that it is hierarchical."[25] All people, whether ancient or mod-

---

24. Lewis, *Out of the Silent Planet*, ch. 4, 28.

25. Lewis, *Discarded Image*, 222.

ern, medieval or enlightened, have their presuppositions, and they cannot help but bring those presuppositions with them into their study of the cosmos. In *Miracles*, Lewis suggests that differing views of cosmological hierarchy correspond to different views regarding hierarchy *per se*. Our Supernaturalist forebears, imagining themselves in a literally hierarchical universe, with God at its summit, regarded other forms of hierarchy positively; modern Naturalists, however, see both differently: "[J]ust as, in a democracy, all citizens are equal, so for the Naturalist one thing or event is as good as another, in the sense that they are all equally dependent on the total system of things."[26] Lewis avoids a "chicken and egg" discussion of the two, but his suggestion is clear: both the Medievals and Moderns, the Supernaturalists and the Naturalists, have models of the universe, and these models relate, unavoidably, to the value judgments they make about and within that universe.

The deepest lessons to be learned from *The Discarded Image* and *Out of the Silent Planet*, then, are not scientific but spiritual, not technological but theological, not physical but philosophical. If the universe in which we live is ordered and rational, if it possesses design and purpose, then, whether we put the Earth or the sun at the center, we can have faith that our own beliefs and actions within that universe matter, and that one thing is not necessarily as good as another. We are not merely morally inconsequential clusters of cells adrift in space; rather, we are rational moral agents, *hnau*, placed in the Heavens with a purpose. In a cosmos so logically and lovingly shaped, our choices not only have consequences; those consequences serve a

---

26. C. S. Lewis, *Miracles* (London: William Collins, 2016), 9.

greater whole that transcends scientific measurement. This is what Lewis means when he speaks of the *Tao* in *The Abolition of Man*: "It is the Way in which the universe goes on, the Way in which things everlastingly emerge, stilly and tranquilly, into space and time. It is also the Way which every man should tread in imitation of that cosmic and supersonic progression, conforming all activities to that great exemplar."[27]

When Weston and Ransom arrive on Malacandra, neither thinks he can learn anything from the indigenous inhabitants. Soon however, Ransom sheds his self-protective biases; Weston, meanwhile, continues to dismiss the inhabitants as savages. Ransom learns and grows, while Weston becomes more entrenched in his own prejudices. One of the reasons the past century has fostered so many Westons who count the development of human society as an absolute good on which no limits should be placed is that we have cut ourselves off from the very ancient philosophical wisdom that we desperately need if we are to properly assess our scientific progress. Ironically, the reason we have cut ourselves off from that wisdom is that we consider our ancestors to be less enlightened than we because they lacked the very technology we cannot control. Knowledge of the *Tao*, or our ordered cosmos, is desperately needed—both to enrich Christian discipleship as we seek to live with wisdom, and to hold out as Good News to those unbelievers weary of a nihilistic technocracy that views the universe with Weston's cold pragmatism.

But there is an even deeper, more pressing lesson that Lewis has to teach us today. As dual heirs of the Enlight-

---

27. C. S. Lewis, *The Abolition of Man* (London: Fount, 1978), 15–16.

enment and Romanticism, we tend to think of good and evil as subjective emotions rather than objective realities. We have forgotten the reality of a state in which we are in harmony with the God-created cosmos without and the God-implanted conscience within. Vice marks a breach of that harmony, a disordering and misdirection that skews our desires and leaves us open to the base passions that control people like Devine and the faulty reasoning that enables people like Weston to justify great evil.

Paul beseeches the believers of Rome not to conform themselves to the world but to be transformed by the renewing of their minds (Rom. 12:2). Today, we risk conformity to a world that has lost any sense of transcendent purpose, meaning, and order. To conform to such an anti-teleological model is to leave oneself open to the kind of utopian thinking that drives Weston. If the cosmos is meaningless, then it is up to us to impose meaning on it, as Weston attempts to do through his obsession with species survival. "Life is greater than any system of morality," says Weston; "her claims are absolute."[28] This vitalist obsession is one shared by many of our leaders today, whether in Silicon Valley or Washington, DC. But if we will, like Ransom, allow our reductive, existentialist vision of the cosmos to be transformed and renewed, if we can perceive once again a goodness in unity, a truth in order, and a beauty in hierarchy, then we too might find a new courage to join the hunt.

Weston chooses to be on the side of the Bent One rather than Maleldil because he considers the former to be active ("he fight, jump, live") and the latter to be passive

---

28. Lewis, *Out of the Silent Planet*, ch. 20, 174.

("all talkee-talkee"). It was for this very reason that Romantic poets William Blake and Percy Bysshe Shelley considered Milton's dynamic, energetic, rebellious Satan, not his static, immobile, monarchical Jehovah, to be the true hero of *Paradise Lost*. Lewis wrote his *Preface to Paradise Lost* (1942) in order to correct this misreading. I would agree that Milton's Satan seems more active than his God, but that is only because he is governed by disordered desire, without control, focus, or purpose. His passions overflow, but turn against themselves in the end. The Oyarsa of Malacandra makes a similar judgment of Weston: "Let me see if there is anything in your mind besides fear and death and desire."[29] In fact, the Oyarsa *does* see more than he expected in Weston, when the latter explains that his motivation is to propagate the human race: "your will is less bent than I thought. It is not for yourself that you would do all this."[30] Weston's love of his kindred is, the Oyarsa concedes, a law known to all *hnau*—but the Bent One has made Weston willing to break all other laws in service of it, and to say so openly. For this reason, the "bent" Weston is a greater danger than the "broken" Devine, who is simply greedy. Weston's inordinate desire and inordinate commitment to one genuine good over against all others puts him on his dynamic Satanic path. Ransom's attempted translation of one line of Weston's speech—"it is better to be alive and bent than to be dead"—seems a conscious echo of Milton's Satan's famous dictum: "Better to reign in Hell, than serve in Heav'n."

---

29. Lewis, *Out of the Silent Planet*, ch. 20, 172.

30. Lewis, *Out of the Silent Planet*, ch. 20, 176.

Milton's God may seem more passive than his Satan, but that is only because the Almighty Creator has dignity, solemnity, and gravitas. He is controlled, focused, and purposeful—not because he is a cosmic tyrant, but because he is omnipotent, omnipresent, and omniscient—the Unmoved Mover. Instability versus stability, rage versus calm, chaos versus rest, reckless activity versus regal composure—these would be more accurate dichotomies for Milton's Satan and God than "active versus passive." These are all virtues in which Christians should seek to grow as we are renewed in the image of our Creator (Col. 3:10)—not simply because our Creator explicitly commands us to do so, but because those commands reinforce truths declared to us daily in the warp and woof of creation.

On a more mundane level, many today, Christians included, echo Milton's Satan and Lewis's Weston not simply by rebelling against God or actively pursuing sin, but in our perpetual busyness and distraction. Could we only stop and contemplate, with David, the majesty of the cosmos—as Ransom does on his journey to Malacandra—we might see that the heavens do indeed speak forth the glory of God and proclaim the beauty of his handiwork (Ps. 19:1). The pagans of Rome are without excuse, Paul explains, because God's power and majesty are clearly written in the cosmos he created (Rom. 1:20). Yet we suppress this. We miss God's presence and glory in creation because we have lost the ability to stop, look, and listen, and to receive non-human creation for the gift that it is.

By admiring Milton's Satan, Lewis argues, we give our "vote not only for a world of misery, but also for a world of lies and propaganda, of wishful thinking, of incessant autobiography."[31] The same holds true for those who admire Weston—and there *are* many who do, even if they do not recognize it. Weston may seem noble, with his philanthropic plan for perpetuating the human race through interplanetary conquest, but, in his desire to carry out that plan at all costs, he surrenders truth and reality to lies, propaganda, and wishful thinking. The Oyarsa even concludes that Weston does not actually love humanity: "You do not love any one of your race—you would have let me kill Ransom. You do not love the mind of your race, nor the body. Any kind of creature will please you if only it is begotten by your kind as they now are. It seems to me, Thick One, that what you really love is no completed creature but the very seed itself: for that is all that is left."[32] The same is true of many who claim to be driven by the future of the human race today, who care only for their nebulous imagined humanity of the future, not real human beings as they find them. We, like Weston, are egoists trapped in an egocentric universe of our own construction.

If we would break out of Weston's egoism, we must also break out of his egocentric universe. That does not mean we must forget everything we have learned from cosmology and the telescope. It means, rather, that we must, like Ransom, regain a medieval sense of awe, wonder, and humility before the beauty and majesty of God's ordered cosmos. We must remember that we are not apes hanging in space, but *hnau* dancing in the Heavens—and

---

31. C. S. Lewis, *A Preface to Paradise Lost* (New York: Oxford University Press, 1961), 102.

32. Lewis, *Out of the Silent Planet*, ch. 20, 177.

not just *hnau*, but humanity, placed in Maledil's infinitely wise choreography at the center of the dance. Only thus will we be able to see again the deeper spiritual realities that lurk behind and within the physical, material realities perceived with our senses. Only then, will we recognize the battle—even the battle*field*—for what it is and the stakes for what they are.

But beware: with renewed vision comes the need for renewed volition. For the Christian with eyes to see, our earth *is* enemy-occupied territory, and we must choose this day whom we will serve: Maledil or the Bent One.

II

THE EDUCATION OF DR RANSOM:
FIRST STEPS FROM PEDESTRIAN TO PENDRAGON

Joe Rigney

I've long said that my preferred method for teaching C. S. Lewis is the book club, ideally one in which we read sections aloud, commenting as we go. This is because, as Lewis's friend Owen Barfield supposedly once put it, "What Lewis thought about everything was secretly present in what he said about anything." A book club provides the perfect opportunity to explore the back roads of Lewis's thought, jumping from what he says in one book to what he says in another. More than that, it opens the doorway to exploring other great authors, leaping from a paragraph in Lewis to the works of Plato or Dante or Shakespeare or Milton.

But, alas, a chapter is not a book club. As a result, we can only acknowledge in passing Lewis's subversion of the scientistic mythology of H. G. Wells, his love of the medieval cosmos and his attempt to recover it through his fiction, and the philosophical and literary influences that lie beneath the Ransom Trilogy. Thankfully, there are marvelous studies on each of these themes, which I am happy to commend to the reader.[1]

But this is a book of "Essays on Christian Living from the Ransom Trilogy." In referring to these three novels as "the Ransom Trilogy" rather than the more common "Space Trilogy," the editors have done a wonderful service, for one of the main purposes of these books is to show the maturation of the main character, Dr. Elwin Ransom. Introduced to him as the Pedestrian on the trilogy's opening page, we follow Ransom as he becomes a courageous Pilgrim on Malacandra and as he learns war and sits with kings on Perelandra, before becoming the Pendragon, the bridge between Deep Heaven and the Silent Planet that delivers England in *That Hideous Strength*. My aim in this chapter is to show the first essential steps along the journey from Pedestrian to Pendragon, a journey in which Ransom must learn to master himself, to train his emotions, and to obey God in the face of his fears.

---

1. Two of the best studies on the Ransom Trilogy are my fellow contributor Christiana Hale's *Deeper Heaven: A Reader's Guide to C. S. Lewis's Ransom Trilogy* (Moscow: Romans Road, 2020) and Sanford Schwartz's *C. S. Lewis on the Final Frontier: Science and the Supernatural in the Space Trilogy* (Oxford: Oxford University Press, 2009). In addition, I draw heavily from *Perelandra* in my own book *Lewis on the Christian Life: Becoming Truly Human in the Presence of God*, Theologians on the Christian Life (Wheaton: Crossway, 2018).

THE PEDESTRIAN'S FEAR

"What are you so afraid of, Ransom of Thulcandra?"[2]

So says the Oyarsa of Malacandra when Ransom meets him for the first time. It is an apt question, for Ransom's journey throughout the novel is one marked and driven by fear.

We are introduced to him as the Pedestrian, a shabby Cambridge don on a walking tour in the middle of England. Good-hearted, but timid, he intervenes to help a poor woman retrieve her son when he is late coming home from work. Ransom's motives are mixed—on the one hand, he does want to help the old woman; on the other, he does hope that in doing so, he'll find himself among men of his own class and be offered a bed for the night.

Ransom's fears begin after Weston and Devine drug him. Upon waking, he overhears their conversation and determines to make a run for it. Though weakened by the drug, "terror was behind him" and he makes it to the front door before he is caught and knocked unconscious.[3] When he comes to, his terror gradually increases. His body is lighter than it ought to be, the sky and stars have an unnatural splendor that suggests to him that something is wrong with his eyes, and the moon (or what he takes to be the moon) is of an impossibly large size. His entire experience is one of extreme disorientation, and though a hundred mental habits rise to his head, he is nevertheless trembling and thoroughly frightened—"not with

---

2. C. S. Lewis, *Out of the Silent Planet* (London: HarperCollins, 2005), ch. 18, 152.

3. Lewis, *Out of the Silent Planet*, ch. 2, 19.

the prosaic fright that a man suffers in a war, but with a heady, bounding kind of fear that was hardly distinguishable from his general excitement: he was poised on a sort of emotional watershed from which, he felt, he might at any moment pass into delirious terror or into an ecstasy of joy."[4] As he slowly comes to grips with the fact that the "moon" is not the moon, his apprehension rises until Weston enters the room and Ransom's nerves give way to a bottomless dismay as he sobs and gasps in desperation.

Weston's confirmation that the "moon" is in fact the Earth overwhelms Ransom with terror. "At the moment he was unconscious of everything except his fear. He did not even know what he was afraid of: the fear itself possessed his whole mind, a formless, infinite misgiving."[5]

Ransom's next bout with terror occurs about a fortnight into their journey, when he overhears Weston and Devine discussing what is to be done with him when they arrive on Malacandra. Ransom is to be given to the *sorns*— the inhabitants of Malacandra—perhaps as a human sacrifice. This reawakens Ransom's fear as he considers what is to come.

> His mind, like so many minds of his generation, was richly furnished with bogies. He had read his H. G. Wells and others. His universe was peopled with horrors such as ancient and medieval mythology could hardly rival. No insect-like, vermiculate or crustacean Abomina-

---

4. Lewis, *Out of the Silent Planet*, ch. 3, 23.

5. Lewis, *Out of the Silent Planet*, ch. 4, 25.

ble, no twitching feelers, rasping wings, slimy coils, curling tentacles, no monstrous union of superhuman intelligence and insatiable cruelty seemed to him anything but likely on an alien world. The sorns would be ... would be ... he dared not think what the sorns would be. And he was to be given to them. Somehow this seemed more horrible than being caught by them. Given, handed over, offered. He saw in imagination various incompatible monstrosities—bulbous eyes, grinning jaws, horns, stings, mandibles. Loathing of insects, loathing of snakes, loathing of things that squashed and squelched, all played their horrible symphonies over his nerves. But the reality would be worse: it would be an extra-terrestrial Otherness—something one had never thought of, never could have thought of.[6]

Here we have layers of terror, from the prospect of death, to the fact of being handed over by his own countrymen, and then, hovering over it all, the unimaginable horrors furnished to his imagination by the science fiction writers of his day and the puerile fears of insects and snakes, bubbling up from the repressed subconscious of childhood.

Ransom again manages to endure and subdue these fears. They are sharply reawakened after arriving upon Malacandra and he sees the *sorns* at a distance. Fleeing in terror and confusion, his fear of *sorns* is modified, away from the Wellsian insectile fantasies to "an earlier, almost

---

6. Lewis, *Out of the Silent Planet*, ch. 5, 39.

infantile complex of fears. Giants—ogres—ghosts—skeletons: those were its key words. Spooks on stilts, he said to himself; surrealistic bogey-men with their long faces."[7] Finding himself lost, hungry, and thirsty in the woods of Malacandra, Ransom feels danger all around him and collapses into "a flood of self-pity" and exhaustion.[8]

And Ransom's fears continue. Encountering a *sorn* in the woods, he flees in fear and encounters a *hross* in the water. Discovering that the *hross* is rational, he journeys to the village of the *hrossa*, where he is hosted for many weeks. But as pleasant as his stay with the *hrossa* is, fear of the *sorns* and apprehension that they might discover him is never far from Ransom's mind. And though Ransom is eventually able to master his fears, dread and anxiety follow him all the way to his audience with Oyarsa, where he admits that his entire journey has been marked by "terrible fear."[9]

MASTERING FEAR THROUGH AWE AT THE COSMOS

So then, if Ransom's journey in this book is fundamentally about the passion of fear, what can we learn from him about how to overcome our own fears, anxieties, apprehensions, and terrors? First, we ought to consider the role of awe, wonder, and curiosity in combating terror and fear. While Ransom's kidnapping and journey through space produces that initial "formless, infinite misgiving,"[10] and it ought to have been a period "of terror and anxiety for

---

7. Lewis, *Out of the Silent Planet*, ch. 8, 55.

8. Lewis, *Out of the Silent Planet*, ch. 8, 58.

9. Lewis, *Out of the Silent Planet*, ch. 18, 154.

10. Lewis, *Out of the Silent Planet*, ch. 4, 25.

Ransom,"[11] his fear soon gives way to severe delight at the endless day and endless night that mark the two sides of the spaceship. "Each was marvellous and he moved from the one to the other at his will, delighted."[12]

> In the nights, which he could create by turning the handle of a door, he lay for hours in contemplation of the skylight. The Earth's disk was nowhere to be seen, the stars, thick as daisies on an uncut lawn, reigned perpetually with no cloud, no moon, no sunrise, to dispute their sway. There were planets of unbelievable majesty, and constellations undreamed of: there were celestial sapphires, rubies, emeralds and pin-pricks of burning gold; far out on the left of the picture hung a comet, tiny and remote: and between all and behind all, far more emphatic and palpable than it showed on Earth, the undimensioned, enigmatic blackness. The lights trembled: they seemed to grow brighter as he looked...
>
> But the days—that is, the hours spent in the sunward hemisphere of their microcosm—were the best of all. Often he rose after only a few hours' sleep to return, drawn by an irresistible attraction, to the regions of light; he could not cease to wonder at the noon which always awaited you however early you were to seek it. There, totally immersed in a bath of pure ethereal co-

---

11. Lewis, *Out of the Silent Planet*, ch. 5, 32.

12. Lewis, *Out of the Silent Planet*, ch. 5, 33.

lour and of unrelenting though unwounding brightness, stretched his full length and with eyes half closed in the strange chariot that bore them, faintly quivering, through depth after depth of tranquility far above the reach of night, he felt his body and mind daily rubbed and scoured and filled with new vitality.[13]

These two paragraphs are part and parcel of the spiritual transformation that Ransom undergoes on his journey to Mars:

> A nightmare, long engendered in the modern mind by the mythology that follows in the wake of science, was falling off him. He had read of "Space": at the back of his thinking for years had lurked the dismal fancy of the black, cold vacuity, the utter deadness, which was supposed to separate the worlds. He had not known how much it affected him till now—now that the very name "Space" seemed a blasphemous libel for this empyrean ocean of radiance in which they swam. He could not call it "dead"; he felt life pouring into him from it every moment. How indeed should it be otherwise, since out of this ocean the worlds and all their life had come? He had thought it barren; he saw now that it was the womb of worlds, whose blazing and innumerable offspring looked down nightly even upon the Earth with so many eyes—and

---

13. Lewis, *Out of the Silent Planet*, ch. 5, 33–34.

here, with how many more! No: Space was the wrong name. Older thinkers had been wiser when they named it simply the heavens—the heavens which declared the glory—the

> happy climes that ly
> Where day never shuts his eye
> Up in the broad fields of the sky

He quoted Milton's words to himself lovingly, at this time and often.[14]

To recover this older, medieval vision of the cosmos is indeed one of the main reasons that Lewis wrote this novel. As Ransom says in the Epilogue, "What we need for the moment is not so much a body of belief as a body of people familiarized with certain ideas. If we could even effect in one per cent of our readers a changeover from the conception of Space to the conception of Heaven, we should have made a beginning."[15]

Through the Ransom Trilogy as a whole, Lewis is essentially offering to us two competing imaginative visions of the universe—one a despairing and terrifying nightmare engendered by scientific mythology and carried forward by greed, lust for power, and technological mastery of man's environment and eventually man himself, and the other an ordered cosmos, shot through with meaning, purpose, and life, in which fear and terror have a place,

---

14. Lewis *Out of the Silent Planet*, ch. 5, 34–35.

15. Lewis, *Out of the Silent Planet*, ch. 22, 198.

but are eventually swallowed by awe and wonder at the Truth, Beauty, and Goodness in which we live and move and have our being.

HUMBLED BY REALITY

Second, while Ransom does absorb this older vision of the cosmos via "sweet influence," it would be a mistake to view the spiritual effect as automatic. After all, Weston and Devine journey through the same Heavens as Ransom and are subject to the same influence, but without receiving the spiritual benefit. Which brings me to the second factor we ought to consider in Ransom's education—the role of humility. Put simply, Ransom is willing to be instructed by reality, to allow his misconceptions about the cosmos and Malacandra and its inhabitants to be corrected.

For example, we're told that Ransom's imagination led him "to expect nothing on a strange planet except rocky desolation or else a network of nightmare machines."[16] Ransom's mind has been shaped by what Lewis elsewhere calls the Scientific Outlook or "Wellsianity" (after H. G. Wells).[17] Its features include an inhospitable Darwinian cosmos, "nature red in tooth and claw," and extraterrestrials that look upon humans the way that we look upon insects. Because of his tacit embrace of the Wellsian vision, Ransom is surprised when he discovers that Malacandra is in fact beautiful, a possibility that never entered into his

---

16. Lewis, *Out of the Silent Planet*, ch. 7, 48.

17. C. S. Lewis, "The Funeral of a Great Myth" in *Christian Reflections* (New York: HarperOne, 2014), 82–93, and "Is Theology Poetry?" in *The Weight of Glory: And Other Addresses* (New York: HarperOne, 2001), 118–40.

speculations about it. But despite his false expectations, Ransom allows reality to reshape his vision, to open his mind to possibilities previously undreamed of.

Ransom again demonstrates humility, as his initial impressions of the primitive society of the *hrossa* give way to a recognition that their knowledge far exceeds his expectations. Not only do they have scientific knowledge of planets and space, but they even instruct Ransom in religion, giving him "a sort of *hrossian* equivalent of the shorter catechism."[18] While Ransom is surprised by this instruction (and indeed, perhaps a little annoyed at times), he nevertheless receives it with humility, attempting to incorporate his newfound knowledge of *hnau* (rational species), *eldila* (angels), and Oyarsa (the presiding angel of a planet) into his existing understanding of the world. His humility contrasts sharply with Weston and Devine, who insist on regarding the inhabitants of Malacandra as primitive, superstitious, and only slightly more intelligent than beasts.

As the chains of the Scientific Outlook slowly fall off of Ransom's imagination, he continues to grow in wisdom, particularly the wisdom of facing both pleasure and death. While making preparations for a hunt, Ransom's conversation with Hyoi turns to the question of sex, love, and procreation. Ransom is surprised to learn that the *hrossa* are naturally continent and monogamous, making love for only a few years of their lives and only with one mate. While lovemaking is as pleasurable to them as it is for humans, the *hrossa* do not insist on gratifying their desires with the same reckless abandon as fallen humans.

---

18. Lewis, *Out of the Silent Planet*, ch. 11, 83.

Instead, a *hross* is content to look for a mate, court her, then beget young, rear them, and then to remember all of it such that it boils inside him and he makes it into poems and wisdom. Puzzled, Ransom asks, "But the pleasure he must be content only to remember?" Hyoi responds:

> A pleasure is full grown only when it is remembered. You are speaking, *Hmān*, as if the pleasure were one thing and the memory another. It is all one thing.… What you call remembering is the last part of the pleasure, as the *crah* is the last part of a poem. When you and I met, the meeting was over very shortly, it was nothing. Now it is growing something as we remember it. But still we know very little about it. What it will be when I remember it as I lie down to die, what it makes in me all my days till then—that is the real meeting. The other is only the beginning of it. You say you have poets in your world. Do they not teach you this?[19]

The incessant demand for a pleasure, what Lewis elsewhere calls the desire for "Encore," is something that must be resisted and mastered in order to enable the fullness of life. As Hyoi says, "how could we endure to live and let time pass if we were always crying for one day or one year to come back—if we did not know that every day in a life fills the whole life with expectation and memory and that

---

19. Lewis, *Out of the Silent Planet*, ch. 12, 89–90.

these *are* that day?"[20] Here again is a form of fear—the fear of missing out, of passing time, of loss of joy.

Ransom then asks about the *hnakra*, the carnivorous aquatic beast that lives in the Malacandrian waters. Hyoi acknowledges that the *hnakra* does sometimes kill *hrossa*. But a few deaths roving the world does not make a *hnau* miserable:

> "I do not think the forest would be so bright, nor the water so warm, nor love so sweet, if there were no danger in the lakes. I will tell you a day in my life that has shaped me; such a day as comes only once, like love, or serving Oyarsa in Meldilorn. Then I was young, not much more than a cub, when I went far, far up the handramit to the land where stars shine at midday and even water is cold. A great waterfall I climbed. I stood on the shore of Balki the pool, which is the place of most awe in all worlds. The walls of it go up for ever and ever and huge and holy images are cut in them, the work of old times. There is the fall called the Mountain of Water. Because I have stood there alone, Maleldil and I, for even Oyarsa sent me no word, my heart has been higher, my song deeper, all my days. But do you think it would have been so unless I had known that in Balki hnéraki dwelled? There I drank life because death was in the pool. That was the best of drinks save one."

---

20. Lewis, *Out of the Silent Planet*, ch. 12, 91–92. Emphasis added.

"What one?" asked Ransom.

"Death itself in the day I drink it and go to Maleldil."[21]

Not only do the *hrossa* not lust for pleasure, they also do not fear death. Instead, danger and the prospect of death make life sweeter. In fact, we discover in the epilogue that, except for the few whom the *hnakra* gets, no *hross* dies before his time. Death is as predictable as birth, and because their corpses are "unbodied" by Oyarsa and they do not doubt their immortality, "Death is not preceded by dread nor followed by corruption."[22]

This courage in the face of death was taught them by Oyarsa. Long ago, the Bent Eldil of Thulcandra assaulted Malacandra, bringing cold death such that nothing could live on the surface of the planet. With Oyarsa's help, the *sorns* and *hrossa* and *pfifltriggi* dug the *handramits,* the canals and seabeds in which they all live. But the real threat to the Malacandrians was not from the cold death, but from the temptations placed in their minds by the Bent One. The Bent One appealed to their fear and sought to make them as humans are now—"wise enough to see the death of their kind approaching but not wise enough to endure it."[23] But Oyarsa cured them, and they left fear behind them, and with fear, murder and rebellion. Even

---

21. Lewis, *Out of the Silent Planet*, ch. 12, 92–93.

22. Lewis, *Out of the Silent Planet*, Postscript, 205.

23. Lewis, *Out of the Silent Planet*, ch. 20, 179.

the weakest do not fear death, and because they embrace the ways of Maleldil, they have peace.[24]

BENT COURAGE

But Ransom's new perspective on reality is not sufficient alone to conquer his fears. His imaginative reorientation must be accompanied by action, by concrete acts of duty in the face of fluctuating fear. Throughout the novel, we witness Ransom overcome his timidity, his reluctances, and his fear through a sense of duty and presence of mind. When he second-guesses his decision to seek out Harry at the Rise (out of a sense of potential embarrassment), the fact that "he had committed himself to a troublesome duty on behalf of the old woman" overcomes his fear of looking like a fool.[25] When madness threatens to overtake him in his flight from the *sorns*, "he applied himself vigorously to his devotions and his toilet."[26] Ransom is forced to learn to endure temporary delusions. Rather than seeking to suppress and remove the delusions (which would likely only enflame them), he learns "to stand still mentally, as it were, and let them roll over his mind."[27] Fear, it seems, is a wave that must be endured.

But the importance of duty and resolution really comes into focus in his final journey to Oyarsa. In many ways, this journey is the culmination of Ransom's education in courage. To understand why, we must first grasp

---

24. Lewis, *Out of the Silent Planet* ch. 20, 179.

25. Lewis, *Out of the Silent Planet*, ch. 1, 5.

26. Lewis, *Out of the Silent Planet*, ch. 9, 59–60.

27. Lewis, *Out of the Silent Planet*, ch. 9, 60.

the importance of an oft-misunderstood episode in the book—Ransom's participation in the *hnakra* hunt. The events are relatively straightforward: Ransom is given a place of honor with Hyoi and Whin in one of the forward boats. As they search for the *hnakra*, an *eldil* comes to them with a message: Ransom should go to Oyarsa. Ransom, "in obedience to something like conscience," wants to kill the *hnakra* first. Just then, the *hnakra* appears and the hunt is on. After a brief but intense battle, the *hnakra* is killed and the three embrace one another on the shore. But the celebration is cut short by a rifle blast as Hyoi is killed by Weston and Divine. After a brief discussion, Whin sends Ransom on his way to Oyarsa.

What is often highlighted in this episode is Ransom's courage. Before the hunt, afraid that his fear will get the best of him, Ransom resolves to be courageous, to "show that the human species also were *hnau*."[28] This resolution is attributed to "something in the air he now breathed, or in the society of the *hrossa*." Like the sweet influence of the Heavens in the space ship, the air of Malacandra and his friendship with the *hrossa* have begun to work the martial spirit into him. "Something long sleeping in the blood" awakes in Ransom.[29] And, of course, the success of the hunt solidifies Ransom's place among his courageous companions: "He was one with them.... They were all *hnau*. They had stood shoulder to shoulder in the face of an enemy, and the shapes of their heads no longer mattered.

---

28. Lewis, *Out of the Silent Planet*, ch. 13, 96.

29. Lewis, *Out of the Silent Planet*, ch. 13, 97.

And he, even Ransom, had come through it and not been disgraced. He had grown up."[30]

So far, so good. But what is frequently missed in this episode is that Ransom's courage, while genuine, is also tainted. It is, to use the language of the story, a *bent* courage. Courage, like many virtues, can go wrong in two opposite ways. The obvious way is by deficiency, what we call cowardice. But the less obvious is by excess, what we often call recklessness or daring. And in overcoming the former, Ransom succumbs to the latter.

The key element is the command of the *eldil*. Here is the full message:

> "It is the Man with you, Hyoi," said the voice. "He ought not to be there. He ought to be going to Oyarsa. Bent *hnau* of his own kind from Thulcandra are following him; he should go to Oyarsa. If they find him anywhere else there will be evil."[31]

In response to this message, Hyoi and Whin move to immediately obey, giving up their share in the hunt. But Ransom resists. Some part of him "urged him to hold on to his new-found manhood; now or never—with such companions or with none—he must leave a deed on his memory, instead of one more broken dream."[32] What had earlier awoken in Ransom was not merely courage, but a

---

30. Lewis, *Out of the Silent Planet*, ch. 13, 100.

31. Lewis, *Out of the Silent Planet*, ch. 13, 98.

32. Lewis, *Out of the Silent Planet*, ch. 13, 99.

desire for glory, a dream that "the fame of *Hman hnakrapunt* might be handed down to posterity in this world that knew no other man."[33] It was not conscience that held Ransom to the hunt, but something like it.[34] And in obeying this bent conscience-like dictate, Ransom disobeys Oyarsa, and above him, Maleldil, and the result is that death and evil befalls his friend, just as the *eldil* had warned. In other words, delayed obedience is disobedience.

Hyoi's death unleashes a torrent of grief and shame in Ransom. He blames himself and offers to turn himself over to Weston and Devine in order to avoid further evil. But Whin sees through to the true problem. "I have been thinking. All this has come from not obeying the *eldil*. He said you were to go to Oyarsa. You ought to have been already on the road."[35] Again, courage, like all virtues, must first be obedient.

Ransom again resists, this time out of fear of his reputation among the *hrossa*: " Your people will think I have run away because I am afraid to look in their faces after Hyoi's death."[36] But Whin again sees the issue clearly. "It is not a question of thinking but of what an *eldil* says. This is cubs' talk. Now listen, and I will teach you the

---

33. Lewis, *Out of the Silent Planet*, ch. 13, 97.

34. We can liken this to how, in *Perelandra*, it is something like reason—a "spurious rationalism"—that suggests to Ransom that he should immediately taste the ecstasy-inducing gourd he has just discovered, even though he is now entirely sated. Ransom intuits that this apparently reasonable suggest is in fact not so (C. S. Lewis, *Perelandra*, (London: Harper Collins, 2005), ch. 3, 46-47.

35. Lewis, *Out of the Silent Planet*, ch. 13, 103.

36. Lewis, *Out of the Silent Planet*, ch. 13, 102.

way." Though Ransom felt that in killing the *hnakra*, he had grown up, he was still speaking "cubs' talk." Courage must be subordinated to a higher standard—a lesson that Ransom learns the hard way.

DUTY IN THE FACE OF CHANGING MOODS

And so Ransom begins his journey to Oyarsa, repressing whining impulses of regret and self-accusation as well as irrational instincts to give himself up to Weston and Devine. For Ransom has a new sense of purpose. Having seen the tragedy wrought by reliance on his own judgment, he makes "a strong resolution, defying in advance all changes of mood," and purposes to complete the journey to Meldilorn. And the mood changes come quickly. The first is the reminder that he is "now walking of his own free will into the very trap that he had been trying to avoid since his arrival on Malacandra."[37]

The second mood change is the reassertion of "the old terrestrial fears of some alien, cold intelligence, super-human in power, sub-human in cruelty."[38] Having lived with the *hrossa* and learned their view of the cosmos, he contemplates "a strange but not inconceivable world; heroism and poetry at the bottom, cold scientific intellect above it, and overtopping all, some dark superstition which scientific intellect, helpless against the revenge of the emotional depths it had ignored, had neither will nor power to remove."[39]

---

37. Lewis, *Out of the Silent Planet*, ch. 14, 106.

38. Lewis, *Out of the Silent Planet*, ch. 14, 106.

39. Lewis, *Out of the Silent Planet*, ch. 14, 106–7.

Lying behind this statement are two distinct cosmic visions. The first and most obvious is the specter of H. G. Wells. The Wellsian vision had augmented Ransom's original fears of the *sorns* and had driven his thirst to understand the social structures of Malacandra and the three races that inhabit it. By virtue of his imaginative training (via Wells and others), Ransom had associated "superhuman intelligence with monstrosity of form and ruthlessness of will." Thus, throughout his time with the *hrossa*, he had been at great pains to deduce whether the *hrossa* rule the *sorns* or the *sorns* rule the *hrossa*. Ransom even alludes to Wells's *Time Machine*, a story in which in the future the human race divides into two species—the carnivorous Morlocks and the innocent Eloi they raise as their food supply.[40] At one point, Ransom had ominously suspected that the *sorns* might be doing the same with the *hrossa*.[41] It is this fear that recurs now on his journey to Meldilorn. While it was impossible to imagine Hyoi, Whin, and the *hrossa* worshiping at a blood-stained idol, it was conceivable that "the *hrossa* were under the thumb of the *sorns*, superior to their masters in all the qualities that human beings value, but intellectually inferior to them and dependent on them."[42]

But in addition to the Wellsian foil, Lewis is also improvising on Plato, taking up and transposing the ideal

---

40. H.G. Wells, *The Time Machine* (New York: Bantam Classics, 1984).

41. Lewis, *Out of the Silent Planet*, ch. 10, 70.

42. Lewis, *Out of the Silent Planet*, ch. 14, 106.

Socratic social order as set forth in *The Republic*.⁴³ In that work, an adversarial debate about the meaning of justice becomes a tense but friendly discussion of the same theme through an act of imagination—the exploration of the ideal city of justice. Through his conversation with Glaucon and Adeimantus, Socrates sets forth a three-tiered city, consisting of philosopher-kings ruling the lower artisan classes through the warrior-guardians in the middle tier. It's not difficult to see the Wellsian Morlocks and Eloi as a Darwinian distortion of this Socratic ideal city.

But more importantly, the Malacandrian social order itself bears a striking resemblance to Plato's city. The matriarchal *pfifltriggi*, digging gold and silver out of the earth and crafting marvelous works in stone, correspond to the Socratic artisan class. The *hrossa*—poets and warriors hunting *hnakra* and raising crops—correspond to the Socratic guardians. The *sorns*, with their systematic scientific inquiry and knowledge of the cosmos and ways of Maleldil, are clearly the counterpart to the Socratic philosopher-kings. Or at least, almost. For the Malacandrian social order is not a hierarchy of *sorns* over *hrossa* over *pfifltriggi*, as in

---

43. Plato, *The Republic* (New York: Basic Books, 2016). Lewis even leaves a little Socratic Easter Egg when Ransom arrives at the cave of Augray: "The light within was an unsteady one and a delicious wave of warmth smote on his face. It was firelight. He came into the mouth of the cave and then, unsteadily, round the fire and into the interior, and stood still blinking in the light. When at last he could see, he discerned a smooth chamber of green rock, very lofty. There were two things in it. One of them, dancing on the wall and roof, was the huge, angular shadow of a *sorn*: the other, crouched beneath it, was the *sorn* himself" (Lewis, *Out of the Silent Planet*, ch. 14, 111–12). This is a clear allusion to Socrates' Allegory of the Cave, complete with firelight, distorted shadows on the wall, and the real things themselves.

Plato, but instead three distinct unfallen species, each with its own distinct traits, preferences, and vocations, all living in submission to Oyarsa, and through him, to Maleldil. Thus, Ransom finds himself repeatedly frustrated in attempting to overlay the Malacandrian social order onto his terrestrial expectations, whether Wellsian or Socratic.

FROM PEDESTRIAN TO PILGRIM

Which brings us back to Ransom and his change of moods. Having lived among the *hrossa* and imbibed the martial spirit, and having been chastened by his failure to immediately obey the *eldil*, Ransom finds his whole outlook changed. He looks back upon his initial time on Malacandra as

> a nightmare, on his own mood at that time as a sort of sickness. Then all had been whimpering, unanalysed, self-nourishing, self-consuming dismay. Now, in the clear light of an accepted duty, he felt fear indeed, but with it a sober sense of confidence in himself and in the world, and even an element of pleasure. It was the difference between a landsman in a sinking ship and a horseman on a bolting horse: either may be killed, but the horseman is an agent as well as a patient.[44]

This sense of duty and resolution steels Ransom on his journey up into the thin air of the Malacandrian *harandra*,

---

44. Lewis, *Out of the Silent Planet*, ch. 14, 107.

where lack of oxygen plays tricks on his mind and his imagination again becomes unruly.

In fact, this journey into unknown danger, undertaken from a sense of clear duty, is where Ransom's story has been building all along. He is no longer a Pedestrian, wandering the hillsides of England; he is a Pilgrim, his face set toward the Malacandrian Jerusalem. He is no longer merely a Patient, tossed about by circumstances and the whims of others. He is an Agent, willing himself forward in the face of changing moods and passions and fears.

And here again we see Lewis transposing Plato into a Christian key. For the ideal city in Plato's *Republic* is an impossibility; Socrates says as much. But it is also a macrocosm of the human soul, enabling us to more clearly see the virtues of temperance, courage, wisdom, and justice. As Lewis notes in *The Abolition of Man*:

> We were told it all long ago by Plato. As the king governs by his executive, so Reason in man must rule the mere appetites by means of the 'spirited element'. The head rules the belly through the chest—the seat, as Alanus tells us, of Magnanimity, of emotions organized by trained habit into stable sentiments. The Chest-Magnanimity-Sentiment—these are the indispensable liaison officers between cerebral man and visceral man. It may even be said that it is by this middle element that man is man: for by his intellect he is mere spirit and by his appetite mere animal.[45]

---

45. C. S. Lewis, *The Abolition of Man* (New York: HarperOne, 2001), 24–25.

So also, Ransom's journey to Mars has restored to him his Chest. His time among the *hrossa*, his frustrated musings on Malacandrian social order, his successes and failures along the way—all of them have worked together to train his emotions and to make him into a true Man, a true *hnau*. As Oyarsa tells him, "You are guilty of no evil, Ransom of Thulcandra, except a little fearfulness. For that, the journey you go on is your pain, and perhaps your cure: for you must be either mad or brave before it is ended."[46] Ransom has taken the first step on his journey from Pedestrian to Pendragon.

And perhaps, if Lewis has been successful, so have we the readers. As Ransom says to Oyarsa, "Bent creatures are full of fears," and the modern world is as disorienting as any journey to another planet might be.[47] Like Ransom, we too often cannot see because we don't know what we're looking at. Our imaginations have also been trained by dark myths and enchantments that deceive us into reducing all of reality into its material components and thereby denying the supernatural, and with it, all Truth, Goodness, and Beauty.

Lewis's aim in the Ransom Trilogy is to give us "sweet influence" from other centuries, to feed our imaginations with an older, truer, and richer vision of reality, if we will but be instructed by it. And so, like Ransom, we too must cultivate awe at the world, allowing human wonder to fuel the quest for Christian wisdom. We must humble ourselves before reality itself and become like cubs, willing to

---

46. Lewis, *Out of the Silent Planet*, ch. 21, 183.

47. Lewis, *Out of the Silent Planet*, ch. 18, 156.

be imaginatively catechized and instructed by the Christian tradition. And we must take up the yoke of immediate and complete obedience to God as he has revealed himself to us in the Scriptures. For the fundamental lesson of Ransom's journey in *Out of the Silent Planet* is the same as that of Ecclesiastes. "The end of the matter; all has been heard. Fear God and keep his commandments, for this is the whole duty of man" (Ecclesiastes 12:13).

Indeed. And we take up this duty in light of the wonders that Ransom tells Oyarsa, the great and terrible things that Maleldil has dared in wrestling with the Bent One in Thulcandra. For the things into which *eldila* long to look have been revealed to the saints, and Maleldil the Young is indeed Lord of the Silent Planet.

III

MEN ARE FROM MARS:
MASCULINITY IN *OUT OF THE SILENT PLANET*

Colin Smothers

C. S. Lewis wrote his Ransom Trilogy amid a flurry of literary excitement surrounding scientific advancement in planetary observation, particularly the planet Mars. This excitement had already inspired works like H. G. Wells's *War of the Worlds* (1898) and Edgar Rice Burroughs's *A Princess of Mars* (1911). But Lewis, ever the old soul, did not write *Out of the Silent Planet* and its sequels to stoke futurism or float novel scientific theories. Just the opposite, in fact. Lewis chose the planetary settings of Mars, and subsequently Venus and Earth, to remind the world of fundamental—even forgotten—truths about human nature, masculinity, femininity, and marriage that he saw eroding in the early 1940s.

Ever since mankind has scientifically observed the night sky, the planets have captivated our curiosity. Ancient civilizations catalogued five planets visible to the naked eye that we know today as Mercury, Venus, Mars, Jupiter, and Saturn. Compared to the relative fixedness of the stars, the appearance and mobility of the planets (literally the "wanderers," *planetes* in Greek) inspired speculation about their essence, particularly how their movement and nature might relate to people and events on earth. These speculations gave birth to mythologies built on the "sympathies, antipathies, and strivings"[1] of each planet, which were numbered alongside the sun and the moon to bring the number of "wanderers" to seven. As Lewis argues in *The Discarded Image*, the character of these seven "planets" deeply influenced the medieval imagination. And as Michael Ward has demonstrated in his seminal *Planet Narnia*, this medieval cosmology loomed large in Lewis's own mind, providing him with rich soil in which to cultivate a compelling exposition of mankind's gendered existence.

MEN ARE FROM MARS, WOMEN ARE FROM VENUS

One of the besetting sins Lewis observed and frequently addressed in his writing was the slow yet steady push toward androgyny and male-female interchangeability, a trend that has only accelerated since. Lewis understood that a society's failure to maintain and celebrate distinctions in the sexes paves the way for civilizational collapse.[2]

---

1. C. S. Lewis, *The Discarded Image* (Cambridge: Cambridge University Press, 2013), 92: "In medieval science the fundamental concept was that of certain sympathies, antipathies, and strivings inherent in matter itself."

2. A strange bedfellow making this same point decades later is femi-

Lewis addressed this theme, for instance, in his essay "Priestesses in the Church," where he opposed those in the Church of England who were pushing for female ordination. Lewis understood that the insistence that equality between the sexes means their interchangeability was nothing short of a revolution.[3] Mankind has always acknowledged and respected the implications of male-female difference, and Lewis knew that if the revolutionaries had their way, their efforts would indelibly compromise bedrock institutions like the church and family.

Similar thoughts are found in *The Pilgrim's Regress*, Lewis's allegory of his own intellectual pilgrimage to the faith. Toward the beginning of his journey, John, Lewis's protagonist and *locum tenens*, finds himself in Eschropolis, literally the "city of filth and obscenity." In this city, "the girls had short hair and flat breasts and flat buttocks so that they looked like boys: but the boys had pale, egg-shaped faces and slender waists and big hips so that they looked like girls."[4] Eschropolis is a decadent place full of disillu-

---

nist Camille Paglia, whose 1990 Yale dissertation-turned-book *Sexual Personae: Art and Decadence from Nefertiti to Emily Dickinson* examined historical movements toward androgyny. At a Battle of Ideas forum, she gave a talk, "Lesson from History: Transgender Mania is Sign of Cultural Collapse," in which she made this point: "The movement towards androgyny occurs in late phases of culture, as a civilization is starting to unravel. You can find it again and again and again through history."

3. For a more in-depth treatment, see Colin J. Smothers, "The Fallacy of Interchangeability," *Eikon* 1, no. 1 (Spring 2019): 8–14, https://cbmw.org/2019/06/05/the-fallacy-of-interchangeability/.

4. C. S. Lewis, *The Pilgrim's Regress* (Grand Rapids: Eerdmans, 2014), 41.

sioned ne'er-do-wells who have sworn off beauty and even reality itself, including the reality of their own sex. When John flees from this place in disgust, he is pelted with feces and called after derisively, "Puritanian!"

At one level, I think this is how we should read Lewis's Ransom Trilogy: as an aid to escaping ugly Eschropolis and embracing the distinctive goods of masculinity, femininity, and matrimony. To do so, the reader must go on a journey like John's with another of Lewis's protagonists, Ransom. The first stop, and the subject of the rest of this chapter, is masculine Mars.

THE MARTIAN *PATHOS*

It would be hard to overstate the importance of the setting for *Out of the Silent Planet*. If the reader fails to grasp the connection between the *where* of the main action (the planet Malacandra, or Mars), and the *what* of one of the book's major themes (masculinity), he will miss much. It will help, then, to be acquainted with not just the *mythos* of Mars—this is what most people think of as Greek or Roman mythology—but also its historic *pathos*.[5]

The ancient Greeks called the red planet Ares, son of Zeus and god of war and courage. We follow the Romans in calling it Mars, son of Jupiter and the god of war and

---

5. Lewis encourages the reader to connect the Martian setting with Roman mythology near the end of *Out of the Silent Planet*. When Ransom finally comes to understand that he has been on the planet he knows as Mars, it is through an alien depiction of their solar system that demonstrates a shared understanding of the planets' characters: "their mythology, like ours, associates some idea of the female with Venus" (C. S. Lewis, *Out of the Silent Planet* [London: HarperCollins, 2005], ch. 17, 141).

agriculture. Legend had it that Romulus and Remus were sons of Mars, and their warlike and agricultural personalities characterized early Roman society (or vice versa). Mars was often represented by a spear and shield and associated with iron. The Medievals assigned a planetary symbol to Mars: a circle with an arrow, representing a spear, at an erect, forty-five-degree angle—today the universal symbol for the male sex.

Lewis elaborates on the *pathos* of Mars in *The Discarded Image:* "Mars makes iron. He gives men the martial temperament, 'sturdy hardiness,' as the Wife of Bath calls it. But he is a bad planet, *Infortuna Minor*. He causes wars."[6] Today, our word "martial" is used most often in this latter sense, synonymous with "warlike." But when Lewis evokes the Martian *pathos* in *Out of the Silent Planet*, warlikeness is only one aspect. "Martianity," as Lewis calls it, goes much deeper—and it has everything to do with masculinity.[7] To immerse oneself in the former is to inspire and inform—in fact, even to form—the latter.

Lewis's poem "The Planets" is evocative in this regard. Lewis personifies Mars as a brash and happy mercenary, suggesting that the martial spirit is morally neutral, able to fight for good *or* evil. Here we have already uncovered a healthier approach to the current discourse around masculinity: the problem of so-called "toxic masculinity" is not masculinity itself, but to what end it is deployed. This tempers Lewis's description of Mars as a "bad planet" in

---

6. Lewis, *The Discarded Image*, 106.

7. C. S. Lewis, Letter to Arthur C. Clark, January 20, 1954; cited in Ward, *Planet Narnia*, 80.

The Discarded Image. As Michael Ward has noted, sin can warp the martial virtues into vices like "cruelty, trouble, haughtiness, gracelessness, mercenariness, insolence, coldness."[8] But this isn't to discard the martial virtues. They are encouraged through "Martianity." We have already mentioned "sturdy hardiness." This martial temperament fortifies a myriad of virtues, including "righting wrongs, rescuing the meek, laughter, beauty, keenness, blitheness, happiness, achievement, courage, strength."[9] In *Out of the Silent Planet*, Lewis aims to re-catechize his readers through the *mythos* and *pathos* of virtuous—and, just as importantly, vicious—masculinity.

MALACANDRA ON MASCULINITY

In *Out of the Silent Planet*, Ransom, a Cambridge don, is kidnapped to Mars, known by its inhabitants as Malacandra. His kidnappers, Weston and Devine, intend to hand Ransom over to the Martians for their own gain. Weston embodies masculine vice in his megalomaniacal quest of scientific inquiry and advancement, no matter who or what stands in his way. Devine is a partner in crime, out for the Martian gold—"sun's blood"—that occurs on the planet in the abundance.

On their journey, Ransom resolves to escape. On board the spacecraft, he grabs a knife—a martial "spear"—to carry in concealment. Lewis intends a foreshadowing here: Martian proximity will transform Ransom. Like Lewis himself, Ransom was a veteran of the Great War,

---

8. Ward, *Planet Narnia*, 78.

9. Ward, *Planet Narnia*, 78.

but he had since grown accustomed to a life of books and ease. Yet fear awakens in Ransom a "bellicose mood" as he comes to grips with his own agency: "the knife could pierce other flesh as well as his own."[10] He resolves to eschew passivity, breaking away from Weston and Devine and fleeing into the Martian wilderness, where he spends nearly the whole rest of the book.

Martial Terrain

Lewis describes Malacandra in terms that rather unsubtly evoke masculinity. Aside from the stony landscape suggesting "sturdy hardiness," Ransom notices the waves, which remind him of "water that he had seen shooting up under the impact of shells in pictures of naval battles," because they are "too high for their length, too narrow at the base, too steep in the sides" and look like "turreted walls."[11] The terrain is "too jagged and irregular for buildings, too thin and steep for mountains," "with needling shapes of pale green, thousands of feet high"—a theme repeated even in the hills, which were "too narrow, too pointed at the top and too small at the base." He sees tree-like vegetation that looks like a "clump of organ-pipes" with stalks that "rose smooth and round, and surprisingly thin, for about forty feet: above that, the huge plants opened into a sheaf-like development."[12]

---

10. Lewis, *Out of the Silent Planet*, ch. 6, 41.

11. Lewis, *Out of the Silent Planet*, ch. 7, 49.

12. Lewis, *Out of the Silent Planet*, ch. 7, 50.

Across the Malacandrian landscape, Ransom notices "perpendicularity—the same rush to the sky."[13] Lewis returns to this theme frequently. Ransom perceives the mountains in a way that Lewis describes as intentionally phallic: "Some ended in points that looked from where he stood as sharp as needles, while others, after narrowing towards the summit, expanded again into knobs or platforms."[14] Early on, Lewis allows Ransom to digest this theme for the reader:

> Here, [Ransom] understood, was the full statement of that *perpendicular* theme which beast and plant and earth all played on Malacandra— here in this riot of rock, leaping and surging skyward like solid jets from some rock-fountain, and hanging by their own lightness in the air, so shaped, so elongated, that all terrestrial mountains must ever after seem to him to be mountains lying on their sides. He felt a lift and lightening at the heart.[15]

The Martian landscape is full of sharp lines and perpendicularity that draw one upwards and out of oneself. Lewis does not intend to convey something base to draw sniggers, but to imbue the atmosphere with a distinctly masculine feel. The leaping and surging landscape corresponds to the inherent "externality" of masculinity.

---

13. Lewis, *Out of the Silent Planet*, ch. 8, 55.

14. Lewis, *Out of the Silent Planet*, ch. 9, 61.

15. Lewis, *Out of the Silent Planet*, ch. 9, 62.

Martial Inhabitants

Malacandra's inhabitants likewise evoke the martial spirit. During his sojourn, Ransom encounters three rational species (*hnau*) on Malacandra, each embodying some aspect of traditional masculine vocation. The *sorns* are tall, lean creatures who live as shepherd-philosophers in caves in the highest livable climes. The *hrossa* are otter-like creatures who live as warrior-poets and hunter-farmers in the warmer valleys by the lakes and streams. Ransom spends the most time with the *hrossa*, experiencing his greatest martial transformation amongst them. He spends the least amount of time with the third species, the *pfifltriggi*, who live in the mountains as miners and metalworking craftsmen. In these rational creatures of Malacandra, Ransom encounters leadership, protection, and provision—the essence of traditional masculine vocation. Here is "Martianity": it is much more than war; it is "sturdy hardiness" applied to culture-making.

MARTIANITY AND MASCULINITY

Masculinity is notoriously difficult to define,[16] partly because one can truly appreciate masculinity only alongside

---

16. G. K. Chesterton insists that words that are hard to define are not necessarily vague or unimportant, but perhaps some of the most important words we use: "Much of our modern difficulty, in religion and other things, arises merely from this: that we confuse the word 'indefinable' with the word 'vague.' If someone speaks of a spiritual fact as 'indefinable' we promptly picture something misty, a cloud with indeterminate edges. But this is an error even in commonplace logic. The thing that cannot be defined is the first thing; the primary fact.... The indefinable is the indisputable.... There are popular expressions which everyone uses and no one can explain; which the wise man will accept and reverence, as he reverences desire or darkness

its complement, femininity. To fully know the meaning of masculine, one must have a concept of feminine. To know "hard," one must be able to comprehend "soft." How can "day" be understood without "night"? "Land" without "sea"? It is no accident that we arrive at the roots of the created order, "male and female he created them," after the pattern of the rest of creation—heaven and earth, sun and moon, land and sea, masculine and feminine.

Lewis reflects on the elusive yet profound meanings of masculinity and femininity in the center of this trilogy, at the end of *Perelandra*, when Ransom encounters the two *Oyéresu* of the planets so far visited. These spiritual guardians emblemize Mars and Venus, masculinity and femininity, respectively. But as spirits, they are not male and female, which means their masculinity and femininity are owing to some other, deeper channel, which is hard for Ransom to put his finger on:

---

or any elemental thing. The prigs of the debating club will demand that he should define his terms. And, being a wise man, he will flatly refuse. This first inexplicable term is the most important term of all. The word that has no definition is the word that has no substitute. If a man falls back again and again on some such word as 'vulgar' or 'manly,' do not suppose that the word means nothing because he cannot say what it means." G. K. Chesterton, *Charles Dickens* (Cornwall: House of Stratus, 2001), 1. Ransom himself experiences something similar when later attempting to describe his voyage to Venus, which Lewis (the narrator) says must be "rather too vague ... to put into words." Ransom replies, "On the contrary, it is words that are vague. The reason why the thing can't be expressed is that it's too definite for language" (C. S. Lewis, *Perelandra* [London: HarperCollins, 2005], ch. 3, 33).

> He has said that Malacandra was like rhythm and Perelandra like melody. He has said that Malacandra affected him like a quantitative, Perelandra like an accentual, metre. He thinks that the first held in his hand something like a spear, but the hands of the other were open, with the palms towards him.[17]

Rhythm and melody. Prominence and receptivity. Impressions, yes, but impressions that run deep to the very grooves of the created order—indeed, for Lewis, deeper even than maleness and femaleness.

An exact definition of masculinity is elusive for another reason: masculinity is not self-referential. It is outwardly directed. It must be productive, active, oriented to something other than itself for it to bear fruit and to experience meaningful consummation. Returning to the essence of traditional masculine vocation, leadership is meaningful only in relation to those led, protection to those protected, provision in relation to those provided for. Lewis takes this concept one step further by allowing the various species on Malacandra to intertwine in a harmonious way, demonstrating this others-directedness: the *sorns* keep books and records for the *hrossa* and invent beneficial instruments useful to all, the *hrossa* permit the *sorn* shepherds to graze their flocks in their fields, and the *pfifltriggi* provide resources and craftsmanship for the *sorn* inventions.

Lewis touches on this theme of outwardness in relation to masculinity in his book *Mere Christianity* when he

---

17. C. S. Lewis, *Perelandra*, ch. 16, 253.

discusses headship in marriage. Even back in the 1950s, when his radio broadcasts were organized for publication, Lewis acknowledged the unpopularity of the Christian teaching of male headship in marriage.[18] (This fact alone should cause us to consider his intentionality in including this unpopular teaching, nevertheless, in his account of a *mere* Christianity). In defense of the historic Christian doctrine on marriage, Lewis anticipates two questions: Why does there need to be a "head" in marriage instead of pure equality? And why does it have to be the man?

His first answer gets to the nature of the one-flesh union and the necessity of husband and wife staying together—the necessity of permanence—even in the face of deep disagreement. If there are two heads in a marriage, and not one, inevitably there will arise two directions that tend to pull the marriage apart. (And we wonder why our egalitarian age, which ridicules headship, is riddled with divorce!)

But when answering the second question as to why the man must be the head and not the woman, Lewis calls the arrangement "unnatural" when wives rule over their husbands. Why is it unnatural? Lewis writes, "The relations of the family to the outer world—what might be called its foreign policy—must depend, in the last resort, upon the man, because he always ought to be, and usually

---

18. "So much for the Christian doctrine about the permeance of marriage. Something else, even more unpopular, remains to be dealt with. Christian wives promise to obey their husbands. In Christian marriage the man is said to be the 'head.' " C. S. Lewis, *Mere Christianity* (London: William Collins, 2016), 112.

is, much more just to outsiders."[19] In this, we see Lewis reflecting, probably both consciously and subconsciously, on the connection between masculinity, manhood, and outwardness, as compared to the inwardness of femininity. This difference is rooted in the very nature of the sexes, which can be observed both biologically and temperamentally, and how this difference is expressed linguistically. Consider how our bodies are differently organized for sexual reproduction. Men reproduce externally, women internally. The Designer is not arbitrary. God creates the man from the ground to work and keep the ground; he builds the woman from the side of the man to help the man and to "house" future men and women. Externality and internality are not accidental to male and female. Form and function are mutually illuminating: even the sexless *Oyarsa* that Ransom sees on Perelandra exhibit forms that hint at their differences—Malacandra wielding a spear, and Perelandra with open palms.[20] Prominence and receptivity, respectively.

The masculine "sturdy hardiness," this "prominence," after all, is *for* something other than itself. Masculinity is *for* femininity, and vice versa. Masculinity is outwardly di-

---

19. Lewis, *Mere Christianity*, 113–14.

20. I think this inward-outward paradigm helps makes sense of Paul's instruction to Titus when he tells him to command the older women to teach the younger women to be "working at home" (Titus 2:5). Christians historically have not seen this as an absolute command—see, for instance, the Proverbs 31 woman—but instead speaks to the callings and giftings, indeed the posture, of the wife *vis-à-vis* her husband, whose vocational orientation is naturally more outward as related to the home.

rected *for* something. It is the arrow aimed in a particular direction with a particular purpose.

MASCULINITY ON MALACANDRA

It is his encounter with all the above—the Martian atmosphere and inhabitants—that prompts Ransom's transformation into a martial man. At times the transformation is subtle, like when Ransom first arms himself on the ship, or when he first drinks from the Martian stream and is "steadied" against his delusions and fears.[21] But other times his transformation is more profound and has something to teach us about masculinity—especially in courage, fatherhood, and self-sacrifice.

Courage

The most obvious transformation Ransom undergoes on Malacandra is growth in courage. The decisive moment comes at the end of Ransom's time with the *hrossa* when he is invited to join the hunt for *hnakra*, a leviathan-like creature that epitomizes danger and deadliness:

> A short time ago, in England, nothing would have seemed more impossible to Ransom than to accept the post of honour and danger in an attack upon an unknown but certainly deadly aquatic monster. Even more recently, when he had first fled from the *sorns*, or when he had lain pitying himself in the forest by night, it would hardly have been in his power to do what he was intending to do to-day. For his intention was

---

21. Lewis, *Out of the Silent Planet*, ch. 9, 59.

clear. Whatever happened, he must show that the human species also were *hnau* [rational creatures]. He was only too well aware that such resolutions might look very different when the moment came, but he felt an unwonted assurance that somehow or other he would be able to go through with it. It was necessary, and the necessary was always possible. Perhaps, too, there was something in the air he now breathed, or in the society of the *hrossa*, which had begun to work a change in him.[22]

In this episode, Lewis draws together several threads of "sturdy hardiness." Ransom puts on the invigorating mantel of courageous necessity: "Something long sleeping in the blood awoke in Ransom. It did not seem impossible at this moment that even he might be the *hnakra*-slayer"— that is, the dragon slayer.[23] But that is exactly who Ransom is, and what Ransom does. He is the one who throws the decisive spear to slay the leviathan. Lewis mimics and teaches through the One true story: the serpent's head must be crushed by a son of man for man's redemption.[24]

---

22. Lewis, *Out of the Silent Planet*, ch. 13, 95–96.

23. Lewis, *Out of the Silent Planet*, ch. 13, 97.

24. Notably, this same "dragon-likeness" is used by the inhabitants of Malacandra to represent the *Oyarsa* of Thulcandra, the silent planet, Earth—that is, Satan, the Bent One. In the angelic fall of this universe, there was a great war, in which Satan was resisted by the other *Oyarsa*—a dragon opposed by Martian war. Furthermore, we see in the *hnakra*-slaying a foreshadowing of Ransom's violent, head-crushing encounter with the Bent One in *Perelandra*.

Ransom's newfound courage contrasts him to Weston and Devine. Their cowardly, bent manhood shatters the joy of this transformational hunt. From the shadows of the forest, they have been watching it all unfold, and they take the opportunity to shoot, from cowardly cover, Hyoi, Ransom's *hrossa* friend. Unlike Ransom, they do not face their foes. They hide, and their cold, hard, mercenary strength is employed for evil. The problem does not lie with their masculinity, but with its aim and agency.

After the hunt, on his way to visit the *Oyarsa* of Malacandra, Ransom reflects on the transformation he has undergone during his time on Mars:

> He looked back on that time as on a nightmare, on his own mood at that time as a sort of sickness. Then all had been whimpering, unanalysed, self-nourishing, self-consuming dismay. Now, in the clear light of an accepted duty, he felt fear indeed, but with it a sober sense of confidence in himself and in the world, and even an element of pleasure. It was the difference between a landsman in a sinking ship and a horseman on a bolting horse: either may be killed, but the horseman is an agent as well as a patient.[25]

Activity over passivity, duty over self-absorption, courage over fear. These are the obvious tones Lewis means to strike in his positive presentation of masculinity and Ransom's growth toward a full and mature manhood.

---

25. Lewis, *Out of the Silent Planet*, ch. 14, 107.

Lewis wrote in *Mere Christianity* that the idea of the knight is "one of the great Christian ideas."[26] Is this merely Lewis the romantic falling prey to cultural tropes and stereotypes? Is there anything inherently manly about courage, or courageous about masculinity? This connection is, sadly, something less obvious to us than it was to Lewis, traveled as he was in the ancient paths.

"Act like men"—so says the Apostle in 1 Corinthians 16:13; "quit you like men" in the King James. The underlying Greek is *andrizomai*, a verbal form built off the word not for humanity in general (*anthropos*), but for the human male, *aner* (genitive *andros*). Some English translations opt to mute the linguistic connection to masculinity, perhaps to help the reader understand that this command is directed to the whole church, not just the men. These versions translate Paul's command "be courageous" (e.g. NIV) or "be brave" (NKJV). Now, these translations do communicate a true sense of the word. Paul really is telling the whole Corinthian church to have courage. But by severing it from its literal meaning and original connection to manliness, something important is lost that our pre-egalitarian age understood instinctively.

---

26. Of course, the present author agrees entirely with this: "The idea of the knight— the Christian in arms for the defence of a good cause—is one of the great Christian ideas. War is a dreadful thing, and I can respect an honest pacifist, though I think he is entirely mistaken. What I cannot understand is this sort of semi-pacifism you get nowadays which gives people the idea that though you have to fight, you ought to do it with a long face and as if you were ashamed of it" (Lewis, *Mere Christianity,* 119). See also C. S. Lewis, "The Necessity of Chivalry," in *Present Concerns: Journalistic Essays* (London: HarperOne, 2017), 1-6.

The Latin vulgate renders 1 Corinthians 16:13 *viriliter agite*, "act manfully." The connection to our word "virility," which is built on the Latin word for man (*vir*) and classically relates to manful strength and courage, is obvious. Of the four cardinal virtues ("virtue," another word derived from *vir*)—prudence, justice, fortitude, and temperance—it is fortitude (Gk. *andreia*) that is closest to the idea of masculinity. This virtue embodies strength and endurance and the tenacity to remove obstacles in the way of rectitude, whether internal or external to the man. All of this requires resolution, determination, valor, boldness, and daring. Here we are close to the heart of masculinity: mastery, including self-mastery, for a greater purpose outside of oneself, facing down fear and foe on behalf of the weak. While all are called to faith and love over fear (cf. 1 John 4:18), men are particularly called to lead in courage. This is why they are endowed by their Creator with masculine strength. When men are cowards, society suffers.

When Ransom lands on Mars, he is a frightful, self-absorbed coward. But by the time he meets with the Malacandrian *Oyarsa*, he is a courageous warrior. The masculine atmosphere has had its way. But more importantly, Ransom's newfound courage is not some kind of growth in a self-help exercise leading to greater self-actualization. Lewis hints at the purpose of his masculine transformation in the *Oyarsa*'s exhortation to Ransom about the evil intent of Weston and Devine: "Watch those two bent ones. Be courageous. Fight them."[27] Ransom's courage, his masculinity, is to be directed, to be aimed as a "hired glad-

---

27. Lewis, *Out of the Silent Planet*, ch. 21, 183.

iator," for the good and opposed to evil. Here is the "why" of courageous masculinity: the vigilant fight for others

Responsible Fatherhood

Another masculine theme present in *Out of the Silent Planet*—which perhaps appears so briefly as to have been little commented on—is that of responsible fatherhood.

Before Ransom goes on his great hunt, he learns and grows during his time living amongst the *hrossa*. In his attempt to better understand the Martian inhabitants, he finds himself in a conversation with his new friend Hyoi about food and competition on Malacandra. This conversation leads him to ask about the relationship between sexual pleasure and reproduction. (Already Lewis brings together what our expressive-individualistic age has attempted to separate: sex and children.) Ransom is trying to understand how scarcity is handled on Malacandra, so he asks what happens if a *hross* has more children than he can feed. This question confuses Hyoi. Their society does not have more children than they can provide for. Ransom asks if sex is pleasurable, then why wouldn't some *hrossa* engage beyond their own capacity to care for the young produced. Is hedonistic sexual promiscuity, ubiquitously associated with hyper-masculine machismo today, part of the martial spirit? By no means! Instead, Ransom discovers that the *hrossa* are naturally monogamous, and that promiscuity is treated as a perversion. Even having two wives is a cautionary tale, not a reality, on Mars. Why? Because masculine fatherhood includes responsibility, which itself begets further joy that augments the original pleasure, not diminishing it. As Hyoi explains to Ransom: "When [the *hross*] is young he has to look for his mate; and then he has to court her; then he begets young; then he rears them; then he remembers all this, and boils it inside him and makes it into poems and wisdom."[28]

This responsibility, once again, contrasts Ransom with Weston. Weston's ambitious scientism warps him into a malicious utilitarian for whom mankind is an abstraction. The *Oyarsa* rebukes him for this: "You do not love any one of your race—you would have let me kill Ransom. You do not love the mind of your race, nor the body. Any kind of creature will please you if only it is begotten by your kind as they now are. It seems to me, Thick One, that what you really love is no completed creature but the very seed itself: for that is all that is left." This is the essence of a selfish masculinity: it is only seed, never planted, never coming to fruition on behalf of another. Weston knows this sets him against Maleldil, the Creator of all, the one who made Nature complementary and fecund. But Weston doesn't care: "Me no care for Maleldil. Like Bent One better: me on his side"[29]

Fatherhood belongs to the essence of what Ransom encounters on Malacandra as constitutive of masculinity—man *for* another, for the protection and provision of another.[30] This attribute relates to a final martial theme, perhaps the most important of all: self-sacrifice.

---

28. Lewis, *Out of the Silent Planet*, ch. 12, 89.

29. Lewis, *Out of the Silent Planet*, ch. 20, 179.

30. This is not to say that all men have to be fathers to be true men, but that fatherliness is a part of true masculinity, as J. Budziszewski argues in his important book, *The Meaning of Sex* (Wilmington: ISI, 2014)

Men are from Mars

Self-Sacrifice

At the beginning of *Out of the Silent Planet*, Ransom finds himself drugged and kidnapped as a direct result of (albeit begrudging) self-sacrifice. Having been on a walk through the countryside, Ransom encounters a woman who is very worried about her son, and she enlists Ransom to search for him in a nearby dilapidated estate. Even though this request presents many obstacles, all of which are contrary to his original desire for a quiet countryside walk, Ransom presses on. He is startled to find the boy struggling in the hands of Weston and Devine, and he intervenes. Thwarted in their sinister plans, Weston and Devine change tack, settling for Ransom instead. Ransom's life for the boy's— —a fitting beginning for a character so named.

Lewis returns to this theme at the end of the novel, in Ransom's conversation with the *Oyarsa*. Trying to better understand the earthlings, the *Oyarsa* asks Ransom what motivated their interplanetary journey. Ransom explains that he was brought against his own will, but the others, Weston and Devine, are self-interested: Devine is solely in it for the riches, while Weston is on a quasi-transhumanist, techno-futurist mission. Ransom warns the *Oyarsa*: "[Weston] does not know there is any Maleldil. But what is certain, Oyarsa, is that he means evil to your world. Our kind must not be allowed to come here again. If you can prevent it only by killing all three of us, I am content."[31]

In this courageous act, Ransom's masculine transformation fully matures. He began his time on Mars with the instinct of self-preservation, which Lewis hints at in an inner dialogue early on during Ransom's wilderness wan-

---

31. Lewis, *Out of the Silent Planet*, ch. 18, 156.

dering: "He drew his knees up and hugged himself; he felt a sort of physical, almost a filial, love for his own body.... 'We'll look after you, Ransom ... we'll stick together, old man.' "[32] But this self-preserving instinct, which we should not condemn—indeed, it is the foundation of neighbor love (Matt. 7:12; Eph. 5:29)—grows to include others and begins to eclipse the self. "Greater love hath no man than this, that a man lay down his life for his friends" (John 15:13, KJV).

Once again, Weston is the foil. Whereas Ransom courageously offers his own life to the *Oyarsa*, Weston selfishly offers only Ransom. The *Oyarsa* acknowledges this cowardice, this unmanliness, for what it is: "You would give him up to the evil you feared. To-day, seeing him here, to save your own life, you would have given him to me a second time, still thinking I meant him hurt."[33]

It is here that I must respectfully disagree with my co-contributor, the eminent Michael Ward, who has done more perhaps than any other to open eyes to the deeper themes of Lewis's trilogy. In *Planet Narnia,* Ward writes: "The principal Martial element that *Out of the Silent Plan-*

---

32. Lewis, *Out of the Silent Planet*, ch. 8, 58.

33. Lewis, *Out of the Silent Planet*, ch. 20, 171. Lewis connects this understanding with Weston's own philosophy: "Life is greater than any system of morality; her claims are absolute. It is not by tribal taboos and copy-book maxims that she has pursued her relentless march from the amoeba to man and from man to civilization." This is "bravery" untethered to any shape of morality. This is untethered ambition. "You do not love the mind of your race, nor the body," the Oyarsa responds to Weston. "It seems to me, Thick One, that what you really love is no completed creature but the very seed itself: for that is all that is left." Lewis, *Out of the Silent Planet*, ch. 20, 177.

et does *not* contain is an active Christological character."³⁴ But isn't this exactly what Ransom is in the end—an active Christological character? He is the courageous ransom whose willingness in self-sacrifice temporarily saves even his enemies. Could Lewis have been any clearer than when he named him Ransom? "For even the Son of Man came not to be served but to serve, and to give his life as a ransom for many" (Mark 10:45).

Paul makes clear the Christological connection between self-sacrifice and biblical manhood in Ephesians: "Husbands, love your wives, as Christ loved the church and gave himself up for her" (Eph 5:25). Giving himself for his beloved, ransoming himself for another—here we have finally reached the pinnacle of masculinity and man's greatest calling: self-sacrifice. This is why the picture of the chivalrous knight floods the imagination when one thinks of a more noble masculinity. What is a soldier but one serving others, even unto death? Lewis concluded that his presentation of Mars in "The Planets" was "the finest piece of anti-war propaganda I had struck!"³⁵ "Martianity," mature masculinity, is the disciplined warrior enlisted in the cause of righteousness, who is fearless and courageous, even to the point of death on behalf of his beloved. Bravery, after all, is what commends one to Maleldil.³⁶ Ransom is most Christlike when he is most manly, most coura-

---

34. Michael Ward, *Planet Narnia*, 80.

35. W. H. Lewis, *Brothers and Friends: The Diaries of Major Warren Hamilton Lewis*, ed. Clyde S. Kilby and Marjorie Lamp Mead (San Francisco: Harper & Row, 1982) 169. I owe the finding of this quotation to Ward, *Planet Narnia*, 272n27.

36. Lewis, *Out of the Silent Planet*, ch. 18, 156.

geous, *for others*. And any man would do well to embrace the same for his beloved.

CONCLUSION

In a world increasingly unwilling to say what a woman is, let alone a man—but nevertheless certain it is masculinity that lies at the root of so many societal ills—Lewis presents a thrilling, compelling vision of a masculinity that can save the world.

Yes, masculinity is a "mercenary," able to do great good and great evil, but it is absolutely necessary to the flourishing of man, woman, and child.[37] It was, after all, a courageous, masculine savior who went to the cross as a ransom for many—for the joy set before him. "Like handiwork he offers to all—earns his wages and whistles all the while. White-feathered dread Mars has mastered."[38] Even death itself.

So let us encourage not a measured masculinity, but a full-throated, happy, courageous, fatherly, self-sacrificing manhood in all members of the martial sex. And let us have Lewis's brilliant trilogy encourage another generation toward that glorious end, until and beyond Christ's return in martial glory.

---

37. Lewis, "The Planets," 27.

38. Lewis, "The Planets," 28.

PERELANDRA

IV

ENJOYMENT AND CONTEMPLATION:

THE GREEN LADY, SELF-KNOWLEDGE, AND GROWTH IN MATURITY

Christiana Hale

It has long been said that knowledge of reality must often begin with knowledge of oneself. To understand the world around us, we must first understand ourselves. Who are we? What are we for? What one says about their own identity fundamentally changes what one will say about the rest of reality—about God, the universe, and everything in it. And yet, in order to truly understand ourselves, must we not first start with something outside of ourselves? John Calvin, the great Reformer, recognized how interconnected these two things—knowledge of self and knowledge of God—are:

> Nearly all the wisdom we possess, that is to say, true and sound wisdom, consists of two parts: the knowledge of God and of ourselves. But, while joined by many bonds, which one precedes and brings forth the other is not easy to discern.[1]

To know oneself truly is to know oneself as a human being, a creature made in the image of God, but fractured and bent by sin. And so, if we are created in His image, we must know Him whose image we bear. Self-knowledge cannot exist in a vacuum, divorced from any context. In a world that argues for the individual's complete control of their identity, the Christian knows from whom he derives his being—we do not create ourselves. And so our stance on the epistemology of the self is a stance that rests on this very foundation.

C. S. Lewis, as he often does, manages to put into clear words concepts that many are familiar with, yet have a hard time describing. In Lewis's essay "Meditation in a Toolshed," he discusses the difference between two different kinds of epistemology or "knowing," utilizing the analogy of a beam of light shining through a crack in the wall of a woodshed:

> I was standing today in the dark toolshed. The sun was shining outside and through the crack at the top of the door there came a sunbeam.

---

1. John Calvin, *Institutes of the Christian Religion*, ed. John T. McNeill, trans. Ford Lewis Battles, 2 vols. (Louisville: Westminster John Knox Press, 1960), 1:35.

From where I stood that beam of light, with specks of dust floating in it, was the most striking thing in the place. Everything else was almost pitch-black. I was seeing the beam, not seeing things by it.

Then I moved, so that the beam fell on my eyes. Instantly the whole previous picture vanished. I saw no toolshed, and (above all) no beam. Instead I saw, framed in the irregular cranny at the top of the door, green leaves moving on the branches of a tree outside and beyond that, 90 odd million miles away, the sun. Looking along the beam, and looking at the beam are very different experiences.[2]

As one stands inside the darkness of the shed, there are two options for how you interact with the beam of light: you can either stand off to the side and look at the beam of light, or you can stand in the beam and look along it. The first kind of observation is Contemplation: you step out of an experience to analyze or look at something as something separate from yourself. In Contemplation, you look at the beam of light *as* a beam, as a peculiar entity. The second kind, looking along the beam, is Enjoyment. When you look along the beam of light, it enables you to see through the walls of the shed to the outside world. And as you do so, you are not really thinking about the beam of light at all, but rather you are primarily cognizant of what the beam of light enables you to see and experience.

---

2. C. S. Lewis, "Meditation in a Toolshed," in *God in the Dock* (Grand Rapids: Eerdmans, 2014), 230.

But this presents a question: who understands the beam of light better? The one who looks at it? Or the one who sees by it?

• • •

The words tumble from the writer's fingers, flashing across the page in a barely legible hand. No stopping. No breathing. Just words flying. Making sense? Hardly. But they tumble out nevertheless. Is the writer thinking about each word as it makes its mark? Is he carefully analyzing the syntax, the logical cohesion, the rhetorical punch? No. Even spelling is cast aside for something far more potent, strong, inexorable. The words come because they have to. The writer strains, as a woman suffering birth pangs. He is "with book, as a woman is with child."[3] Any writer can tell you this: there are times when the writing feels more as if it is being born than written. He writes because that is all he can do. The writer knows that to *not* write isn't an option. And when this fit is upon him, any analyzing—stopping, thinking, rewriting, editing, pondering—is as far from his thoughts as putting up the pen entirely. Where is the passion in that? The unguarded baring of one's mind in the burst of unhindered inspiration—maybe the words are worthless. Garbage. Drivel. No matter. The purely creative moment is its own reward. Maybe a gem of wisdom or a certain turn of phrase will make it into a final draft, but for right now, in this moment, the writer writes out of sheer enjoyment of the thing. He is inside. And to step outside

---

3. C. S. Lewis, *Till We Have Faces* (Orlando: Harcourt, 1984), 247.

would be to destroy something delicate and rare, especially in our time—looking along the beam.

In this example of Enjoyment, little to no analysis happens at the time. The author doesn't step back and look at his writing as a critic or an editor in that moment. He simply moves on to the next word and the next and the next, receiving the waves as they come toward him, not thinking about whether the waves bring good or ill, not stopping to wonder if what he is accomplishing is worth anything. That time will come later. Perhaps never, if what he has written is destined for nothing more than a dusty notebook or an unopened Word file on his computer. In the moment, he simply experiences and enjoys. There are other analogies, other examples. Any artist can surely relate, but so too any true human being, if they have ever had any experience where they have simply been, to use a modern phrase, "in the moment." However, in our age of social media and influencers and Instagrammers, this experience is a rarer one. We so easily slip into Contemplation, particularly of ourselves.

Sit on a park bench and feel a spring breeze on your face. Watch the sun play in puddles on a sidewalk. Take that first sip of morning coffee with just the right amount of cream, not too hot or cold. Let the strains of a Mendelssohn concerto flow over you, a tidal wave of sound and melody. What do all of these experiences have in common? You look along them, rather than at them. They enable you to see something deeper, something more than meets the eye. When you take that first sip of coffee, the fact that it sends warmth straight down to your toes and contentment into your soul isn't simply the result of chemicals reacting in a certain way, heated to a certain temperature. As soon as you start thinking of that, you are no longer purely participating in enjoyment—contemplation has crept in. In a similar fashion, as soon as you become self-aware of your own enjoyment, as soon as you see yourself sipping that coffee, viewing that sunset, eating that meal, as soon as the selfie is taken, contemplation is now the focus.

Lest this seem like a diatribe against contemplation, Lewis himself does not in fact argue for enjoyment over and against contemplation as a means of attaining true knowledge, especially of oneself. Rather, he launches a defense against one of his most rabid enemies: materialistic reductionism. In Lewis's time, as well as our own, the prevailing ditch was not one of despising contemplation as a means of knowing truly, but rather the opposite. Scholars and elites, those who have never tasted fruit ripe off the vine, are the ones who claim the most intimate knowledge of what that fruit is. They can outline and map and explain and dissect. They can draw diagrams. Run chemical experiments. Tell you why, when the fruit is mashed and fermented and aged and strained and put into casks and then bottles and then swirled just so in a glass shaped just like this, the chemicals will align in such a way that berries or chocolate or orange blossom burst on the tongue. And those who simply drink, who bring a bottle to a friend's retirement party, to toast and share and *drink* to a life well-lived—how could they really know what wine is? The temptation to dismiss experience and enjoyment as a lesser path to true knowledge is a hallmark of modernity, a key tenet of materialistic reductionism. If the material world is all there is, then surely the way to truly know something is to analyze its material make-up?

If the deepest, most foundational truth is only material, then enjoyment is of necessity a lesser means of obtaining true knowledge.

• • •

Before diving into how Lewis unpacks these concepts of enjoyment and contemplation in *Perelandra*, we must set the backdrop of his entire endeavor. Perelandra itself, the planet Venus, is more than just a setting for a story. Throughout the Ransom Trilogy, Lewis demonstrates his deep affection for and understanding of the medieval model of the cosmos, primarily through his use of the planetary personalities. This idea was a key element of the medieval cosmos and the one in which Lewis saw the greatest creative and imaginative potential.[4] The planets of the medieval cosmos are vibrant, personal, vivacious, and unique. All of the literary, religious, mythological, and historical connotations of each planet work together as one upon the imagination in such a potent and yet surreptitious way that it gives a whole new meaning to the word "atmosphere." "Modern readers sometimes discuss whether, when Jupiter or Venus is mentioned by a medieval poet, he means the planet or the deity. It is doubtful whether the question usually admits of an answer.... All three things—the visible planet in the sky, the source of the influence, and the god—generally acted as a unity upon his mind."[5] And Lewis nowhere demonstrates his abilities in this area

---

4. C. S. Lewis, *The Discarded Image* (Cambridge: Cambridge University Press, 1964), 14.

5. Lewis, *The Discarded Image*, 104–5.

more vividly than in his depictions of the planet Venus. The very air of Perelandra works upon the reader from the moment we splash down with Ransom into the warm waters of the Lady of Love. How is it that as readers we, together with Ransom himself, long to return to the burnished skies and watery islands of the Morning Star? How is it that we smell in dreams a scent that has no name but awakens the longing that man was born with? Lewis deftly weaves together not just a backdrop, but a setting that is itself a character in the story. The fact that Ransom's conversations with the Green Lady about knowledge, enjoyment, and contemplation occur on Perelandra is not incidental. The atmosphere itself infuses everything.

When Ransom arrives on Perelandra, he arrives as one being reborn. Venus is inextricably tied to the maternal, the life-giving fruitfulness of motherhood. Thus, it is no surprise that Ransom himself only arrives on Perelandra through a physical and spiritual rebirth. In his description of Ransom's arrival on Perelandra, Lewis does his best to depict what it might be like for a full-grown man to be reborn physically. Ransom is encased in the coffin-like casket that was the vehicle used to transport him through the heavens on his journey to Perelandra. As he plunges into the atmosphere of Perelandra and lands in its waters, the casket becomes soft and pliable: "All this time he [Ransom] must have been making faint, unconscious efforts to move his limbs, for now he suddenly found that the sides of his prison-house yielded to pressure." His casket becomes first an amniotic sac, before turning into a "viscous substance," a substance that he realizes is white. And when the substance clears away, the overwhelming confusion of light and color and perspective is disorienting. In place of the casket he experiences "an indescribable confusion of color—a rich, varied world in which nothing, for the moment, seemed palpable. There was no casket now. He was turned out—deposited—solitary. He was in Perelandra."[6]

The significance of Ransom's re-birth on Perelandra is intimately connected to the following conversations about knowledge, specifically through enjoyment and contemplation. Ransom, from his first moments on Perelandra, is not the same man he was. After his rebirth, he eats of the fruit of Perelandra, an experience as revelatory as it is symbolic. He tastes true translunary pleasure for the first time. Later, he declares that he has been "breast-fed by the planet Venus herself."[7] The coupling of pure motherhood with untainted pleasure forms the backdrop against which Ransom's awareness of both enjoyment and contemplation takes shape.

• • •

On the heels of his first meeting with the Green Lady, Ransom finds himself inadvertently introducing her to the concept of contemplation, an idea clearly foreign to her. This passage is worth quoting at length:

> "I see it now," she said presently. "It is very strange to say one is young at the moment one is speaking. But to-morrow I shall be older. And then I shall say I was young to-day. You are quite

---

6. C. S. Lewis, *Perelandra* (London: HarperCollins, 2005), ch. 15, 234.

7. Michael Ward, *Planet Narnia: The Seven Heavens in the Imagination of C. S. Lewis* (New York: Oxford University Press, 2008), 170.

right. This is great wisdom you are bringing, O Piebald Man."

"What do you mean?"

"This looking backward and forward along the line and seeing how a day has one appearance as it comes to you, and another when you are in it, and a third when it has gone past. Like the waves."

"But you are very little older than yesterday."

"How do you know that?"

"I mean," said Ransom, "a night is not a very long time."

She thought again, and then spoke suddenly, her face lightening. "I see it now," she said. "You think times have lengths. A night is always a night whatever you do in it, as from this tree to that is always so many paces whether you take them quickly or slowly. I suppose that is true in a way. But the waves do not always come at equal distances. I see that you come from a wise world ... if this is wise. I have never done it before—stepping out of life into the Alongside and looking at oneself living as if one were not alive. Do they all do that in your world, Piebald?"[8]

Up until her meeting with Ransom, the Green Lady's experience has been one of pure enjoyment—she takes things as they come, fully immersing herself in the joys and pleasures that are in front of her, never stepping outside of that state of immediacy to contemplate how things might

---

8. Lewis, *Perelandra*, ch. 5, 68–69.

be different or to view her own self from "outside." In one sense, this is a great blessing. Until she meets Ransom, it would seem that she has not experienced the pang of disappointment, of expecting one thing but receiving another, of hoping for a certain outcome only to have those hopes dashed. She hasn't "stepped outside" of the beam of light in order to consider whether she should be happy or disappointed. She hasn't looked at herself at all.

When the Green Lady first considers the idea of contemplation, of stepping into the "Alongside" and looking at oneself, she sees it as wisdom or a growth in maturity. "I was young yesterday," she says.[9] This idea, while novel to her, seems in her eyes to be wise. Though some doubt follows immediately on the heels of her affirmation: "... if this is wise."[10] Her uncertainty itself shows a kind of child-like wisdom that unnerves Ransom. He is frequently tempted to compare the Green Lady herself to a child, her innocence and certain naivete giving the impression of simplicity. But Ransom time and again wrestles with reconciling two seemingly opposite characteristics: innocence and deep wisdom; child-like, yet full of authority; at once both like a woman, yet unlike any human woman Ransom had seen:

> The alert, inner silence which looked out from those eyes overawed him; yet at any moment she might laugh like a child, or run like Artemis or dance like a Mænaed.... There was in her face an

---

9. Lewis, *Perelandra*, ch. 5, 68.

10. Lewis, *Perelandra*, ch. 5, 69.

authority, in her caresses a condescension, which by taking seriously the inferiority of her adorers made them somehow less inferior—raised them from the status of pets to that of slaves.[11]

Yet while the Green Lady initially sees contemplation as a good thing, Weston's arrival on the scene soon reveals its temptations. Weston, playing the role of Satan in the Garden of Eden, focuses his efforts at temptation toward disobedience on this sort of self-awareness. He attempts to pry open the crack that Ransom put in the Green Lady's epistemology. Whether a good or bad thing initially, this is where Weston launches his attack. Weston's temptation, like Satan's in Eden, centers on her knowledge, questioning God's commands and seeking to get her to do the same. "Has God really said?" is the recurring question. In various ways and through various means, Weston, now the "Un-man," undermines the one prohibition. And his primary weapon as he does so is the Green Lady's view of *herself*.

Much like Screwtape's in *The Screwtape Letters*, the Un-man's tactic is to pull Tinidril's gaze away from Maleldil and toward herself. At first, he attempts old fashioned vanity. This backfires spectacularly when Tinidril is intrigued by, but not enraptured with, her own beauty. She is yet too guileless to succumb to mere vanity over her physical beauty. And so the Un-man shifts tactic. He seeks instead to introduce a particular kind of contemplation into the Green Lady's psyche—constant contemplation of the Self.

---

11. Lewis, *Perelandra*, ch. 5, 74–75.

In several places throughout his writings, Lewis applies the concepts of contemplation and enjoyment to our knowledge of ourselves. How do we typically know ourselves? Is it primarily through enjoyment or contemplation? Is it possible to do both at once? Lewis offers some insight:

> The enjoyment and the contemplation of our inner activities are incompatible. You cannot hope and also think about hoping at the same moment; for in hope we look to hope's object and we interrupt this by (so to speak) turning round to look at the hope itself. Of course the two activities can and do alternate with great rapidity; but they are distinct and incompatible.[12]

As soon as we look at ourselves being faithful, rather than looking toward the object of our faith, that faith has faltered. As soon as we are more concerned with looking at *ourselves* being charitable than with the enjoyment of the act of charity itself, has not that charity been stripped of something like its essential virtue? This self-examination that was, remember, so novel to Tinidril when she first met Ransom contains within it a deadly poison, quick to kill virtue as a tender plant withers in the desiccating ray of a magnifying glass. Is this indeed wisdom?

Yet, while this poison can be quick to kill virtue, it is in equal measure dangerous against vice and sin. In this sense, self-examination or contemplation of the self is an almost vital component in the process of a Christian's

---

12. Lewis, "Meditation in a Toolshed," 232.

sanctification. While Lewis criticizes those who would see contemplation as a more valid way of seeing the world and states that "the surest way of spoiling a pleasure [is] to start examining your satisfaction,"[13] elsewhere in his writings he sees this as a serious weapon to be used against lust and vice. In Joe Rigney's book *Lewis on the Christian Life* he posits that "sometimes our pleasures need to be spoiled."[14] Contemplation, when turned toward the right object, has the power of awakening us to the realities of our own sins and follies. Lewis nowhere applies this idea more obviously, perhaps, than in *The Screwtape Letters*. Throughout the devil Screwtape's advice to his nephew on tempting "the patient" to sin and vice, his emphasis frequently rests on the patient's perception of both himself and others. Of course, since this advice comes from a devil, the Christian reader needs to view the mirror image of the advice to see what Lewis is saying about the true Christian life:

> In all activities of mind which favour our [demonic] cause, encourage the patient to be unselfconscious and to concentrate on the object, but in all activities favourable to the Enemy [i.e. God] bend his mind back on itself. Let an insult or a woman's body so fix his attention outward that he does not reflect "I am now entering into the state called Anger—or the state called Lust."

---

13. Lewis, *Surprised by Joy: The Shape of My Early Life* (Florida: Harcourt, Brace, & Company, 1956), 218–19.

14. Joe Rigney, *Lewis on the Christian Life: Becoming Truly Human in the Presence of God*, Theologians on the Christian Life (Wheaton: Crossway, 2018), 143.

Enjoyment and Contemplation

> Contrariwise let the reflection "My feelings are now growing more devout, or more charitable" so fix his attention inward that he no longer looks beyond himself to see our Enemy or his own neighbours.[15]

In the above example, Screwtape encourages his nephew to draw the patient into contemplation of his own self only when he is being virtuous. As we saw above, nothing kills virtue so quickly as the self's contemplation of that very virtue. However, on the flip side, some lusts and vices are equally susceptible to the death-ray of self-awareness. "Stepping outside the experience allows us to gain perspective, to diffuse the passion of the moment so that we can, as they say, 'get a grip.' "[16] Herein lies a peculiar danger of self-examination: it is, to some degree, inescapable. We must ingest this poison. As Christians, we *must* look to our own selves lest we also be tempted (Gal. 6:2). And so we have a perfect knife's edge for the devil to prowl along. This is why Screwtape is so keen to keep the patient's focus on his "inner life." If the constant focus of a man is on his own self, not as others see him, but as he himself perceives the inner workings of his own mind and motivations, this narrowness of his perception eventually excludes truth itself.

> Keep his mind off the most elementary duties by directing it to the most advanced and spiritual ones. Aggravate that most useful human char-

---

15. Lewis, *The Screwtape Letters* (New York: Macmillan, 1982), 29–30.

16. Rigney, *Lewis on the Christian Life*, 143.

acteristic, the horror and neglect of the obvious. You must bring him to a condition in which he can practice self-examination for an hour without discovering any of those facts about himself which are perfectly clear to anyone who has ever lived in the same house with him or worked in the same office.[17]

So what does this have to do with the Green Lady and the Un-man's temptation toward disobedience? The connection lies in Ransom's first conversation with Tinidril where he introduces the very concept of self-awareness and self-examination. A crack has opened, whether for good or ill, in Tinidril's way of knowing and understanding reality. Where all was enjoyment before, she has now considered the possibility of stepping "outside." There is now a rift, a separation between Tinidril herself and her experiences. It is now possible for her to not just see obedience as the inevitable outworking of Maleldil's will, but as a choice or action of the individual. Tinidril rejoices in this revelation as a glory and an awe-inspiring mystery:

> "I thought," she said, "that I was carried in the will of Him I love, but now I see that I walk with it. I thought that the good things He sent me drew me into them as the waves lift the islands; but now I see that it is I who plunge into them with my own legs and arms, as when we go swimming. I feel as if I were living in that roofless world of yours where men walk undefended

---

17. Lewis, *Screwtape Letters*, 16.

> beneath naked heaven. It is a delight with terror in it! One's own self to be walking from one good to another, walking beside Him as Himself may walk, not even holding hands. How has He made me so separate from Himself? How did it enter His mind to conceive such a thing? The world is so much larger than I thought. I thought we went along paths—but it seems there are no paths. The going itself is the path."[18]

For the first time, Tinidril contemplates the Creator/creature distinction, the possibility, however remote, that a creature could decide to "cling to a good" and turn aside from the good given.[19] And it is this revelation that the Un-man uses in his temptation, as he preys upon Tinidril's innocence and twists her ideas of obedience into something theatrical and verging on disingenuous.

The devil is crafty and strategic in his deception. The Un-man doesn't shift his strategy in a way that simply exchanges moral vanity for physical vanity. That would be far too simple and likely just as successful as the first attempt. The Green Lady is too aware of her own identity, Maleldil's identity, and the relationship between Maleldil and all creatures to be taken in by bald-faced flattery. Rather, the Un-man seeks to exchange a physical mirror for a metaphorical one in which Tinidril can not only admire her own virtue, but actually imagine herself performing virtu-

---

18. Lewis, *Perelandra*, ch. 5, 81.

19. Lewis, *Perelandra*, ch. 6, 99–100.

ous acts in the future. And all of these virtuous acts center around her identity as Woman and Mother.

The Un-man doesn't want Tinidril to see obedience itself. He wants her to see *herself* walking in obedience. Rather than look at Maleldil's will, he wants her to look at *herself* interacting with Maleldil's will. The Un-man clearly graduated with honors from "Screwtape University." Screwtape's advice to his nephew is worked out, nearly to devastating consequences, in the Un-man's temptation of Tinidril:

> Your patient has become humble; have you drawn his attention to the fact? All virtues are less formidable to us [the devils] once the man is aware that he has them, but this is specially true of humility. Catch him at the moment when he is really poor in spirit and smuggle into his mind the gratifying reflection, "By jove! I'm being humble," and almost immediately pride—pride at his own humility—will appear.[20]

Pride is the cavernous abyss that lurks almost unseen next to every exercise in self-examination. Pride is the enemy of true obedience, the insidious infestation corrupting all fallen man's virtues. From the very beginning, pride has tripped us up. "Has God indeed said?"

Ransom truly understands the severity of the danger that Tinidril is in when he sees the effect that the Un-man's stories have on her. All the Un-man's stories target Tinidril's identity as woman and mother as well as her

---

20. Lewis, *Screwtape Letters*, 62–63.

perception of what obedience truly is. "What emerged from the stories was rather an image than an idea—the picture of the tall, slender form, unbowed though the world's weight rested upon its shoulders, stepping forth fearless and friendless into the dark to do for others what those others forbade it to do yet needed to have done."[21] The Un-man subtly and cleverly seeks to redefine what it means to be an obedient woman. He tells stories of risks taken for the good of loved ones, sufferings undergone on behalf of friends or family, grand sacrifices where it seemed the woman was the only one with eyes to see what needed to be done and stood strong in the face of revilement for her actions. Through every tale runs the idea that true obedience can only be performed through difficulty, through persecution, that obedience needs to be grand in order to be real. Meanwhile, the entire time, the Un-man seeks to turn the camera's focus back to the self. And Ransom is horrified when he sees this beginning to affect the Green Lady. This passage is worth quoting at length, because it highlights the two-pronged danger of the Un-man's temptation: self-awareness and looking toward the future:

> The expression on her face, revealed in the sudden light, was one that he had not seen there before. Her eyes were not fixed on the narrator: as far as that went, her thoughts might have been a thousand miles away. Her lips were shut and a little pursed. Her eyebrows were slightly raised. He had not yet seen her look so like a woman of our own race; and yet her expression was one he

---

21. Lewis, *Perelandra*, ch. 10, 154.

had not very often met on earth—except, as he realized with a shock, on the stage. "Like a tragedy queen" was the disgusting comparison that arose in his mind.... A very *good* tragedy queen, no doubt. The heroine of a very great tragedy, very nobly played by an actress who was a good woman in real life. By earthly standards, an expression to be praised, even to be revered: but remembering all that he had read in her countenance before, the unselfconscious radiance, the frolic sanctity, the depth of stillness that reminded him sometimes of infancy and sometimes of extreme old age while the hard youth and valiancy of face and body denied both, he found this new expression horrifying. The fatal touch of invited grandeur, of enjoyed pathos—the assumption, however slight, of a role—seemed a hateful vulgarity. Perhaps she was doing no more—he had good hope that she was doing no more—than responding in a purely imaginative fashion to this new art of Story or Poetry. But by God she'd better not! And for the first time the thought "This can't go on" formulated itself in his mind.[22]

Prior to Ransom's arrival on Perelandra, it seems that disappointment was an unknown concept to Tinidril. Because enjoyment was her default mode of experiencing reality, stepping outside of the moment to look at what "might have been" or "what wasn't" or "what might be"

---

22. Lewis, *Perelandra*, ch. 10, 155–56.

Enjoyment and Contemplation

is an entirely novel concept. It hasn't occurred to her to look ahead, to look forward to what wasn't but what might be. She is a creature doing exactly what Screwtape would hate—living entirely in the present moment, which is the only place true obedience lies.[23] And this is why the Un-Man must launch his attack at not only the Green Lady's perception of her own self, but also at her perception of time. She must be tempted to look forward, to look at the "unrealities" of the future, and this, combined with her new awareness of herself as an actor in this plot, is the poisonous mix that presents a real danger, a danger that Ransom realizes must be stopped.

What is the purpose of all of these threads? How do they twist together into a whole? There are two primary points to take away, two areas where the dangers of both the wrong kind of enjoyment and the wrong kind of contemplation lurk.

True humility is the rudder by which one can steer clear of the primary dangers of contemplation when turned toward the self. True humility knows how to contemplate in the right way—neither too long nor too deep, especially when pleased with the view. But pride is not merely an inflated view of the self; it is also a pointed or all-encompassing view of the self. It doesn't matter if you think you are a worm—are you always looking at your worm-like self? Do you think you are no good? How much time do you spend thinking about your no-good self? False humility likes to pretend that all it has to do to be truly humble is think lowly thoughts about the self. But the problem is, it's still the *self* being thought about. Deep humility rejoices in its

---

23. Lewis, *Screwtape Letters*, 70.

smallness and then stops looking at itself altogether. Its focus is primarily outward, looking at the next thing to be done, the next act of obedience, the next person to serve.

Which leads to the second application—obedience and the future. True obedience, as Screwtape warns Wormwood, is found only in the present. It is not enough to be planning to be obedient at some distant point in the future, a future that may or may not come to exist. Our Christian calling is to be obedient now. What is God calling us to *now*? What is the act of obedience in front of us *now*? True obedience is an epistemological certainty that defies contemplation. The eyes of faith enable us to look at the present as ripe with eternity. But as soon as we stop and look *at* our obedience, we have almost certainly ceased in our act of obedience. Though there is a definite place for contemplation of the present moment, the dangers of contemplation lurk around every corner. Look too closely, contemplate too deeply, and you've driven away the very thing you sought to understand. In the end, all of our contemplating of ourselves or our own thoughts or our own actions cannot hope to contend with the simple joy of obedience in the present moment. To say with the Green Lady "I am His beast, and all His biddings are joys."[24]

Who understands obedience more—the one who has spent years writing a treatise on the subject, analyzing and dissecting, or the one who has stayed faithfully at their post, doing hard work, day in and day out, with little thanks and no applause? But perhaps, you may protest, the scholar was *called* to such a work, and obedience therefore was tied into both enjoying and contemplating.

---

24. Lewis, *Perelandra*, ch. 6, 89.

Very well. But such instances are rare. The one who truly understands the nature of obedience is in fact the one who has been obedient in the trenches, despite all temptations to the contrary.

While we live in an age of seemingly endless temptations to turn contemplation toward our own selves, it is never more imperative that we keep Malacandra's words to Ransom at the end of *Perelandra* at the front of our minds: "Be comforted, small one, in your smallness. He lays no merit on you. Receive and be glad. Have no fear, lest your shoulders be bearing this world. Look! it is beneath your head and carries you."[25] To know ourselves truly we must know the Lord who made us. And to know Him truly is to walk in His ways, enjoying Him forever as we walk in obedience to His Word. "If ye love me, keep my commandments. And I will pray the Father, and he shall give you another Comforter, that he may abide with you for ever; even the Spirit of truth; whom the world cannot receive, because it seeth him not, neither knoweth him: but ye know him; for he dwelleth with you, and shall be in you" (John 14:15-17, KJV).

---

25. Lewis, *Perelandra*, ch. 16, 249.

V

THE DEVIL WENT DOWN TO VENUS:

LESSONS FROM THE UN-MAN

Bethel McGrew

On January 31, 2024, American Navy Reserve veteran Michael Cassidy was charged with a felony—a hate crime, no less. What was the nature of this crime? The previous December, he had destroyed a statue of Satan in the Iowa state capitol building. More specifically, he had decapitated it, then carted off its remains in a garbage bag. In straightforward fashion, he had reported his misdeed to capitol security, received his citation, and gone merrily on his way. Initially, he was charged with a fourth-degree misdemeanor. But because he had clearly stated that he was motivated against the "blasphemous" statue by his devout Christianity, this charge was subsequently upgraded to the third-degree felony of hate crime. He was not simply accused of destroying property, but of doing it out of hatred for the owners' religion, and thereby violating their civil rights. As I write, the subsequent discourse remains extremely lively, with some calling Cassidy a hero and others calling him a threat to pluralism, democracy, and the American way.

So which is Cassidy, hero or villain? Among C. S. Lewis readers, several of us couldn't help thinking there might be a clue in the climactic passage of *Perelandra*, where Ransom fights and defeats his nemesis, the Un-man. Once an eloquent scholar, the Un-man is now possessed by a demon, if not by Satan himself. Though it still wears the professor's human body like a skinsuit, it is utterly inhuman. The Un-man puts on two legs the Augustinian idea of Evil as a lack of Goodness—no positive content of its own, only deprivation, a perpetual *un*. As Ransom confronts this sickeningly familiar humanoid figure, he is overcome with a novel experience: the feeling of "perfectly unmixed and lawful hatred."[1] He realizes that he needn't feel any guilt for this. He no longer needs to worry that he is "failing fully to distinguish the sinner from the sin." His enemy is not merely a corrupted creature, but "corruption itself." In a moment that would otherwise be horrific, this epiphany fills him with joy—the joy of "finding at last what hatred was made for." Lewis compares it to the joy of a boy with an ax who finds a tree, or a boy with a box of colored chalks who finds a pile of white paper. After being told "No," he can't chop here, he can't color there, at last he has found the proper use for his frustrated tools.

---

1. C. S. Lewis, *Perelandra* (London: HarperCollins, 2005), ch. 12, 193–94.

So Ransom rejoices "in the perfect congruity between his emotion and its object."[2]

Granting that the stakes of Ransom's mission are far higher than the stakes for Michael Cassidy's, the parallel is not entirely inapt. After all, the state is attempting to pin the crime of "hate" on Cassidy's chest. But if there was any hate in Cassidy's action, it was a hate that, like Ransom's, had found its proper object—not against the corrupted Satan-worshipers who had left the idol in the capitol, but against the pure "corruption itself" of the idol, and that evil Thing in whose likeness it was fashioned.

The Un-man is not Lewis's only Satanic villain, nor his most popular. That distinction would easily go to Jadis, the Witch-Queen who invades Narnia at its genesis and plays Satan to Aslan's Christ. Unlike the Un-man, she is beautiful, majestic, and other-worldly. Yet that other-worldliness places her at a remove from the reader, in the "once upon a time" realm of fairytale. The villains of the Ransom Trilogy lack this quality, though in their rhetoric they share some of the same delusions of grandeur. They are politicians, scientists, scholars, all too disturbingly *this*-worldly. Their philosophical arguments, as Ransom thinks to himself in *Perelandra*, "might just as well

---

2. Ransom experiences the same thing with pleasure on Perelandra. Whereas in the Un-man he meets corruption itself, in the pleasure of the young planet he experiences "Pleasure itself." With the Un-man, he finds himself surprised at his own perfect hatred; when experiencing the immense pleasure of Perelandra, he is "haunted, not by a feeling of guilt, but by a surprise that he had no such feeling" (Lewis, *Perelandra*, ch. 3, 39).

have occurred in a Cambridge combination room."[3] This makes their descent into demonic possession all the more chilling to watch. But the most frightening of them all is the Un-man, formerly known as Professor Edward Rolles Weston. In considering the warning signs of his descent, the nature of evil as manifested through his possession, and the response demanded of Ransom, there is much that Christians today may take to heart as we take the measure of our enemies—and our Enemy.

• • •

When we first meet Weston in *Out of the Silent Planet*, he is fulsomely introduced to Ransom as "*The* Weston," the "great physicist" who "has Einstein on toast and drinks a pint of Schrodinger's blood for breakfast."[4] Making the introduction is Dick Devine, who plays his own minor villainous role before disappearing and reemerging later as Lord Feverstone in *That Hideous Strength*. Ransom has interrupted Weston and Devine's plot to kidnap a mentally handicapped boy in their spaceship, little knowing what they're up to or that he will soon take the boy's place. Before he knows it, he is slowly waking up in a drugged haze, half-eavesdropping on their schemings. "The boy was ideal," Weston is sulking. "Incapable of serving humanity and only too likely to propagate idiocy. He was the sort of boy who in a civilized community would be

---

3. Lewis, *Perelandra*, ch. 7, 106.

4. C. S. Lewis, *Out of the Silent Planet* (London: HarperCollins, 2005), ch. 1, 9.

automatically handed over to a state laboratory for experimental purposes."[5]

Lewis thus quickly establishes what type of scientist Weston is—a type whose notions of space travel would have been mocked by the intelligentsia, but whose social Darwinism would have been very much at home in elite circles of the early 1900s (and a hundred years later is now making something of a comeback). Weston is the hero of his own story, willing to risk his own life in the "great cause" of seeding humanity across the vastness of space. Of course, he was going to violate the disabled boy's human rights along the way, and, failing that, will now violate Ransom's. But in his defense, he tells us that "small claims must give way to great."[6] Only the "small-minded" could argue against his cause based on something so quaint as the rights of the individual, or even "a million individuals." One must sometimes crack an egg or a million to make an omelet, after all. (This would become a familiar Lewisian villain theme. Compare with Jadis in *The Magician's Nephew*: "The weight of the world is on our shoulders. We must be freed from all rules. Ours is a high and lonely destiny"— a line that strikes young Digory Kirke as he listens, because his power-hungry Uncle Andrew has said the very same thing, albeit less grandly.)[7] For Weston, his particular "high destiny" consists of leading the human race to colonize and, if necessary, enslave as many new worlds as necessary to ensure humanity's perpetual propa-

---

5. Lewis, *Out of the Silent Planet*, ch. 2, 17.

6. Lewis, *Out of the Silent Planet*, ch. 4, 27–28.

7. C. S. Lewis, *The Magician's Nephew* (London: Penguin, 1965), 61.

gation. Wherever "inferior" species are encountered, they must naturally be subjugated, just like inferior men. Thus, paradoxically, he sees himself as a humanist, even as he disdains human rights. And where other "humanists" like him could only dream, "In Professor Weston the power had at last met the dream."[8]

That dream is decisively thwarted on Malacandra, where Weston loses his professorial dignity in humiliating debate with the planet's severe celestial guardian, Oyarsa. As Oyarsa kills Weston's dream (for now), the angel also exposes his contradictions, by asking in what sense Weston can be said to "care for man" when he is so ready to dispose of any innocent individual man who stands in his way. Oyarsa perceives that Weston has taken "love of kindred" as his single guiding virtue at the expense of all other virtues, "bent" to the point that it has become "folly."[9] Weston doesn't even love anything about the distinctive human form, indicating that he wouldn't care if mankind "evolved" into some unrecognizable new shape on another planet. What, then, is there left of man for him to love?

Oyarsa judges this to be the work of "the lord of the silent world," or "the Bent One"—that is, Satan.[10] When asked why Satan might have done this, Weston is offended, like any good Satanist. "Me think no such person," he answers in his broken Old Solar.[11] "[M]e wise, new man—

---

8. Lewis, *Perelandra*, ch. 6, 97.

9. Lewis, *Out of the Silent Planet*, ch. 20, 178.

10. Lewis, *Out of the Silent Planet*, ch. 20, 177.

11. Lewis, *Out of the Silent Planet*, ch. 20, 178.

no believe all that old talk." But when Oyarsa explains that Maleldil (God) has taught Malacandrians to accept death peacefully instead of chasing immortality on other planets, Weston retorts, "Me no care Maleldil. Like Bent One better: me on his side."[12] Hypothetically, of course.

Exactly how Weston goes on to acquire a new spaceship after Oyarsa's servants disable his first one is unclear. But, not to be defeated, he lands on Perelandra to resume his devilish quest, as grandiose and long-winded as ever. Yet he doesn't seem quite the same to Ransom. His face has something "subtly unfamiliar" about it. He's also acquired an unsettling new fluency in the Old Solar language, which he mysteriously attributes to "guidance, you know, guidance."[13] All sorts of things are "coming into his head." He believes he is being "prepared" as a "fit receptacle" for ... something.[14]

This preparation, Weston explains, has led him to depart from his "old conception of a duty to Man as such."[15] Between the events of *Out of the Silent Planet* and *Perelandra*, Weston adopts a new philosophy. He now sees that "Man in himself is nothing."[16] Of course, Oyarsa foresaw that this was the inevitable next phase of Weston's arc. As Dostoevsky observed, no one who hates man in particular

---

12. Lewis, *Out of the Silent Planet*, ch. 20, 179.

13. Lewis, *Perelandra*, ch. 7, 114.

14. Lewis, *Perelandra*, ch. 7, 114.

15. Lewis, *Perelandra*, ch. 7, 109.

16. Lewis, *Perelandra*, ch. 7, 109.

can truly claim to love mankind in general.[17] And into the vacuum that his hatred has created, a new Spirit, capital "S," has rushed in. Not that Weston wants to think of it as a "Person," of course. Even now, he prides himself on not falling for "anthropomorphism."[18] Yet he does think of it as very much "alive,"[19] and though he doesn't use the word "worship,"[20] he worships it—this "great, inscrutable Force,"[21] this "blind, inarticulate purposiveness."[22] Where he once worked for himself, for science, and for humanity, he now works for "Spirit itself," on a new and unabashedly religious "mission" to spread "spirituality"

---

17. These are the words of Ivan in *The Brothers Karamazov*: "'I love humanity,' he said, 'but I wonder at myself. The more I love humanity in general, the less I love man in particular. In my dreams,' he said, 'I have often come to making enthusiastic schemes for the service of humanity, and perhaps I might actually have faced crucifixion if it had been suddenly necessary; and yet I am incapable of living in the same room with any one for two days together, as I know by experience. As soon as any one is near me, his personality disturbs my self complacency and restricts my freedom. In twenty-four hours I begin to hate the best of men: one because he's too long over his dinner; another because he has a cold and keeps on blowing his nose. I become hostile to people the moment they come close to me. But it has always happened that the more I detest men individually the more ardent becomes my love for humanity.'" Fyodor Dostoyevsky, *The Brothers Karamazov*, trans. Constance Garnett (New York: Random House, 1900), 64.

18. Lewis, *Perelandra*, ch. 7, 111.

19. Lewis, *Perelandra*, ch. 7, 110.

20. Lewis, *Perelandra*, ch. 7, 112.

21. Lewis, *Perelandra*, ch. 7, 111

22. Lewis, *Perelandra*, ch. 7, 109.

wherever he is guided.²³ So devoted is he to that Spirit that he would betray every part of his old identity, even "print[ing] lies as serious research in a scientific periodical," if that was required.²⁴

Lewis has some obvious philosophical foes in the crosshairs in this characterization of Weston in *Perelandra*. All the talk of "Spirit" seems like a fairly direct shot at Hegel, for instance.²⁵ A letter to Arthur C. Clarke suggests that he has no particular scientists in mind in his portrayal of Weston's plans to populate other planets, but rather a particular idea he saw developing in science fiction:

> I don't of course think that at the moment many scientists are budding Westons: but I do think (hang it all, I live among scientists!) that a point of view not unlike Weston's is on the way. Look at Stapledon (*Star Gazer* ends in sheer devil wor-

---

23. Lewis, *Perelandra*, ch. 7, 109.

24. Lewis, *Perelandra*, ch. 7, 115.

25. A representative quotation from the inaugural address of Hegel's *Lectures on the History of Philosophy*: "To combat the shallowness, to strive with German earnestness and honesty, to draw Philosophy out of the solitude into which it has wandered—to do such work as this we may hope that we are called by the higher spirit of our time. Let us together greet the dawn of a better time in which the spirit, hitherto a prey to externalities, may return within itself, come to itself again, and win space and room for a kingdom of its own, where true minds will rise above the interests of the moment, and obtain the power to receive the true, eternal and divine, the power to consider and to grasp the highest." Georg Wilhelm Friedrich Hegel, *Lectures on the History of Philosophy*, vol. 1, trans. Elizabeth Sanderson Haldan (Lincoln: University of Nebraska Press, 1995), xiii.

ship), Haldane's *Possible Worlds* and Waddington's *Science and Ethics*. I agree Technology is *per se* neutral: but a race devoted to the increase of its own power by technology with complete indifference to ethics does seem to me a cancer in the universe. Certainly if he goes on his present course much further man can *not* be trusted with knowledge.[26]

It seems fair to say that the human race did indeed continue on that course, although the consequences have perhaps been both more mundane and more sinister than Lewis predicted. Man doesn't look poised to conquer new planets by force any time soon. People have simply grown numb to the ethical costs of our tech, provided it makes our lives on this planet more convenient. There's no need for an evil cabal to eliminate those who, as Weston describes the idiot boy, are "incapable of serving humanity." Ordinary men and women choose to do so in ordinary doctors' offices every day. Scientists today have the power to grow embryos in a lab, but nobody has yet managed to generate anything fantastically devilish with this knowledge, though the madder ones might try. The technology is simply "bent" in its essence, in the human life that is quietly discarded every day while everyone collectively looks the other way.

---

26. C. S. Lewis, Letter to Arthur C. Clarke, December 7, 1943, in *The Collected Letters of C. S. Lewis*, vol. 2, *Books, Broadcasts, and the War 1931–1949*, ed. Walter Hooper (London: William Collins, 2004), 690.

Still, there are those mad few still dreaming Weston's dreams, like pop science historian Yuval Noah Harari. Here he is addressing the World Economic Forum:

> By hacking organisms, elites may gain the power to reengineer the future of life itself, because once you can hack something, you can usually also engineer it, and if indeed we succeed in hacking and engineering life, this will be not just the greatest revolution in the history of humanity. This will be the greatest revolution in biology since the very beginning of life four billion years ago. For four billion years, nothing fundamental changed in the basic rules of the game of life. All of life, for four billion years—dinosaurs, amoebas, tomatoes, humans, all of life was subject to the laws of natural selection and to the laws of organic biochemistry, but this is now about to change. Science is replacing evolution by natural selection with evolution by intelligent design. Not the intelligent design of some God above the clouds, but our intelligent design, and the intelligent design of our "clouds": the IBM cloud, the Microsoft cloud, these are the new driving forces of evolution. And at the same time, science may enable life, after being confined for four billion years to the limited realm of organic compounds, science may enable life to break out into the inorganic.[27]

---

27. World Economic Forum, "Will the Future Be Human? – Yuval Noah Harari," January 25, 2018, https://www.youtube.com/

Granted, Harari's flights of fantasy depend on a fundamentally materialistic view of the universe, meaning that the danger is not so much that they will actually come true, but that dangerous forces could be harnessed (or, perhaps, channeled) by men who believe they can. And sometimes, as with tech entrepreneur and venture capitalist Bryan Johnson, such men seem to be their own first victims. At the time of writing, Johnson is obsessively devoted to a bizarre antiaging quest he calls "Operation Blueprint," which is at once hilarious and frightening. Using methods including a transfusion of his teenage son's blood, Johnson is attempting to remain, quite literally, forever young.[28] As he put it in a much-quoted podcast interview, "The only thing I believe in is I don't want to die."[29] Johnson may lack Weston's scholarly eloquence, but they resemble each other in that their blind quest for immortality leads both men to—paradoxically—hold their own humanity terrifyingly cheap. This leaves them, as Johnson puts it, "wide open" to whatever might replace it:

> We're right now in a moment, in the last moment, where things kinda have been how they

---

watch?v=hL9uk4hKyg4&.

28. See Andrea Michelsen, "This multimillionaire entrepreneur infused himself with blood from his 17-year-old son in a quest to stay young forever," *Business Insider*, May 22 2023, tps://www.businessinsider.com/millionaire-bryan-johnson-swapped-blood-with-teenage-son-young-blood–2023–5?op=1&r=US&IR=T.

29. Rich Roll, "The $2M Longevity Protocol: Bryan Johnson's Biohacking Blueprint," January 29, 2024, https://www.youtube.com/watch?v=roHeUk7ApUo& (00:14).

have been, but they're about to change radically. And in this new future, we can't predict what's gonna happen. We no longer have that ability. And so we're living in a zeroth world, and so Gen Zero is a group of multi-ethnic, multinational people who rise up, and they say, "We are willing to courageously step into the future. And we're willing to divorce, open to divorce from ourselves all human norms, all human customs, all human thought. And we're willing to say, we're wide open. About everything. Absolute blank slate."[30]

Can we expect Harari or Johnson to turn up demon-possessed sometime soon? Perhaps not. But for their own sakes, we can at least hope they fail to keep an audience.

Of course, it's in the nature of speculative fiction that Weston's transformation is radically accelerated, though Ransom doesn't yet know it as he attempts to set robust Christian theology against the professor's literally devilish nonsense. Weston dismisses it all as "the old accursed dualism," where God and the Devil are two separate entities.[31] But doesn't Ransom know that God and the Devil are one? And so, in a nauseating flash, Weston's possession is complete, as he "calls that Force" into himself completely. But just before he is taken over, something like "the old Weston" comes out, frantically pleading, "Ransom, Ran-

---

30. Roll, "The $2m Longevity Protocol," 2:14:51–2:15:35.

31. Lewis, *Perelandra*, ch. 7, 115.

som! For Christ's sake don't let them …"[32] It won't be the first time Ransom seems to glimpse the old Weston. But it may be the last time he actually does.

• • •

Gradually, Ransom begins to awaken to the awful truth, as he eavesdrops on the first temptation of the Green Lady and senses a looming disaster. Something that sounds both like and unlike Weston is tempting her.[33] But it doesn't fully sink in until the next day, beginning with the sickening discovery of a mutilated frog—the first "dead or spoiled" thing Ransom has seen in Perelandra.[34] As a small theological side note, this scene vividly illustrates how animal death could plausibly have followed the fall of Satan rather than the fall of Adam. The frog's mutilation is not remotely trivialized. It's an "intolerable obscenity," as awful as "the first lie from a friend on whose truth one was willing to stake a thousand pounds."[35] In the moment, Ransom thinks "It would be better … for the whole universe never to have existed than for this one thing to have happened."[36] At the same time, it's considered as a thing apart from the crowning corruption that the Bent One still means to work on those made in Maleldil's image.

---

32. Lewis, *Perelandra*, ch. 7, 116.

33. Lewis, *Perelandra*, ch. 8, 130.

34. Lewis, *Perelandra*, ch. 9, 132.

35. Lewis, *Perelandra*, ch. 9, 132.

36. Lewis, *Perelandra*, ch. 9, 132.

After this first shock, Ransom walks on and is shocked afresh by a whole trail of mutilated frogs leading to the Un-man, in the act of slicing open yet another one with its fiendishly long fingernails. And here, with his first good look at the Un-man's blankly stupid face in broad daylight, Ransom finally understands that it is no longer Weston he is looking at. The thing wearing Weston's skin gives him a "devilish" smile, but not devilish in a sinister or cunning sense. In a sickening way, it could even be described as "innocent." It's the smile of evil that has not defied good, but rather "ignored it to the point of annihilation."[37]

The Un-man's nasty qualities are lingered on and developed to chilling effect. Lewis sets his Satan apart from Marlowe's suave Mephistopheles or Milton's tragically brooding Lucifer. (He even telegraphs in Ransom's voice that this is precisely his intent.) This Satan *can* be graceful and eloquent, when the moment suits. It even offers arguments to the Green Lady that are more subtly dangerous than Satan's arguments in *Paradise Lost*, because they appeal to the Green Lady's virtues where Milton's Satan appeals to Eve's vices. However, in Lewis's storyworld, subtle grace and eloquence are not of the devil's essence. Unlike many villains who play stupid on the outside but are really dastardly clever beneath, Lewis's Satan is, beneath it all, an idiot. The Un-man functions like a well-programmed artificial intelligence, able to ape human words and actions fluently. But its default mode is inane cruelty—like that one boy who spends his recess methodically tearing off butterflies' wings. When it's not trying to tear apart any small animal it can find (which Ransom becomes practiced at

---

37. Lewis, *Perelandra*, ch. 9, 135.

defending), it's playing with its own genitalia (implied) or mechanically repeating Ransom's name for hours on end. "Sin makes you stupid," goes the cliché, but Lewis here takes cliché and turns it into truly compelling speculative fiction. Weston's brilliance was once his pride, fueling his signature grandiose speeches. Now, he has been spiritually lobotomized, a puppet for banal evil in its purest form. Most terrifyingly, his memories have been replaced with the Bent One's memories, as in the bone-chilling moment when it recalls Our Lord's crucifixion with a loud "*Eloi, Eloi, lama sabachthani*," and somehow Ransom knows that it is speaking perfect first-century Aramaic. "The Unman was not quoting. It was remembering."[38]

But does some spark of "the old Weston" yet live? There are moments when Ransom wonders, when the creature starts pitifully rambling in what might be a captive Weston's voice. "I'm down in the bottom of a big black hole," it (he?) mumbles. "No, I'm not, though. I'm on Perelandra. I can't think very well now, but that doesn't matter, he does all my thinking for me …"[39] Ransom debates internally about what exactly he's hearing, never sure if this really is Weston's voice or just a devilish prank. Lewis flirts here as elsewhere with a form of annihilationism, speculating that what used to be Weston may now be nothing more than an everlasting decayed mumble, like the woman in *The Great Divorce* who is nothing more than an everlasting grumble.[40]

---

38. Lewis, *Perelandra*, ch. 12, 190.

39. Lewis, *Perelandra*, ch. 10, 159.

40. "The question is whether she is a grumbler, or only a grumble. If

This much Ransom does know: Whatever hatred he once felt for Weston is now gone, so completely that it feels only natural to "pray fervently for his soul."[41] Watching closely during one of the temptation sessions, he happens to notice that Weston's old pack looks just like his own, and this small detail almost brings him to tears, because it suddenly reminds him "that Weston had once been a man, that he too had once had pleasures and pains and a human mind."[42] Later, on the edge of the story's climax, this wavering almost gets him killed. As they ride giant fishes into a storm, old Weston's babbling voice surfaces one last time. In a swift motion of compassion, Ransom reaches out a hand to his old enemy. "Say a child's prayer if you can't say a man's," he urges. "Repent your sins. Take my hand."[43] But it is the Un-man who takes it.

• • •

The problem of how to love one's enemies occupied Lewis's thought deeply, as we know from his letters. One written to his brother Warren—Warnie—in May 1940 particularly sheds light here. The rise of Hitler greatly troubled War-

---

there is a real woman—even the least trace of one—still there inside the grumbling, it can be brought to life again. If there's one wee spark under all those ashes, we'll blow it till the whole pile is red and clear. But if there's nothing but ashes we'll not go on blowing them in our own eyes forever. They must be swept up." C. S. Lewis, *The Great Divorce* (London: HarperCollins, 2002), 77.

41. Lewis, *Perelandra*, ch. 10, 160.

42. Lewis, *Perelandra*, ch. 10, 168.

43. Lewis, *Perelandra*, ch. 13, 215.

nie, who was wrestling with the question of how exactly one was to love "the Gestapo-man." Lewis writes back that he prays every night for the people he is most tempted to despise, including Hitler and Stalin and a few unknown names, presumably drawn from the brothers' acquaintances circle (with the amusing N.B. that "I don't mean that I'm tempted to hate them equally, of course!")[44] Enemy love is non-optional, that much is clear, but he tells Warnie he has expended much thought in his effort to "make it real." His main insight is that loving the enemy does not mean pretending the enemy is *lovable*. Nor does it mean downplaying his sins. It means Agapë love, choosing to will the enemy's best good:

> It's the old business about "loving the sinner and hating the sin" wh. becomes alive to me when I realise that this is what I do to myself all the time. In fact I provisionally define Agapë as "steadily remembering that inside the Gestapo-man there is a thing wh. says I and Me just as you do, which has just the same grounds (neither more nor less) as your 'Me' for being distinguished from all its sins however numerous, which, like you, was made by God for eternal happiness—remembering, and always acting for the real interests of that thing as far as you can."[45]

---

44. C. S. Lewis, Letter to His Brother, May 4, 1940, in *Collected Letters*, 2:408.

45. Lewis, Letter to His Brother, May 4, 1940, in *Collected Letters*, 2:409.

He then considers a suggestion Warnie has apparently made that perhaps the Gestapo-men might be literally possessed. This, he suggests, would only make the task easier:

> Suppose your eyes were opened and you cd. see the Gestapo man visibly fiend-ridden—a twisted and stunted human form, covered with blood and filth, with a sort of cross between a mandrill and a giant centipede fastened onto it? Surely you, and the human remains, become almost allies against the horror which is tormenting you both, him directly and you through him?[46]

Here Lewis sketches in abstract what he would soon make concrete with Ransom and the Un-man. Ransom is at least willing to be an ally to Weston, or to Weston's "human remains." However, he realizes in the end that Weston's possession has progressed to full damnation, the "further stage" this letter also goes on to outline. When once the fiend's victim has passed the point of no return to humanity, then (and only then) we are finally permitted to hate him. But Lewis insists we must never assume that a man has passed that point as long as he's alive, great as the temptation may be. It is still possible, and indeed commanded, to pray for his soul, even though we needn't pray that he will escape justice if he continues as he is. These reflections ring prophetic in hindsight when considering the cases of individual Nazis who did, in fact,

---

46. Lewis, Letter to His Brother, May 4, 1940, in *Collected Letters*, 2:409.

make full confessions and repentance before facing their just earthly punishment. Alas, for poor Weston, there will be no coming back.

• • •

The Christian today can apply these insights generously, to enemies close or distant. Where *The Great Divorce* offers a Dantean tour of how people can lose their souls through personal vices, *Perelandra* shows how the Bent One works through a combination of personal vice and evil ideology, making the Un-man an especially apt figure of study as we consider our ideological foes. We might think about men and women who seem quite literally hellbent on marshalling recruits into the New Sexual Revolution. A palpably demonic spirit often hangs about these people's presentation and social media propaganda. There is nothing they have chosen to share with us that stirs up warm feelings or appears remotely lovable. Sometimes they have even made a deliberate effort to appear as bizarre and unsettling as possible. They have been Un-manned.

In my own experience as a writer who frequently plunges into such waters online, I've occasionally found myself a target of intense vitriol from people like this who find my work most unwelcome. Earlier this year, I made an unsuccessful attempt to engage with a whole group of such people who had showed up to spoil a detransitioned friend's lonely protest outside a branch of Planned Parenthood. The contrast between them and my friend, as well as the Catholic pro-lifers calmly taking shifts in our modest picket line, was—quite literally—like night and day. One Catholic woman even expressed concern for the counter-protestors' safety as they dashed carelessly across the busy street. I also found it humbling to watch my non-Christian friend return nothing but grace when her enemies came at her with mockery, even earnestly insisting she didn't hate any of them. There was one especially troubled man in his 30s who wore dark glasses and a green dress printed with sea turtles. Like Ransom struck by Weston's pack, I was strangely moved by this dress—such an innocent design, so cheerfully loud, so obviously not made for the unhappy soul wearing it.

Discussing the protest later, my friend said that if someone "not in their right mind" attacks her, then "who am I to be angry at them? They aren't the monster, the mental illness or the trauma or the pain is the monster. That's what we hate. That's what we fight. Not people." In spirit, this felt impressively Lewisian, though Lewis would sharpen it with the language of "sinner" and "sin," and would also have no qualms about "fighting" either, even if we are only allowed to "hate" the latter. Admittedly, this is a challenge when these sorts of aggressive sinners seem to harness such a vindictive—even satanic—spirit. I did not feel especially saintly or open-hearted as I watched them bully my friend. But then, Lewis also reminds me that I don't have to. In the end, for Ransom, as knightly guardian of the Green Lady and her planet, both fighting and hatred will have their place. He will fight the sinner, hating his sin, and eventually hating the Thing sin makes of him. While Lewis's exhortation to love our enemies is sorely needed in the present moment, so too is his counsel that, sometimes, concrete opposition to the forces of evil is called for. Before their final confrontation, Ransom spends a long time piously trying to convince himself that physical violence against the Un-man cannot possibly be what Maleldil wants from him: "It stood to reason that a struggle with the Devil meant a *spiritual* struggle ... the notion of a physical combat was only fit for a savage."[47] It dawns on him, though, that Perelandra knows no difference between physical and spiritual, between truth, myth, and fact. Eventually, physical combat—hand to hand, no less—presents itself as a grim and good necessity. Of course, we are not on Perelandra. We should be slow to identify any particular concrete action we take with the great mythic, spiritual struggle between Good and Evil. And though righteous hatred is possible, we should probably never imagine that we experience it fully here on Thulcandra. Yet Ransom's attempts to avoid the inevitable should warn us that it is all too easy to piously insist that "our struggle is not against flesh and blood" (Eph. 6:12) when, really, we are just indulging the basest kind of cowardice, unwilling to face up to the Un-man running amok with its sharp nails drawn.[48] It will bruise Ransom's heel, but he will crush its head, muttering an improvised bit of liturgy: "In the name of the Father, and of the Son, and of the Holy Ghost, here goes ... I mean, Amen!"

---

47. Lewis, *Perelandra*, ch. 11, 176.

48. See Lewis's "Why I Am Not A Pacifist" for a fuller argument of this kind. Interestingly, he suggests there that those who reject physical violence betray themselves as materialists of a sort. "The doctrine that war is always a greater evil seems to imply a materialist ethic, a belief that death and pain are the greatest evils. But I do not think they are." *The Weight of Glory and Other Addresses* (London: William Collins, 2013), 77.

And yet, there's one last bit of grace for old Weston—for what he was, and what he could or should have been. While resting after his ordeal, Ransom takes a day to do "something which may appear rather foolish," yet something it seems to him he "could hardly omit."[49] On discovering that he's able to write with stone in the soft side of a translucent underground cliff, he busies himself in the preparation of a long epitaph for Weston in Old Solar. Gracefully and elegantly, the language lays this "learned *hnau*" to rest, telling briefly how he "gave up learned will and reason to the bent Eldil when Tellus was making the one thousandth nine hundredth and forty-second revolution after the birth of Maleldil, blessed be he."[50] "That was a tomfool thing to do," Ransom thinks as he lies back down. "No one will ever read it. But there ought to be some record. He was a great physicist, after all."[51]

---

49. Lewis, *Perelandra*, ch. 15, 237.

50. Lewis, *Perelandra*, ch. 15, 237–38.

51. Lewis, *Perelandra*, ch. 15, 238.

VI

A TASTE OF PARADISE:
NAMING, RESTRAINING, AND EMBRACING PLEASURE ON PERELANDRA

Rhys Laverty

> *"Every joy is beyond all others. The fruit we are eating is always the best fruit of all"*
> —The Green Lady, *Perelandra*[1]

Why set a story in paradise? Tolstoy famously opens *Anna Karenina* by quipping that "All happy families are alike; each unhappy family is unhappy in its own way." There is an edge to Tolstoy's line: unhappy families may be unhappy, but at least they are interesting. Happy ones are a bore. Compelling narratives surely involve conflict, which requires unhappiness, dissonance, threats to be overcome. Even the simplest children's board books involve such: a

---

1. C.S. Lewis, *Perelandra* (London: HarperCollins, 2005), ch. 6, 99.

missing farm animal, an incomplete tea party, a hidden face in a game of peekaboo. When we *do* find stories set in something like paradise, we usually swiftly find that all is not as it seems. Every utopia is a dystopia. If it seems too good to be true, it is—and if it were true, then what a bore.

And then we come to *Perelandra*. Ever since entering the world of Ransom Trilogy readers, I have routinely found *Perelandra* to be the favorite of devotees. *Perelandra* does, of course, involve conflict—indeed, *the* conflict, with *the* Enemy. And yet what I find people most often return to *Perelandra* for is simply to put themselves in Ransom's shoes and to be a fallen creature wandering through an unfallen world—to walk in the Garden in the cool of the day. It is a genuine utopia—"Paradise Retained," some say.[2]

Perelandra opens up an age-old thought experiment: what would life be like in paradise? There are many strands to this, most only hinted at. Yet one to which Lewis gives frequent attention is this: *what would unfallen pleasure be like?*[3]

---

2. This phrase was coined in Victor M. Hamm, "Mr. Lewis in Perelandra," *Thought: Fordham University Quarterly* 20, no. 2 (June 1945), 271.

3. A major question here is whether Lewis at all intended Perelandra to be akin to Eden, the New Creation, or Heaven (that is, the spiritual realm in which God and the angels dwells and where the souls of departed believers are understood to wait until Christ's return). The three are not synonymous in Christian theology. In short, I do not think Perelandra is synonymous with any. Lewis himself wrote, in a letter to Victor M. Hamm:

> The only point I think you are slightly wrong on is that you use the Martian society too boldly as a guide to what Perelandra wd. become later on. But there is no real parallel. The *Incarnation* has

A Taste of Paradise

EXCURSUS: WHY DISCUSS PARADISE AT ALL?

Before considering these questions, we should first handle a potential objection: does discussing the possibilities of paradise not amount to unhelpful—or at least distracting—speculation? We are far east of Eden, after all. We cannot know what unfallen life would have been like in many particulars, likewise with resurrection life. The dangers of such speculation are in view when the Apostle Paul issues his rebuke regarding the resurrection body in 1 Corinthians 15: "But someone will ask, 'How are the

> come in between. Malacandra belongs to the old order in wh. planetary creatures were subjected to the angels: but the angels kneel before Tor. There is no limit to the future glories of the world wh., needing no redemption itself, yet profits by the Incarnation. You get the idea? And, by the bye, I don't mean the idea of a cosmic language as anything more than fiction. (*The Collected Letters of C. S. Lewis*, vol. 2, *Books, Broadcasts, and the War 1931–1949*, ed. Walter Hooper [London: HarperOne, 2009], 780).

Perelandra, then, is closer to a thought experiment than it is to Heaven, Eden, or the New Creation: a world unreached by the Fall, on which rational creatures made in the image of God are brought into being only *after* God himself has become incarnate as an image-bearer on Earth. This gives Lewis an immense amount of freedom with his imagined paradise, and thus I think he avoids having to conform to any of our initially imagined possibilities. Heaven, Eden, and the New Creation are all called to mind at different points—although it seems to me that the thrust of things, particularly in view of Ransom's descriptions of his "transcendent" experiences in the space-coffin and his growth into the wounded yet glorified Pendragon, tends to evoke the New Creation more than either of the others. I am thankful to Jason Lepojärvi for pushing me to think on this issue.

dead raised? With what kind of body will they come?' How foolish!" (15:35 ESV). Jesus clashes with the resurrection-denying Sadducees along the same lines (Matt. 22:23-33). In these instances, speculation leads to denial. Falling off the other side of the horse, however, it is not hard to find those who become incredibly wrapped up in the exacting details of resurrection life: Will we sleep? Will we still go to the bathroom? How old will we be? These are twin errors. But does that mean that there is no benefit to imagining the unfallen life? I do not think so. To demonstrate why, consider another topic that is often dismissed due to excessive speculation: angels.

In Book I of Augustine's *On Christian Teaching*, while discussing theology and preaching, Augustine suddenly says, "At this point there arise questions about the angels."[4] The modern reader asks: *do they?* A sudden gear change for many, but familiar to those who have spent time reading ancient or medieval Christian theology. Why do those writers so often change gear and find it obvious to talk about angels? Well, although excessive angelic speculation is a danger, there is a venerable and useful purpose to reflecting on angels: to road test things we have said about humanity. For example, we may say "human beings are the only rational creatures." We say this in order to distinguish men from animals. *But what about angels?* Aren't they rational creatures too? Perhaps even *more* rational than us? Suddenly, our confident and pastorally well-intentioned statement about the uniqueness of humanity requires fine-tuning. And so we return to the drawing board.

---

4. Augustine, *On Christian Teaching*, trans. R. P. H. Green (Oxford: Oxford University Press, 1997), I.66.

Reflection on paradise is, I suggest, much the same. It causes us to consider our firmly held beliefs about this world against a more perfect foil. This, in fact, is arguably what Christ himself forces the Sadducees to do when they approach him with their tricksy questions about marriage at the resurrection. The Sadducees must consider the mysterious realities of future paradise (Matt. 22:29-30), as must the Corinthians when Paul writes to them about marriage and celibacy in 1 Corinthians 7. Informed reflection upon the nature of paradise, then, can have a great practical impact upon the Christian life.

PLEASURE VS. JOY?

And so, we come to the question of pleasure in *Perelandra*. Many readers will be familiar with Lewis's view of "Joy," and may instinctively think that he would take a dim view of pleasure as a pretender to Joy. Aren't Pleasures those things with which we are "far too easily pleased?"[5] Lewis himself said we must sharply distinguish between Joy, Happiness, and Pleasure,[6] and mused on "whether all pleasures are not substitutes for Joy."[7]

To pit pleasure and Joy against each other absolutely misreads Lewis however. First, Joy is often misunderstood. While profoundly desirable and pleasurable for Lewis, Joy is a *desire*, not a settled and ultimate state of mind. It is often overlooked that Lewis declared that Joy "lost nearly all

---

5. C. S. Lewis, *The Weight of Glory and Other Addresses* (London: William Collins, 2013), 26.

6. Lewis, *Surprised By Joy* (London: Collins, 2012), 18.

7. Lewis, *Surprised By Joy*, 197.

interest" after his conversion, because he had found that for which it longed.⁸ Joy may "outrank" pleasure in some sense in this life by virtue of the fact that its direct object is the highest possible Good—that is, heaven, where God dwells. But Joy itself neither a goal, nor an intrinsic good.

Second: whereas Joy is neither goal nor intrinsic good for Lewis, pleasure is both. In the most thorough study of Lewis's thoughts on pleasure, Stewart Goetz is abundantly clear: Lewis was a hedonist, without qualification.⁹ Perfect Happiness will be a state of eternal Pleasure with God—and this is that for which Joy longs. We really should not need Goetz to tell us this. Lewis discusses pleasure frequently and, in itself, positively. The most substantial treatment is possible the second chapter of *The Four Loves*, which is largely a study of pleasure, diving all into "Need-pleasures" and "pleasures of Appreciation" (an idea to which we shall return).¹⁰

Wesley Kort points out that Lewis saw pleasure as having a similar structure to both Joy and knowledge. For Lewis, "Pleasures are more common, more precisely oriented, and more physical than are experiences of joy."¹¹ Joy, by contrast "is a more specific and intense experience"

---

8. Lewis, *Surprised By Joy*, 276.

9. See "Hedonistic Happiness," the first chapter in Goetz's *A Philosophical Walking Tour with C. S. Lewis: Why It Did Not Include Rome* (New York: Bloomsbury, 2015), 17–67.

10. C. S. Lewis, *The Four Loves* (London: Harper Collins, 2012), 15. See Goetz, "Hedonistic Happiness," 'for the many other places in which Lewis discusses pleasure.

11. Wesley A. Kort, *C. S. Lewis: Then and Now* (Oxford: Oxford University Press, 2001), 124.

that necessarily contains "an element of pain"—*sehnsucht*, that strangely enjoyable sense of lack.

Yet Joy, pleasure, and knowing all "direct attention away from the self"; all place one in the wider world; and all point to higher things, but in different ways.[12] Pleasure relates mainly to precise physical experiences and is a fairly "complete" experience in the moment. One may be left wanting more afterwards, but this differs from Joy in which one is left wanting more *while the experience is still happening*. Neither Lewis nor Kort tries to draw sharp lines between these categories, but Kort's broad distinctions (which are, on one level, fairly intuitive) are sound.

Perelandra, more vividly than any other text, demonstrates the high regard in which Lewis holds pleasure. Gilbert Meilaender describes the novel as Lewis's "picture of the appropriate attitude toward created things."[13] For instance, when Ransom lands in the seas of Perelandra, one of his first experiences is of profound pleasure:

> Though he had not been aware of thirst till now, his drink gave him a quite astonishing pleasure. It was almost like meeting Pleasure itself for the first time. He buried his flushed face in the green translucence, and when he withdrew it found himself once more on top of a wave.[14]

---

12. Kort, *C. S. Lewis: Then and Now*, 125.

13. Gilbert Meilaender, *The Taste for the Other: The Social and Ethical Thought of C. S. Lewis* (Grand Rapids: Eerdmans, 1978), 17.

14. Lewis, *Perelandra*, ch. 3, 36.

This amounts to "a strange sense of excessive pleasure which seemed somehow to be communicated to him through all his senses at once."[15] As soon as Lewis's protagonist arrives in paradise he experiences pleasure—indeed, "Pleasure itself."

Further, the narrator tells us how Ransom describes—or rather, fails to describe—his experiences on Perelandra and his journey there upon his return to Earth. A "sceptical friend" of his, McPhee (surely the same commonsense Scotsman as in *That Hideous Strength*), expresses Sadducee-like mockery toward the idea of the resurrection of the body—the idea of guts and palate but no eating, genitals but no copulation, seems an absurdity.[16] Ransom responds:

> "Oh, don't you see, you ass, that there's a difference between a trans-sensuous life and a non-sensuous life?" That, of course, directed McPhee's fire to him. What emerged was that in Ransom's opinion the present functions and appetites of the body would disappear, not because they were atrophied but because they were, as he said, "engulfed." He used the word "trans-sexual," I remember, and began to hunt about for some similar words to apply to eating (after rejecting "trans-gastronomic") ...[17]

---

15. Lewis, *Perelandra*, ch. 3, 39.

16. Lewis, *Perelandra*, ch. 3, 33.

17. Lewis, *Perelandra*, ch. 3, 33. The shifting connotations of the word "trans-sexual" are, of course, amusing to us readers today.

"Pleasure" is not specifically mentioned here, but is clearly in view. Via Ransom, Lewis offers a "high view" of pleasure. Although it will one day enter a "higher medium" in glory, this will be a *transformation* rather than *negation* of pleasure, engulfment rather than erasure.[18] The pleasures of this world are tethered to those of the world to come, differing from them "not as emptiness differs from water or water from wine but as a flower differs from a bulb or a cathedral from an architect's drawing."[19]

Perelandra, then, is a world in which pleasure exists in its flowered form, rather than as a bulb. Rightly speaking, it is a trans-pleasurable world, in which the delights of the body do not sit at a conflicting angle with those of the soul, but rather run in parallel. The narrator repeatedly describes Perelandra as a world in which there is no trifurcation between myth, truth, and fact, and roots this in "that unhappy division between soul and body which resulted from the Fall."[20] On Perelandra, we experience pleasure as it should have been and will one day be.

LESSONS ON PLEASURE FROM *PERELANDRA*

Having sketched Lewis's positive account of pleasure, let us ask: what reflections does he provoke by exposing us to its perfected form? I want to suggest three closely related reflections that are particularly nourishing for the Christian life. First, we will see that Lewis provides us with a taxonomy for naming different kinds of pleasures. Second,

---

18. C. S. Lewis, "Transposition" in *The Weight of Glory*, 100.

19. Lewis, "Transposition," 109.

20. Lewis, *Perelandra*, 177.

he provides a compelling rationale for the restraint of pleasure. And third, he richly demonstrates the way in which we are meant to embrace pleasure.

I. Naming Pleasure

On Perelandra, Lewis provides a kind of "taxonomy" of different kinds of material pleasures. Ransom's experience of the planet's garden of delights is not monotone.

First, newly arrived on the planet, Ransom encounters what we could call "ecstatic pleasure," in the juice of a delicious yellow gourd. It is hard not to quote this passage at length:

> He had meant to extract the smallest, experimental sip, but the first taste put his caution all to flight. It was, of course, a taste, just as his thirst and hunger had been thirst and hunger. But then it was so different from every other taste that it seemed mere pedantry to call it a taste at all. It was like the discovery of a totally new genus of pleasures, something unheard of among men, out of all reckoning, beyond all covenant. For one draught of this on Earth wars would be fought and nations betrayed. It could not be classified. He could never tell us, when he came back to the world of men, whether it was sharp or sweet, savoury or voluptuous, creamy or piercing. "Not like that" was all he could ever say to such inquiries.[21]

---

21. Lewis, *Perelandra*, ch. 3, 46.

A Taste of Paradise

Next, Ransom encounters what we could call "refreshing pleasure" in the strange bubbles blown by some Perelandrian trees:

> Moved by a natural impulse he put out his hand to touch it. Immediately his head, face and shoulder were drenched with what seemed (in that warm world) an ice-cold shower bath, and his nostrils filled with a sharp, shrill, exquisite scent that somehow brought to his mind the verse in Pope, "die of a rose in aromatic pain." Such was the refreshment that he seemed to himself to have been, till now, but half awake. When he opened his eyes—which had closed voluntarily at the shock of moisture—all the colours about him seemed richer and the dimness of that world seemed clarified. A re-enchantment fell upon him.[22]

Not long after this, Ransom encounters a kind of green berry, thrice the size of an almond, providing what we could call "nourishing" pleasure, which, in contrast to the magnificent gourds, have "the specific pleasure of plain food—the delight of munching and being nourished, a 'Sober certainty of waking bliss.' A man, or at least a man like Ransom, felt he ought to say grace over it; and so he presently did. The gourds would have required an oratorio or a mystical meditation."[23]

---

22. Lewis, *Perelandra*, ch. 4, 52.

23. Lewis, *Perelandra*, ch. 4, 56.

Later, when riding one of the Perelandrian fish in pursuit of the Un-man, Ransom, drinking from the planet's waters, experiences a "quenching" pleasure, saying that "Nothing had ever tasted so good" and describing it as "among the happiest moments of his life."[24]

After his conflict with the Un-man has concluded and he is recovering from his wounds, he encounters what we could call a "life-giving" pleasure in some newfound fruit. Rich clusters of grapes seem to bow themselves down to him, and he feels "breast-fed by the planet Venus herself: unweaned till he moved from that place."[25]

Other readers may well find further categories or subcategories of pleasures throughout *Perelandra*, or quibble about my suggestions. I am not wed to my outline here, and would welcome further development. But the variety of pleasures outlined—ecstatic, refreshing, nourishing, quenching, life-giving—sufficiently demonstrates my main point: Lewis intentionally presents us with different kinds of material pleasure on unfallen Perelandra—mostly to do with eating and drinking—and draws our attention to these differences.

What benefit does Lewis's taxonomy have for the Christian life? First, in depicting this variety of pleasures on an unfallen world, Lewis presents a variety of material

---

24. Lewis, *Perelandra*, ch. 12, 198. I am not entirely sure if this pleasure is distinct from the refreshing pleasure of the bubbles, but "refreshment" and "quenching" seem intuitively different.

25. Lewis, *Perelandra*, ch. 15, 234. This life-giving pleasure seems close in kind to the nourishing pleasure of the berries, but given that the former is like being coddled and breastfed and the latter like sitting down to a hearty meal, I think there is a fair distinction.

pleasure as part of God's good design for reality. If we ever turned our minds to the question of unfallen pleasure, we may be tempted—as Ransom seems to be, briefly, when he tastes the gourds—to imagine that material pleasure in Eden, or in the New Creation, would all be of the ecstatic variety. This is what Freud imagined we all really want: a state of constant orgiastic pleasure, with all other apparent desires being "a disguise for lust."[26] It is not a million miles away from the "utopia" of *Brave New World*, sustained by constant consumption of soma. This perhaps betrays an assumption that pleasure is purely *quantitative*, rather than *qualitative*, with ecstatic pleasure simply being that which is *most* pleasurable, rather than a distinct *kind* of pleasure unto itself. But Lewis (who skewered Freud at regular intervals throughout his life) has none of this. It is not due to the Fall that all kinds of pleasure are not like supping on the yellow gourds. Lewis sees pleasure as coming in infinite variety, rather than varying quantity. All pleasures great and small, the Lord God made them all.

This being the case, then, we should be prompted to see simply acknowledging and "naming" reality, including its pleasures, as part of the Christian life—indeed, as part of simply being human. Lewis sees a "quiddity" in each pleasure—a *this*-ness, standing distinctly above the abyss of non-being, as if proud of what it is. The pleasures of Perelandra do just what Gerard Manley Hopkins said all created things do, as each one

> finds tongue to fling out broad its name;
> Each mortal thing does one thing and the same:

---

26. C. S. Lewis, *The Pilgrim's Regress* (London: Fount, 1977), 88.

Deals out that being indoors each one dwells;
Selves—goes itself; *myself* it speaks and spells,
Crying *Whát I dó is me: for that I came.*[27]

Lewis anticipates here what he would later write regarding pleasures of Appreciation in *The Four Loves*. Such pleasures "make us feel something has not merely gratified our senses in fact but claimed our appreciation by right."[28] Each makes us feel that it "deserves [our] full attention," and there is "even a glimmering of unselfishness in [this] attitude" because we feel motivated to honor the pleasure itself, such as it is.

The act of *naming* such pleasures is an especially human thing. Adam names in Eden, though he is not commanded to. God simply brings the animals to him "to see what he would name them" (Gen. 2:19, NIV). Man cannot but name. He looks around and names the birds of the air, the fishes of the sea, the beasts of the field, the things that creep along the ground; he looks to the sky and names *stratus, cumulus, cirrus*; he digs below and names gold, bdellium, onyx. This is part of the Adamic task, and "Adamic" is precisely what Ransom begins to be on Perelandra—the bulb form, which will flower in *That Hideous Strength*. We see this Adamic naming when we finally meet the King, Tor, at the end of *Perelandra*. As the Green Lady describes to Ransom the region to which Tor was driven by Maleldil during his absence, Tor says "Its name is Lur."

---

27. Gerard Manley Hopkins, "As Kingfishers Catch Fire."

28. Lewis, *Four Loves*, 17.

The *eldila* repeat this, and Ransom realizes "that the King had uttered not an observation but an enactment."[29]

In his exploration of the full garden of earthly delights then, Lewis prompts us to attend to and to name the pleasures with which God blesses us—to hear each one speak "*myself*," to know it, and to reply in our own speech by enacting its name: ecstasy, refreshment, nourishment, quenching, life-giving, and perhaps even more. We delight to name what we enjoy because the naming not merely expresses but completes the enjoyment.[30]

II. Restraining Pleasure

In view of knowing and naming differing pleasures, Lewis gives a curious but compelling rationale for exercising restraint with regard to certain pleasures. More than once, we see Ransom exercise self-control—first with the ecstatic gourds:

> As he let the empty gourd fall from his hand and was about to pluck a second one, it came into his head that he was now neither hungry nor thirsty. And yet to repeat a pleasure so intense and almost so spiritual seemed an obvious thing to do. His reason, or what we commonly take to be reason in our own world was all in favour of tasting the miracle again; the childlike innocence of fruit, the labours he had undergone, the uncertainty of the future, all seemed

---

29. Lewis, *Perelandra*, ch. 17, 266.

30. I am here riffing on Lewis's famous comment regarding praise.

to commend the action. Yet something seemed opposed to this "reason." It is difficult to suppose that this opposition came from desire, for what desire would turn from so much deliciousness? But for whatever cause, it appeared to him better not to taste again. Perhaps the experience had been so complete that repetition would be a vulgarity—like asking to hear the same symphony twice in a day.[31]

Ransom is not driven to restraint by a simple concern for his own sin or virtue, as if to indulge again would mean being dragged away by his own evil desire (Jas. 1:14). Indeed, he realizes he doesn't even *want* to taste again; rather a "spurious rationalism" that sees pleasure as quantitative simply asks, "Why *wouldn't* you taste again?"[32] But because pleasure is *qualitative*, Ransom senses that this *particular kind* of pleasure is one that it would be vulgar to repeat immediately. Restraint is demanded not by a concern for his own soul, but by an intuitive reverence for the pleasure itself.[33] This same reality is what tells him that the nourishing berries demand that one say grace over them,

---

31. Lewis, *Perelandra*, ch. 3, 46.

32. Lewis, *Perelandra*, ch. 3, 47.

33. In this attitude, we sense Lewis's idea of the *Tao*: "the belief that certain attitudes are really true, and others really false, to the kind of thing the universe is and the kind of things we are" (C.S. Lewis, *The Abolition of Man* (New York: Macmillan, 1947), 12). This applies just as much to whether one says "another!" or "no more!" about an ecstatic gourd as it does to whether one says "pretty" or "sublime" about a waterfall.

whereas the gourds demand "an oratorio or a mystical meditation."[34]

There are many Christian motivations for self-control—love of God, love of neighbor, a desire to grow in Christlikeness. Lewis here adds another: to honor the pleasure itself. Once again, it is that "glimmering of unselfishness" we feel toward pleasure of Appreciation. To do this, we must take care in rightly naming pleasures; we must know what we are dealing with, and whether we are in fact engaging in a vulgar repetition that not only corrupts our own soul but that denigrates the pleasurable gift.

In a world of modern Western luxury, we are surrounded by pleasures that most of humanity—including the kings of the past—could only dream of. We swiftly become desensitized to the sheer grandeur of the pleasures at our fingertips: food, travel, entertainment. Technology intensifies this. In the digital age, we *can* listen to the same symphony twice in a day—indeed, as many times as we like, and performed by the greatest conductors and musicians of history. The greatest artefacts of human civilization are only ever a few clicks away, and we can graze through them in half an hour's idle scrolling, leaving each unfinished since we were never really desirous of them to begin with. Every day, we surely taste more things than we realize that we rob of their deserved oratorios, and a single day would not have time enough to give them. A sojourn on Perelandra calls us to pause and ask what kind of pleasure presents itself to us, and to restrain ourselves accordingly.

---

34. Lewis, *Perelandra*, ch. 4, 56.

III. Embracing Pleasure

Having named pleasure and discerned when to restrain it, what then does it mean to perfectly embrace pleasure? In short it is to humbly accept whichever particular pleasure is at hand in any given moment. In loose biblical terms, this is not to say that we opt for "the fleeting pleasures of sin" (Heb. 11:25) that in any moment may distract us; rather, if it is true that "every good and perfect gift is from above" (Jas. 1:17), then we must to ask "which *particular* gift of pleasure have I been given in this *particular* moment?" and to receive it with thanksgiving as "those who know and believe the truth" (1 Tim. 4:3).

The need to accept the pleasure of the moment lies at the heart of Lewis's retelling of the Fall (or lack thereof) in *Perelandra*. The Perelandrian "covenant of works" rests not on a prohibition to not eat from the Tree of Knowledge, but to not dwell or sleep on the Fixed Land. In the concluding "theodicy," the Green Lady explains how she now understands Maleldil's command:

> The reason for not yet living on the Fixed Land is now so plain. How could I wish to live there except because it was Fixed? And why should I desire the Fixed except to make sure—to be able on one day to command where I should be the next and what should happen to me? It was to reject the wave—to draw my hands out of Maleldil's to say to Him, "Not thus, but thus," to put in our own power what times should roll towards us ... as if you gathered fruits together today for tomorrow's eating instead of taking what came. That would have been cold love and

feeble trust. And out of it how could we ever have climbed back into love and trust again?[35]

Lewis uses the shifting seas of Perelandra to illustrate the flux of creaturely life. Tinidril sees that her temptations were pushing her to surrender to Maleldil's providence within the flux. We are used to waves as a metaphor for God's providence amid unpredictable suffering—"He plants his footsteps in the sea, and rides upon the storm."[36] No fell winds blow on Perelandra, and yet there is flux, since this is simply what it means to be a creature. The Green Lady's temptation was not to reject providential suffering, but providential pleasure—the pleasures that Maleldil had ordained for that moment.

Ransom encounters the same temptation. After the refreshing bubbles, he experiences (as with the gourds) the desire for an *encore*.[37] But he resists the tasteless longing, taking his meditations on self-control to a deeper level:

> The itch to have things over again, as if life were a film that could be unrolled twice or even made to work backwards ... was it possibly the root of all evil? No: of course the love of money was called that. But money itself—perhaps one valued it chiefly as a defence against chance, a se-

---

35. Lewis, *Perelandra*, ch. 17, 264–65. I think Lewis here evokes those Israelites who gather too much manna in Exodus 16.

36. William Cowper, "God Moves in a Mysterious Way."

37. Lewis expresses the same idea regarding "*encore*" in *Letters to Malcolm: Chiefly on Prayer* (London: Geofrey Bles, 1964), 41–42.

curity for being able to have things over again, a means of arresting the unrolling of the film.[38]

Repeated pleasure, particularly that afforded by money, is a rejection of the wave currently rolling toward us. It tries to recapture the wave that has just passed. It is base ingratitude, nothing short of wishing ourselves to be God. Such a possibility first occurs to the Green Lady when reflecting on her feelings at meeting Ransom when she expected to find the King:

> One joy was expected and another is given. But this I had never noticed before that at the very moment of the finding there is in the mind a kind of thrusting back, or a setting aside. The picture of the fruit you have *not* found is still, for a moment, before you. And if you wished—if it were possible to wish—you could keep it there. You could send your soul after the good you have expected, instead of turning it to the good you had got. You could refuse the real good; you could make the real fruit insipid by thinking of the other.... One can conceive a heart which ... clung to the good it had first thought of and turned the good which it was given into no good.[39]

---

38. Lewis, *Perelandra*, ch. 4, 54.

39. Lewis, *Perelandra*, ch. 5, 80–81.

A Taste of Paradise

Soon after, this is how Ransom characterizes the Devil himself:

> "You spoke yesterday, Lady, of clinging to the old good instead of taking the good that came."
>
> "Yes—for a few heart-beats."
>
> "There was an *eldil* who clung longer—who has been clinging since before the worlds were made."
>
> "But the old good would cease to be a good at all if he did that."
>
> "Yes. It has ceased. And he still clings."[40]

The significance of this for the Christian life is obvious: we must receive with thanksgiving the joys given, not sour them with wishes for those expected or past. Job knew this: the Lord gives, and the Lord takes away; we receive good from the hand of the Lord, shall we not also receive a different kind of good? Dante knew this too:

---

40. Lewis, *Perelandra*, ch. 6, 99. It must be noted, though we do not have time to explore it, that the Un-man twists this same logic in order to tempt the Green Lady. He is too cunning to openly admit that he rejects the fruit presently given. Rather, he describes Ransom as "One who rejects the fruit he is given for the sake of the fruit he expected or the fruit he found last time" (139). The difference is that the fruit the Un-man speaks of (i.e., being like Maleldil) has *not* actually been given. He attempts to get her to reject the fruit presently given her by convincing her that the withholding of another fruit is, in fact, a concealed offering of the fruit which Maleldil secretly longs for her to take, if only she could become great-minded enough to see it.

> And in His will there is our peace: that sea
> to which all beings move—the beings He
> creates or nature makes—such is His will.[41]

This too feels like a particularly prescient lesson for a technological age. What could be better designed to enable the refusal of a present joy in favor of a past or expected one than the digital world? There, we can relive our past by scrolling through memories or returning to childhood entertainments in pursuit of the lost security and wonder of youth; we can live an alternate present in which our closest companions are not those in the same house or town as us but people on the other side of the world; we can imagine alternative futures in which our deep, dark fantasies are realized; we can ignore the pleasures on offer in the same room for those offered in the digital ether. Yet, without fail, this makes the real fruit given to us in our God-ordained time and place insipid with thoughts of other fruit.

In any moment, there are pleasures to be had, whether great or small. We must embrace each as it comes to us, for it will soon be gone. The tantalizing prospect of "a better offer" constantly presents itself to us, but must be refused—it is the tool of the Enemy. As my fellow contributor Joseph Minich, has noted, enjoyment is a form of spiritual warfare.[42] As we take up the fight, and wield the

---

41. Dante, *Paradiso*, trans. Allen Mandelbaum, Canto 3.85–87, https://digitaldante.columbia.edu/dante/divine-comedy/paradiso/paradiso-3/. We see here one possible source of inspiration for the Perelandran seas.

42. Pilgrim Faith, "Episode 80: Enjoying as Spiritual Warfare," YouTube, November 30, 2023, podcast, https://www.youtube.com/

sword of the Spirit which is the Word of God, we will find that its hilt is decorated with the rare jewel of Christian contentment. This contentment is to heed the words of the Green Lady that head this chapter: "Every joy is beyond all others. The fruit we are eating is always the best fruit of all."[43]

---

watch?v=L9VBrTJP6Bk&list=PLV68MyIL6gMc5ocrY2K7Cn4Jnp-mqm8Z76&ab_channel=DavenantInstitute.

43. Lewis, *Perelandra*, ch. 6, 99.

THAT
HIDEOUS
STRENGTH

VII

SELLING THE WELL AND THE WOOD:
THAT HIDEOUS STRENGTH AND THE ABOLITION OF MATRIMONY

Michael Ward

> *Drop down, ye heavens, from above, and let*
> *the skies pour down righteousness: let the earth*
> *open and bring forth a Saviour*
> — Isaiah 45:8

Having transported readers of his Ransom Trilogy to masculine Mars in the first novel and to feminine Venus in the second, C. S. Lewis begins the third and final book with the word "matrimony," thus adumbrating its theme: the gender principles portrayed celestially in the opening two stories are to be brought down to earth in the mundane marriage of Mark and Jane Studdock. *That Hideous Strength* has accordingly been described by one critic as "a prose epithalamium."[1] Another critic states that there is "a case for saying that marriage itself is central in this work."[2] Marriage is, indeed, central to the novel and, concomitantly, retroactively, to the trilogy as a whole. This essay will examine marriage as Lewis presents it and explore possible reasons why he wished to give it such an extensive imaginative treatment.

It is telling that *That Hideous Strength*'s opening word is not "marriage," but "matrimony." The two terms are commonly regarded as exact synonyms, but there is a distinction between them. "Matrimony" literally means "mother-making" or "mother-condition," whereas "marriage," etymologically considered, contains no reference to offspring. In the decades since Lewis wrote, the idea of marriage as a relationship that is not in principle matrimonial has become increasingly widespread. But Lewis belonged to a generation that took it for granted that marriage normally entailed procreation. A man might keep "a mistress for pleasure," but he would marry "a wife for fruit."[3]

---

1. Joe McClatchey, "The Affair of Jane's Dreams: Reading *That Hideous Strength* as Iconographic Art," in *The Taste of the Pineapple: Essays on C. S. Lewis as Reader, Critic, and Imaginative Writer*, ed. Bruce L. Edwards (Bowling Green: Bowling Green State University Popular Press, 1988), 171. An epithalamium is a poem or song written to celebrate a marriage.

2. Gilbert Meilaender, *The Taste for the Other: The Social and Ethical Thought of C. S. Lewis* (Vancouver: Regent College Publishing, 2003), 148.

3. C. S. Lewis, Letter to Owen Barfield, June 28, 1936, in *The Collected Letters of C. S. Lewis*, vol. 2, *Books, Broadcasts, and the War 1931–1949*, ed. Walter Hooper (London: HarperCollins, 2004), 199.

The "procreation of children" is the first purpose of matrimony, according to the Anglican Book of Common Prayer, the second purpose being "a remedy against sin" and the third "the mutual society, help, and comfort, that the one ought to have of the other." Lewis's former student, Mary Neylan, on whom Jane Studdock is partly based,[4] apparently disliked this ordering because she felt it unduly relegated the "emotional aspects" of marriage. In a letter of 1940, Lewis pushed back against Neylan's priorities, asking her, "What is there to object to in the order in which they [these three purposes] are put?" Good sense demands that "the biological aspect" be listed first, he argued, because

> No one is going to deny that the *biological* end of the sexual functions is offspring. And this is, on any sane view, of more importance than the *feelings* of the parents. Your descendants may be alive a million years hence and may number tens of thousands. In this regard marriages are the fountains of *History.* Surely to put the mere emotional aspects first would be sheer sentimentalism.[5]

Sentimentalism about marriage evidently struck Lewis as sufficiently interesting and important to warrant explora-

---

4. See David Downing, "Is Mary Jane? Mary Neylan as a Model for Jane Studdock in *That Hideous Strength*," *VII: Journal of the Marion E. Wade Center* 36 (2019), online edition, e123-e128.

5. C. S. Lewis, Letter to Mary Neylan, April 18, 1940, in *Collected Letters*, 2:392–97.

tion in his fictional works, where it twice receives attention: in *The Screwtape Letters* (1942), the demon Screwtape repeatedly fails to put "the biological end" at the head of the list of purposes for which "the Enemy" (God) has created marriage,[6] and in *That Hideous Strength* (1945), Jane Studdock is concerned with the third purpose of matrimony and not at all bothered with the other two. Hence the novel's opening lines:

> "Matrimony was ordained, thirdly," said Jane Studdock to herself, "for the mutual society, help, and comfort that the one ought to have of the other." She had not been to church since her schooldays until she went there six months ago to be married, and the words of the service had stuck in her mind.[7]

By starting *That Hideous Strength* in this way, Lewis makes it clear where *Out of the Silent Planet* and *Perelandra* have been leading. The trilogy moves, as Edward Zogby observes, "from archetype to anagoge, from speculation on the universal truth [of gender] to that same truth brought

---

6. Screwtape gets the order backwards when he describes marriage as "a partnership for mutual help, for the preservation of chastity, and for the transmission of life" (Letter 18). Elsewhere, he mentions "spiritually helpful, happy, and fertile marriages" (Letter 20) and "marriages which are made in obedience to the Enemy's designs, that is, with the intention of fidelity, fertility and good will" (Letter 18). Never does Screwtape put fertility first.

7. C. S. Lewis, *That Hideous Strength* (London: HarperCollins, 2003), ch. 1, 1.

into contemporary personal experience."[8] Ransom's visits to Mars and Venus turn out to have been propaedeutic adventures, equipping him to understand the essence of masculinity and femininity respectively so that, back here on earth, he can act as priest and king, drawing couples together in a sacerdotal manner and arranging dynastic unions in a monarchical fashion.[9]

That Ransom is much concerned with marital relationships is revealed during Jane's initial encounter with him in the Blue Room, where she "tasted the word *King* itself with all linked associations of battle, marriage, priesthood, mercy, and power."[10] The two proceed to have a discussion about marriage, with Jane telling him, "I don't think I look on marriage quite as you do," and Ransom replying, "It is not a question of how you or I look on marriage but how my Masters [the *Oyéresu*, the planetary intelligences] look on it."[11] In response to Jane's remarks about the "equality" of husband and wife, Ransom likens equality to clothing and praises "the naked body ... underneath the clothes, ripening for the day when we shall need them no longer"; he talks of the "fruition" of mar-

---

8. Edward G. Zogby, SJ, "Triadic Patterns in Lewis's Life and Thought," in *The Longing for a Form: Essays on the Fiction of C. S. Lewis*, ed. Peter J. Schakel (Eugene: Wipf & Stock, 2007), 26.

9. For more on Ransom's role as a maker of marriages, see my *Planet Narnia: The Seven Heavens in the Imagination of C. S. Lewis* (Oxford: Oxford University Press, 2008), 47–53.

10. Lewis, *That Hideous Strength*, ch. 7, 189.

11. Lewis, *That Hideous Strength*, ch. 7, 194.

riage.[12] His words shake Jane's philosophical foundations, but in a positive way, so that, after the audience is over, she finds herself "in the sphere of Jove."[13] The planetary reference is no casual expression, for Jane is destined to become a mother in the lineage of Jupiter. We know this from the fact that her maiden name is "Tudor." The mythical British or Celtic line (the heritage of Logres) was the one that, as Lewis explains to a correspondent, "goes back through the Tudors to Cadwallader and thence to Arthur, Uther, Cassibelan, Lear, Lud, Brut, Aeneas, Jupiter."[14] By bringing health to the Studdocks' marriage, Ransom is ensuring that this Jovial scion will be born, and England remain under Jupiter's protection.[15]

Ransom's role as a kind of sanctified marriage-guidance counsellor is seen in connection with other relationships too. At the lowest level, he performs this function when he tells the she-bear, "the future Mrs. Bultitude," "Go to your mate."[16] At the human level, he instructs Ivy Maggs, *apropos* her husband Tom, "Go and heal this

---

12. Lewis, *That Hideous Strength*, ch. 7, 196.

13. Lewis, *That Hideous Strength*, ch. 7, 201.

14. Lewis, Letter to Mary Willis Shelburne, January 16, 1954, in *The Collected Letters of C. S. Lewis*, vol. 3, *Narnia, Cambridge, and Joy 1950–1963*, ed. Walter Hooper (London: HarperCollins, 2006), 420.

15. Mark's lineage is also said to be important, though the reason is not disclosed. Merlin speaks of the birth of the new Pendragon as having been prepared in "two lines" (Lewis, *That Hideous Strength*, ch. 13, 384); Frost remarks that "The couple are eugenically interesting" (Lewis, *That Hideous Strength*, ch. 11, 332).

16. Lewis, *That Hideous Strength*, ch. 17, 526.

man,"[17] and, in a comic register, tells MacPhee and Miss Ironwood that "If you two quarrel much more ... I think I'll make you marry one another."[18] At the superhuman level, Ransom becomes a "bridge" across which the planetary powers pass, "the barrier" of "the Seventh Law" having been taken away, so that the angelic and the earthly realms can meet.[19]

Fertile encounters are everywhere celebrated in this novel, be they sexual, between male and female; astrological, between the celestial and the terrestrial; or spiritual, between the divine and the human. This theme of fruitful encounter reflects an aspect of the argument of *The Abolition of Man*, the philosophical counterpart to *That Hideous Strength*, which is that human beings should not be "geldings."[20] "We castrate and bid the geldings be fruit-

---

17. Lewis, *That Hideous Strength*, ch. 17, 527.

18. Lewis, *That Hideous Strength*, ch. 9, 272.

19. Lewis, *That Hideous Strength*, ch. 13, 401–2. "They [the Dark Eldila] had talked of a barrier which made it impossible that powers from Deep Heaven should reach the surface of the Earth," but the NICE "had broken by natural philosophy the barrier which God of His own power would not break" (Lewis, *That Hideous Strength*, ch. 16, 490; ch. 13, 401–2). Lewis does not explain the reason for this "Seventh Law" that prevented the celestial powers from descending, but the fact that it has been broken by Weston and Feverstone, thus bringing about the circumstances in which their own destruction can occur, is an example of the way that nature revenges herself on those who violate her—a major theme in *The Abolition of Man*.

20. C. S. Lewis, *The Abolition of Man* (New York: HarperCollins, 2001), 26. Adopting the position of the ethical "Innovators" (whom he means to critique), Lewis states that "the modern situation permits and demands a new sexual morality: the old taboos served some real

ful," as *Abolition* has it in one of its most famous lines.²¹ In other words, we—that is, we foolish subjectivists—divorce reason from passion and expect people still to be integrated wholes. Subjectivism drives a wedge between the cerebral and the visceral, so that people either evaporate upwards into false spirituality, as if they were angels, or devolve downwards into excessive sensuality, as if they were beasts. Those two sides of human nature must meet and interpenetrate in "the chest," the "seat of magnanimity," for man "by his intellect … is mere spirit and by his appetite mere animal."²² As the coming together of mind and body constitutes the humanity of each person anthropologically speaking, so the coming together of male and female in matrimony is what makes each person biologically speaking.

---

purpose in helping to preserve the species, but contraceptives have modified this and we can now abandon many of the taboos. For of course sexual desire, being instinctive, is to be gratified whenever it does not conflict with the preservation of the species" (33).

21. Lewis, *Abolition of Man*, 26. In a comparable passage in *That Hideous Strength*, Filostrato says to one of his colleagues in the N.I.C.E., "My friend, you have already separated the Fun, as you call it, from the fertility. The Fun itself begins to pass away.… Nature herself begins to throw away the anachronism. When she has quite thrown it away, then real civilisation becomes possible. You would understand if you were peasants. Who would try to work with stallions and bulls? No, no; we want geldings and oxen" (ch. 8, 233).

22. Lewis, *Abolition of Man*, 25. Appropriately, Merlin has an "enormous chest" (ch. 13, 375) and the tinker "a huge hairy chest" (ch. 12, 366), whereas "claws seemed to be tearing [Straik's] chest from inside" (ch. 16, 494) and Fairy Hardcastle, as if testing Mark's humanity, is shown "tapping Mark's chest with her forefinger" (ch. 3, 84).

The Studdocks' conception of matrimony, however, is that it should involve no conception, "or not for a long time yet."[23] Mark and Jane harbor a "laboratory outlook upon love":[24] they rely on unspecified contraceptive devices or methods to suppress their fertility rather than taking direct responsibility for it through chaste conduct.[25] In this respect, they exemplify the modernist ethical stance critiqued in *The Abolition of Man*. Whereas the "cardinal problem" for the "wise men of old" had been "how to conform the soul to reality, and the solution had been knowledge, self-discipline, and virtue," for Mark and Jane "the problem is how to subdue reality to the wishes of men: the solution is a technique."[26]

Mark and Jane "subdue reality" by imposing barrenness upon their young, healthy bodies. They reach for a technical solution to the "problem" of fertility rather than developing moral character appropriate to their physiological natures. Why bother with self-control when contra-

---

23. Lewis, *That Hideous Strength*, ch. 1, 2.

24. Lewis, *That Hideous Strength*, ch. 17, 531.

25. The Pill became available on the National Health Service of the United Kingdom in 1961. In the period in which the novel is set (i.e., the early 1940s), available forms of birth control included condoms, diaphragms, cervical caps, and spermicides. It is of course also possible that the Studdocks practice the withdrawal method ("Onanism," see Gen. 38:8–10); however, given that *That Hideous Strength* is the fictional counterpart to *The Abolition of Man*, which critiques the domination of nature by means of applied science, it seems likely that Lewis is hinting at technological intervention.

26. Lewis, *Abolition of Man*, 77. For a discussion of contraception in *The Abolition of Man*, see my *After Humanity*, 95, 152–56.

ceptives will achieve the desired end more conveniently? Their voluntary sterility, which freed them to have sex before marriage, now frees them, within marriage, to pursue their lifestyle choices unencumbered by the natural consequences of sexual intercourse.

But "nothing can be had without paying," as Lewis tells a correspondent, in connection with what he there calls "birth control."[27] The Studdocks' reliance upon contraception comes with a cost to their relationship. Deliberate infertility, it transpires, is not unrelated to emotional disharmony. Their surname suggests the problem for, as Lionel Adey observes, "'Stud-dock' denotes, in the marriage of Mark and Jane, [that] procreation, indeed passion itself, are in suspension."[28] The OED defines *stud* as "a man of (reputedly) great sexual potency" and *dock* as a verb meaning "to cut short ... to divest of some part or appendage." Mark, though nominally a son of Mars, is a "man of straw"[29] who avoids using "such words as 'man' or 'woman' "[30] and is more interested in entering

---

27. Unpublished letter to Alan Rooke, December 8, 1937, held in the Wade Center, Wheaton College, Illinois: "To keep it [the half-light] going for the sake of the thrill, to *hold off* a growing clarity in order to have the pleasure of fog a bit longer, is ... like birth control.... Nothing can be had without paying."

28. Lionel Adey, *C. S. Lewis: Writer, Dreamer, and Mentor* (Grand Rapids: Eerdmans, 1998), 135. More positively, *dock* could be taken to denote a creek or inlet where a boat rides at anchor.

29. Lewis, *That Hideous Strength*, ch. 9, 250.

30. Lewis, *That Hideous Strength*, ch. 4, 109.

Selling the Well and the Wood

"the Inner Ring at Belbury"[31] than entering into fruitful intimacy with his wife. Not that he dislikes sexual intercourse with her: on the contrary, he'll take it whenever he can get it, an attitude revealed on the occasion when he comes home late and finds Jane waiting for him, distressed and needing comfort: "It was a pity, he thought, that this should have happened on a night when he was so late and so tired and, to tell the truth, not perfectly sober."[32] Jane's sense that she is being alternately exploited and neglected is well founded:

> "Mutual society, help, and comfort," said Jane bitterly. In reality marriage had proved to be the door out of a world of work and comradeship and laughter and innumerable things to do, into something like solitary confinement. For some years before their marriage she had never seen so little of Mark as she had done in the last six months. Even when he was at home he hardly ever talked. He was always either sleepy or intellectually preoccupied.... Only one thing ever seemed able to keep him awake after he had gone to bed, and even that did not keep him awake for long.[33]

The difficulty confronting the protagonists is thus established in the reader's mind and its eventual resolution im-

---

31. Lewis, *That Hideous Strength*, ch. 10, 305.

32. Lewis, *That Hideous Strength*, ch. 2, 49.

33. Lewis, *That Hideous Strength*, ch. 1, 1–3.

plied. This "Modern Fairy-tale for Grown-Ups"—as the sub-title proclaims the story to be—is heading in an obvious direction. Whereas a traditional fairy-tale, for children, might end with a prince and princess kissing demurely on their wedding day, this more contemporary adult fairy-tale ends with a man and a woman about to enjoy "sex *au naturel*,"[34] fructifying for the first time in their lives.[35] Their intercourse here tells us something about the nature of marriage as Lewis understood it, and also—symbolically speaking—about the nature of all human persons, in whom there should be no barrier between reason and passion. Mark and Jane, in learning to have uncontracepted sex, are learning to have chests; their hearts expand as they conceive their own full humanity, mind and body becoming one.[36]

---

34. A term derived from Patrick Coffin's apologia for procreativity, *Sex Au Naturel: What It Is and Why It's Good for Your Marriage* (Steubenville: Emmaus Road, 2010).

35. I suspect we are meant to assume that Mark and Jane will that very night conceive their heir.

36. Lewis repeatedly tells us about Jane and Mark in terms of how their hearts respond to events, indicating as the story progresses that their "chests" are slowly coming alive. Jane's heart "missed a beat" when Dimble mentions the Spanish-like Latin used in Arthurian England (ch. 1, 28)) and "her heart sank" during her conversation with Ransom (ch. 7, 195); but she embraces rabbits and cows "in heart with merry, holiday love" (ch. 7, 201-2) during her train-ride through the countryside and felt her heart "leap and quiver" when hearing the Great Tongue spoken (ch. 10, 312). Mark's heart was "beating wildly" when told about Alcasan (ch. 8, 238); self-knowledge comes over him "with a kind of heart-break" (ch. 11, 338) but the conspiratorial glee of the tinker "warmed the heart" (ch. 14, 430); finally he perceives that, whereas he "was only a Spade", Jane "was a

BRAGDON WOOD

If the Ransom books comprise a sort of triptych that depicts masculinity on Malacandra, femininity on Perelandra, and then matrimony on Thulcandra, the opening chapter of *That Hideous Strength* repeats that threefold picture, except here the first two portraits are reversed: the story unfolds from femininity to masculinity to matrimony. The initial section of Chapter One introduces us to Jane; the second section to Mark; and the third section to Bragdon Wood—and Bragdon Wood is a private, delicately balanced world, a world of wood and water, which is deliberately suggestive of harmonious and fruitful marriage.

The third section of Chapter One is formally unique. It is the only section of the novel in which the narrator appears "on stage," so to speak. The narrator is an interesting character, and much more deserves to be said about him than can be explored here. We are to assume that he is the same "Lewis" who has appeared in the previous two tales, although in this third volume he is never named. His voice is heard at various moments, using the first-person pronoun ("Though I am Oxford bred and very fond of Cambridge ..."; "I share Dr. Dimble's sex and his limitation ..."; etc.), but only in the third section of Chapter One does he actually do anything other than comment on the action. This signifies that what is being depicted here is special, something set apart from the rest of the story, rather as marriage sets apart husband and wife from their other relationships.

Heart" (ch. 17, 502). I am grateful to David Terpstra for putting me onto this thread of imagery.

The narrator makes his way through Bracton College and is admitted to the walled enclosure of Bragdon Wood by a friend who apologizes for locking him in. He then walks for half a mile, listening as he goes to "the sound of running water and the cooing of wood pigeons,"[37] till he reaches the middle of the Wood where he sees steps going down into a well. With respectful restraint, he does not descend these steps, nor even stand on the ancient pavement surrounding the well. Instead, he lies down on the grass, touches the stonework reverently with his fingers, and falls asleep. He is woken by his friend "hallooing to me from a long way off."[38]

The section is densely laden with references to history (both real and fictional)[39] that generate a sense of im-

---

37. Lewis, *That Hideous Strength*, ch. 1, 12.

38. Lewis, *That Hideous Strength*, ch. 1, 15.

39. E.g., Bragdon Wood was where "Sir Kenelm Digby had lain all one summer night and seen a certain strange appearance: where Collins the poet had lain, and where George the Third had cried: where the brilliant and much-loved Nathaniel Fox had composed the famous poem three weeks before he was killed in France" (ch. 1, 15).

Sir Kenelm Digby (1603–1665), courtier and diplomat, had a highly romantic courtship of and marriage to a lady called Venetia Stanley. Lewis's reference to "a certain strange appearance" is perhaps meant to connote the occasion when, in a kind of enchantment, Digby saw Venetia and "when he thought he had taken her by the hand, he found that he grasped nothing but air." The spirit who had assumed his beloved's form assured him "that her soul was pure" and adjured him: "believe what I have said of Venetia Stanley's integrity, and that in despite of all oppositions and both your strongest resolutions, you two must be joined in one sacred knot." *The Life of Sir Kenelm Digby By One Of His Descendants* (London: Longmans, Green, 1896), 63–69.

portance, diuturnity and even mystery. Bragdon Wood is

William Collins (1721–1759) was an English poet whose "Ode Occasion'd by the Death of Mr Thomson" begins "In yonder grave a Druid lies" and ends "In yonder grave your Druid lies"—suitable words to allude to, given Merlin's burial under Bragdon Wood. Thomson was buried near the River Thames at Richmond, not far from the royal residence of Richmond Lodge which had in its grounds a "Merlin's Cave" installed by Queen Caroline, wife of King George II. See "Merlin's Cave and the Hermitage," The Library Blog, Richmond upon Thames Library Services, August 16, 2019, https://libraryblog.lbrut.org.uk/2019/08/merlins-cave-hermitage/.

George II was succeeded by his grandson, George III, who in 1764 made Richmond Lodge the royal family's principal country seat. He had an observatory built there from which he viewed the 1769 transit of Venus. A devout man of deep piety, George III was grieved by his brothers' loose morals and perhaps it is for this reason that he is said by Lewis to have "cried" in Bragdon Wood. He insisted on a new law that forbade members of the royal family from marrying without the consent of the sovereign. The subsequent bill passed as the Royal Marriages Act 1772 and remained in force until it was replaced by the Succession to the Crown Act 2013.

Nathaniel Fox is suggestive of Rupert Brooke and his poem "The Soldier," a poem which repeatedly mentions healthy hearts (or, to put it in Lewisian terms, magnanimous chests): "this heart, all evil shed away,/A pulse in the eternal mind, no less/Gives somewhere back the thoughts by England given;/Her sights and sounds; dreams happy as her day;/And laughter, learnt of friends; and gentleness,/In hearts at peace, under an English heaven." Presumably Fox, like Brooke, was unmarried, even a virgin, but he still has a root, morally speaking, in Bragdon Wood, the symbol of the natural sexual order. Likewise, Ransom, Grace Ironwood, and MacPhee are single, and the Dimbles are childless (indeed Mrs Dimble is "barren"), but nonetheless they all partake of the same ethical world of fertility and chastity. Actual fecundity, Lewis seems to be suggesting, is irrelevant; the crucial issue is whether one is, in principle, open to new life and its freedom or closed to it unless one can manipulate it.

manifestly a sacrosanct sort of place: "the sense of gradual penetration into a holy of holies was very strong."[40]

The use of the word "penetration" and the fact that this site centers on a well might lead us to suppose that Lewis is presenting a symbol of the female body. That is the view of Nancy-Lou Patterson, who takes this "sacred woodland" to be one of the many "feminine images of divine wholeness" in the novel.[41] Patterson's work is generally insightful, but in this particular respect I think it is mistaken. To be sure, the fact that the place is enclosed by a wall is reminiscent of the *hortus conclusus* of the Song of Solomon—"A garden inclosed is my sister, my spouse" (4:12 KJV)—but Bragdon is not an enclosed garden, it is an enclosed *wood*: "The trees were just so wide apart that one saw uninterrupted foliage in the distance."[42] This is no accident. The arboreal imagery should remind us of Mars: "Trees as protectors of life are a recurrent theme" in *Out of Silent Planet*, as Dickerson and O'Hara correctly note.[43] Malacandra is, indeed, full of forests, and of any number of other things that are tall, hard, straight, and perpendicular. Yet, at the same time as being a home to trees, Bragdon is situated on the bank of the River Wynd, contains a

---

40. Lewis, *That Hideous Strength*, ch. 1, 11.

41. Nancy-Lou Patterson, "The Unfathomable Feminine Principle: Images of Wholeness in *That Hideous Strength*," *The Lamp-Post of the Southern California C. S. Lewis Society* 9, no. 1/3 (July 1986), 35.

42. Lewis, *That Hideous Strength*, ch. 1, 12.

43. Matthew Dickerson and David O'Hara, *Narnia and the Fields of Arbol: The Environmental Vision of C. S. Lewis* (Lexington: University Press of Kentucky, 2009), 153.

well and is, so we later learn, "very nearly water-logged."⁴⁴ And this watery imagery should remind us of *Perelandra*, for Venus is a marine world where the "lands swim"⁴⁵ and Ransom effectively learns "to walk on water itself."⁴⁶ If we have been paying attention to the symbolism of the first two novels, we cannot read of wood and water here in *That Hideous Strength* without thinking of masculinity and femininity together.⁴⁷

That Bragdon should be a place simultaneously aqueous and arboreal reinforces the marital theme of the novel. It also reflects many a symbolic landscape that Lewis analyzed in *The Allegory of Love* and other works of scholarship. For instance, the "garden of Granusion" in a poem by Bernardus Sylvestris contains groves that drop odors, a sky-reflecting well, and goddesses "ready for the making of man."⁴⁸ A pair of competing examples

---

44. Lewis, *That Hideous Strength*, ch. 10, 310.

45. C. S. Lewis, *Perelandra* (London: HarperCollins, 2005), ch. 16, 254

46. Lewis, *Perelandra*, ch. 3, 44. For more on water imagery in the Ransom Trilogy, see *Planet Narnia*, 169–75.

47. Wood and water recur repeatedly paired in the novel. For example, "with Ivy he [Mr Bultitude] was perfectly at home - as a savage who believes in some remote High God is more at home with the little deities of wood and water" (ch. 14, 426); "The soul has gone out of the wood and water," according to Ransom (ch. 13, 398). Bragdon Wood appears to owe something to Charles Williams's "Wood of Broceliande" (see *Planet Narnia*, 175-77) and perhaps provides Lewis with something of a prototype for "the Wood between the Worlds" in *The Magician's Nephew* (see *Planet Narnia*, 181, 185-86).

48. Lewis, *Allegory of Love*, 96.

are the territories of Diana and Venus in Lydgate's *Reason and Sensuality*, the former of which is benign ("thys forest vertuous" where "thou shalt no welles fynde / But that be holsom") and the latter allegedly dangerous ("There are trees yonder whose shadow kills a man, and wells where he can drown like Narcissus").[49] Another example occurs in the *Faerie Queene*, where Spenser presents "forces of life and health and fecundity. St. George ... is refreshed with water from the well of life and saved by the shadow of the tree of life. Babies cluster at Charissa's breasts."[50] The "woods and waters" of Spenser's *Epithalamion* (I, 10), a poem Lewis alludes to in *That Hideous Strength*, provide yet one more example of this pair of images in a sexual, indeed nuptial, context.[51]

---

49. Lewis, *Allegory of Love*, 275.

50. Lewis, *Allegory of Love*, 316.

51. When Jane assists Mrs. Dimble in preparing the bedchamber at the Lodge, it "suggested to her literary memory all sorts of things out of sixteenth-century epithalamiums" (ch. 14, 416). The best of these, in Lewis's opinion, was Spenser's, which he calls "matchless" (C. S. Lewis, "Edmund Spenser, 1522–99," *Studies in Medieval and Renaissance Literature* [Cambridge: Cambridge University Press, 1966] 130). It conveys an "intense desire for posterity" who "will people not only earth but heaven," for there is much that is astrological and cosmic in the poem (C. S. Lewis, *English Literature in the Sixteenth Century, Excluding Drama* [Oxford: Oxford University Press, 1954], 373): e.g., "ye high heavens.../Poure out your blessing on us plentiously,/And happy influence upon us raine,/That we may raise a large posterity." In Lewis's own epithalamium, "The Small Man Orders His Wedding," Jove and Aphrodite (i.e., in planetary terms, Jupiter and Venus) supervise the couple's lovemaking, as does "Genius burning through the night/The torch of man's futurity" (C. S. Lewis, *Poems*, ed. Walter Hooper [London: HarperCollins, 1994, 45–47).

Given the symbolism of the first two novels in the trilogy and given Lewis's familiarity with such symbolism in medieval and renaissance literature, there is little doubt that Bragdon Wood signifies something more than a literal portion of the grounds of Bracton College: it is also emblematic of sexual union. Its synecdochic name, "Merlin's Well," indicates again its combination of the masculine and the feminine.

Merlin, the ancient druid, lies beneath Bragdon Wood in a centuries-long sleep. Though he is a magician, his magic is organic and holistic, not intrusive or interventionist. "The old *magia* of Merlin" is said to be something that "worked with the spiritual qualities of Nature, loving and reverencing them and knowing them from within," as distinct from "the new *goeteia*—the brutal surgery from without."[52] For Merlin, "every operation on Nature is a kind of personal contact, like coaxing a child or stroking one's horse.... After him came the modern man to whom Nature is ... a machine to be worked, and taken to bits if it won't work the way he pleases." Merlin "seems to produce his results simply by being Merlin," not by resorting to "forbidden books" or "forbidden arts."[53] He "is friends with the woods and rivers"[54] and is therefore grieved to discover, after he wakes from sleep, that voluntary sterility in marriage has become "so common" in the twentieth century.[55]

---

52. Lewis, *That Hideous Strength*, ch. 13, 395.

53. Lewis, *That Hideous Strength*, ch. 9, 272–73.

54. Lewis, *That Hideous Strength*, ch. 14, 435.

55. Lewis, *That Hideous Strength*, ch. 13, 384.

SALE OF COLLEGE PROPERTY

Since Merlin's Well is the name of a watery woodland that connotes fertile marriage, and since Merlin himself keenly promotes the same, we should understand Bracton College's willingness to *sell* this site for commercial development as profoundly significant. Having introduced readers to Jane, Mark, and Bragdon, Lewis proceeds, in the fourth section of Chapter One, to the meeting at which the Fellows of Bracton discuss the "Sale of College Property." The meeting lasts all day and finally reaches its main point of business, "the question of selling Bragdon Wood":

> It was not called '"the sale of Bragdon Wood." The Bursar called it the "sale of the area coloured pink on the plan which, with the Warden's permission, I will now pass round the table." He pointed out quite frankly that this involved the loss of part of the Wood. In fact, the proposed N.I.C.E. [National Institute of Co-ordinated Experiments] site still left to the College a strip about sixteen feet broad along the far half of the south side, but there was no deception for the Fellows had the plan to look at with their own eyes. It was a small-scale plan and not perhaps perfectly accurate—only meant to give one a general idea. In answer to questions he admitted that unfortunately—or perhaps fortunately the Well itself was in the area which the N.I.C.E. wanted. The rights of the College to access would, of course, be guaranteed: and the Well and its pavement would be preserved by the Institute in a manner to satisfy all the archaeol-

ogists in the world. He refrained from offering any advice and merely mentioned the quite astonishing figure which the N.I.C.E. was offering. After that, the meeting became lively. The advantages of the sale discovered themselves one by one like ripe fruit dropping into the hand.[56]

Matrimony has natural fruit: children. Selling the well and the wood turns out to have "fruit" too, all sorts of advantages deriving from the astronomical sum on offer: "It solved the problem of the wall: it solved the problem of protecting ancient monuments: it solved the financial problem: it looked like solving the problem of the junior Fellows' stipends."[57] If we read this symbolically, the suggestion would appear to be that marriage, when put on a contracepted footing, likewise bears much fruit in terms of money, careers, freedom, accommodation, and so forth.

Lewis was enough of a realist to recognize the advantages provided to married couples by contraception, and as an apologist for Christianity he was prudent enough to perceive that he should steer clear of the issue when writing about marriage directly. Hence, in the preface to *Mere Christianity*, he writes: "I have ... said nothing about birth-control. I am not a woman nor even a married man, nor am I a priest. I did not think it my place to take a firm line about pains, dangers and expenses from which I am protected; having no pastoral office which obliged me to

---

56. Lewis, *That Hideous Strength*, ch. 1, 22.

57. Lewis, *That Hideous Strength*, ch. 1, 22.

do so."⁵⁸ But that was in his non-fiction. Here, in the Ransom Trilogy, he is free to address matters in an exploratory, narrative context, where he can suggest considerations attendant upon certain moral issues and imply a position without explicitly stating it. In his satirical portrait of the Fellows of Bracton and the way they are gradually induced to accept the offer made by the NICE he is subtly depicting the way that one's ethical vision can become clouded by factors that are not, strictly speaking, relevant to the question at hand. He is also able to portray the failure of those on his own side of the debate with a bit of ironic self-mockery:

> The few real "Die-hards" present, to whom Bragdon Wood was almost a basic assumption of life, could hardly bring themselves to realise what was happening. When they found their voices, they struck a discordant note amid the general buzz of cheerful comment. They were manoeuvred into the position of appearing as the party who passionately desired to see Bragdon surrounded with barbed wire.⁵⁹

These "Die-hards" are effectively the same sort of traditionally-minded people who have already appeared in the Ransom Trilogy. In *Perelandra* we hear tell of those "men of that intensely male and backward-looking type who always shrank away from the new good" and "had

---

58. C. S. Lewis, *Mere Christianity* (Glasgow: Collins, 1990), 9.

59. Lewis, *That Hideous Strength*, ch. 1, 23.

continuously laboured to keep woman down to mere child-bearing."[60] The fact that it is the villainous Weston who describes traditionalists in this fashion indicates where Lewis's sympathies lie. That Weston should use the term "*mere* child-bearing" begs the question, as if fertility were some kind of shame or drawback, whereas in fact, as we have seen, fertile marriages are, in Lewis's view, the fountains of history. When Weston becomes "the Un-man," his new name betokens not just his own moral collapse into a sub-human state, but also indicates how his philosophy serves to "un-man" all those who embrace it: subjectivism results, sooner or later, in the abolition of man, whether that manhood be understood anthropologically or biologically.

In *That Hideous Strength*, Bragdon is also effectively abolished. Its sale leads to "the conversion of an ancient woodland into an inferno of mud and noise and steel and concrete."[61] For many of Bracton's Fellows, this is, at least initially, a price worth paying for the benefits that accrue to the College. Although "the kindly earth/With contraceptive tarmac is forbidden to give birth," as Lewis puts

---

60. Lewis, *Perelandra*, ch. 10, 162. Lewis was aware how easily an unmarried man like himself could be characterized as "backward-looking" for questioning the advantages of contraception, and it was for this reason that he never wrote about birth-control in his theological works. "As a bachelor I think I shd. be imprudent in attacking it," he once told a correspondent (Letter to Mrs. Baxter, August 19, 1947, *Collected Letters*, 2:798). Nevertheless, he clearly felt that contraception was an ethical issue of considerable moment and one that he could address in his fiction and poetry.

61. Lewis, *That Hideous Strength*, ch. 4, 113.

it in a poem, it's the cost of doing business.[62] Regrettable, perhaps, but unavoidable. To resist progress would be obscurantist, Luddite, reactionary. The sale is, in effect, a necessary step taken to keep abreast of the times. However, the College soon finds to its utter dismay that it is really and truly "caught in the net of necessity."[63] Bragdon Wood becomes an "obscenity," an "abomination," and there is no escape.[64] We even discover, from the only real scientist in the novel, William Hingest, that "The N.I.C.E. would have had the Wood in any case. They had powers to compel a sale."[65] This suggests that far greater and darker forces are at work than the Fellows' desire for money.

THE USAGES OF SULVA

That Hideous Strength is a story not just of social commentary, but of spiritual warfare. The part played in the story by the demonic "Macrobes" continues a theme announced earlier in the trilogy where we learned that the "Dark Lord, this depraved Oyarsa of Tellus" was "driven back within these bounds centuries before any human life existed on our planet. If he ventured to show himself outside the Moon's orbit he'd be driven back again by main

---

62. C. S. Lewis, "Dear Mr. Marshall, Thank You," in *The Collected Poems of C. S. Lewis: A Critical Edition*, ed. Don W. King (Kent: Kent State University Press, 2015), 397. See also "The Future of Forestry," *Poems*, 75.

63. Lewis, *That Hideous Strength*, ch. 6, 158.

64. Lewis, *That Hideous Strength*, ch. 6, 157.

65. Lewis, *That Hideous Strength*, ch. 3, 66.

force."[66] Satan, "the prince of the power of the air" in biblical terminology (Eph. 2:2), is, in other words, confined to the sublunary realm; it is because Satan dominates Tellus that Earth is "the silent planet," unable to participate in the perpetual *gloria*, the music of the spheres, that otherwise proclaims the glory of God across the cosmos. As Ransom explains:

> Half of [the Moon's] orb is turned towards us and shares our curse. Her other half looks to Deep Heaven; happy would he be who could cross that frontier and see the fields on her farther side. On this side the womb is barren and the marriages cold.... There when a young man takes a maiden in marriage they do not lie together, but each lies with a cunningly fashioned image of the other ... for real flesh will not please them, they are so dainty (*delicati*) in their dreams of lust.[67]

Merlin later takes up this point when, in reference to the Studdocks' childless marriage, he announces, "Of their own will they are barren: I did not know till now that the usages of Sulva were so common among you."[68] (Sulva is the name of the Moon in Lewis's invented "Old Solar" language.)

---

66. Lewis, *Perelandra*, ch. 2, 20.

67. Lewis, *That Hideous Strength*, ch. 13, 377.

68. Lewis, *That Hideous Strength*, ch. 13, 384.

The earthward side of the Moon is the region under Satan's power. It represents a rejection of "otherness," a determination to decline the gift of an alternative locus of reality in all its independent integrity. To quench "the taste for the *other*" is one of the works of Hell.[69] The far side of the Moon's sphere, however, is not so closed in on itself, but open to the radiant heavens where "day never shuts his eye," as Lewis puts it, quoting Milton, in *Out of the Silent Planet*.[70] In an unpublished draft of his poem, "The Planets," Lewis describes the Sun as "the worshipt male,/The earth's husband, all engend'ring."[71] Ransom makes the same point more prosaically in *That Hideous Strength*: "What is above and beyond all things is so masculine that we are all feminine in relation to it."[72] But Mark and Jane do not want that Solar source of fertility to penetrate their relationship. Symbolically speaking, they give the Sun the cold shoulder, preferring the lower side of the Moon and the "fruitless works of darkness" (Eph., 5:11) to which it gives cover.[73] Sexually speaking, they

---

69. C. S. Lewis, *The Problem of Pain* (Glasgow: Collins, 1983), 111.

70. C. S. Lewis, *Out of the Silent Planet* (London: HarperCollins, 2005), ch. 5, 35.

71. "The Planets" unpublished draft version. In the version published in *Lysistrata* 2, no. 1 (May 1935), the Sun is "all beholding."

72. Lewis, *That Hideous Strength*, ch. 14, 437.

73. That Venus will overcome these fruitless works of darkness is suggested at the descent of Perelandra, whose influence comes with the fragrance of "night-scented flowers, sticky gums, groves that drop odours, and with cool savour of midnight fruit" (*That Hideous Strength*, ch. 15, 447).

share Filostrato's disdain for the "One great dirty patch on the far side of her [Sulva] where there is still water and air and forests."[74]

The Studdocks' marital dysfunction is, of course, illustrative of their spiritual recalcitrance for, as Lewis wrote elsewhere, "One of the ends for which sex was created was to symbolize to us the hidden things of God. One of the functions of human marriage is to express the nature of the union between Christ and the Church."[75] The lack of true union between Mark and Jane is overcome as the story progresses, the Studdocks gradually learning to open themselves not only to each other but also to Christ, the Light of the World (John 8:12).

In Mark's case the moment of truth comes when he is required to trample on a crucifix and refuses. He becomes aware of objective value, figured here as "the Straight," and realizes that he must not dishonor "the wooden Christ" nailed to this Tree of Life, even if it should cost him his own life.[76] When his mind turns to Jane "she seemed to him, as he now thought of her, to have in herself deep wells and knee-deep meadows of happiness, rivers of freshness."[77]

Similarly, Jane encounters Maleldil (Christ) in the garden at St Anne's: "A boundary had been crossed. She had come into a world, or into a Person, or into the

---

74. Lewis, *That Hideous Strength*, ch. 8, 237.

75. C.S Lewis, "Priestesses in the Church?" in *God in the Dock: Essays on Theology*, ed. Walter Hooper (Glasgow: Collins, 1979), 92.

76. Lewis, *That Hideous Strength*, ch. 15, 466.

77. Lewis, *That Hideous Strength*, ch. 11, 339.

presence of a Person. Something expectant, patient, inexorable, met her with no veil or protection between."[78] She thinks of Mark as she traverses "the wet lawn" on her way down to the Lodge where their connubial reunion will occur, "and she thought of children, and of pain and death."[79] In *The Abolition of Man*, sacrificial death is the *experimentum crucis* of belief in objective value. Jane, like Mark, finally learns that it is better to die on the right side than live on the wrong side. She embraces the chance to be known no longer as a mistress would be known, for mere pleasure, but as a wife would be known, for pleasure *and* for fruit, for "matrimony," for mother-making. That the story ends on Christmas Eve—or so it is implied—is of course no coincidence.[80]

---

78. Lewis, *That Hideous Strength*, ch. 14, 441.

79. Lewis, *That Hideous Strength*, ch. 17, 533–34.

80. Ivy Maggs's statement, "It's getting ever so near Christmas now" (ch. 12, 361), is suggestive, and Merlin prophesies "that before Christmas this bear [Mr. Bultitude] would do the best deed that any bear had done in Britain" (ch. 13, 389). Snow is thick on the ground "and there was more in the sky" (ch. 17, 500), as the tale approaches its climax. The reference to the men cooking goose and plum pudding (ch. 17, 523) and to the wearing of "festal garments" (ch. 17, 512) (presumably for the feast of the Nativity) would seem to imply that the novel finishes on December 24th, for it is not unknown in English households to have the main celebratory meal on Christmas Eve. The allusion to Psalm 45 when Jane first encounters Ransom and forgets her "father's house" (see Ps. 45:10) is a further nod in this direction, for Psalm 45 is a "Christmas Psalm… a rich, festive Epithalamium", according to Lewis in *Reflections on the Psalms* ((Glasgow: Collins, 1984), 107). The dating Lewis gives to the Preface (i.e., "Christmas Eve"), is also telling. Lewis is perhaps alluding to Shakespeare's description in *Hamlet* of Christmas Eve as that hallowed time when "no

In the final scene, Jane enters the bedchamber where Mark, undressed, awaits her, and as she opens the door we close the book. What passes next between husband and wife is not for us to witness. But what is about to happen might be summed up in a phrase from a poem Lewis wrote about the overcoming of Narcissism, which tells how "Self-Love, brought to bed of Love may die and bear/ Her sweet son in despair."[81]

THE ABOLITION OF MATRIMONY

Mark and Jane thus resist the abolition of matrimony signified by the sale of Bragdon Wood, but the question remains as to why Lewis, who was not himself married when he wrote the trilogy and never became a father, should have been so interested in this topic.

By his own account, Lewis "never propounded a general position about contraception"[82] and was "not prepared to say that it is always wrong,"[83] yet in his entire body of work, both published and unpublished, he consistently refrains from saying anything positive about it. His comments are either studiedly neutral or, more usually, negative. Lewis remarked that he should "not like the job of defending [contraception] against almost un-

---

planet strikes" and "the cock, that is the trumpet to the dawn... singeth all night long" (Act I.i).

81. Lewis, *The Pilgrim's Regress* (London: William Collins, 2018), 196

82. Lewis, Letter to Mrs. Baxter, August 19, 1947, in *Collected Letters*, 2:798.

83. Lewis, Letter to Mrs. Johnson, March 13, 1956, in *Collected Letters*, 3:719.

broken Xtian disapproval."[84] His wording there—"almost unbroken Christian disapproval"—is a glance at the 1930 Lambeth Conference, the assembly of Anglican bishops, which revised the Church of England's teaching on the matter so as to permit the use of contraception under certain very limited conditions. This permission was the first instance of a mainline Christian denomination asserting that marital sexual relations need not always be open to procreation.[85]

This revised ethic has been called "one of the most significant turning points in the history of Anglican sexual politics," and it did not go unchallenged, either from within the Church of England or from without. [86]

The most notable Anglican opponent was Charles Gore, sometime Bishop of Oxford.[87] In his 1930 pam-

---

84. Lewis, Letter to Mrs. Baxter, August 19, 1947, in *Collected Letters*, 2:798.

85. For more on this, see my *First Things* article "C. S. Lewis and Contraception" (November 3, 2022) and my chapter "Mistress for Pleasure or Wife for Fruit?" in *Women and C. S. Lewis: What His Life and Literature Reveal for Today's Culture*, ed. Carolyn Curtis and Mary Pomroy Key (Oxford: Lion, 2015).

86. Timothy Willem Jones, *Sexual Politics in the Church of England, 1857–1957* (Oxford: Oxford University Press 2012), ch. 5, "Contraception, Sex, and Pleasure."

87. Charles Gore (1853–1932) was a distinguished theologian and churchman whose tenure of the Oxford diocese ran from 1911 to 1919, thus overlapping with Lewis's first two years as an undergraduate. Lewis would certainly have known Gore's name, perhaps have known him by sight, though there is no record of Lewis attending services at Christ Church during this period, so it is unlikely he heard him preach.

phlet, "Lambeth on Contraceptives," Gore called the decision "disastrous" and described contraception as "unnatural and wrong in itself."[88] In a line of argumentation that would resonate with Lewis's later defense of the *Tao* in *The Abolition of Man*, Gore contended that "Nature shows signs of revenging itself on a practice which sets it at defiance."[89] We do not have firm evidence that Lewis knew of the pamphlet, but it would seem probable. For one thing, contraception was generally "a hot topic" of the day that even the news-averse Lewis could not escape;[90] for another, Lewis was familiar with and deeply admired Gore's other works. He described his *Jesus of Nazareth* in 1933 as "perhaps the best book about religion I have yet read," advising his friend Arthur Greeves to "get

---

88. Charles Gore, "Lambeth on Contraceptives" (Mowbray, 1930), reprinted in *Touchstone: A Journal of Mere Christianity*, January/February 2023), 24, 27.

89. Gore "Lambeth on Contraceptives," 26.

90. In 1922, he records that his eccentric Aunt Lily, having been impeded by "a crush of prams" when walking through Oxford, had acquired "a lot of leaflets issued by the C.B.C. (Constructive Birth Control): and she was going to drop one into every pram the next time she went into Oxford." Lewis refers to this as "a good joke" but one cannot tell whether he then, in his pre-Christian days, approved of the C.B.C. or not (16 December 1922: *All My Road Before Me: The Diary of C.S. Lewis, 1922-1927*, ed. Walter Hooper [London: Harvest: 1991], 153). In 1923, Lewis records how he "travelled [by train] from Didcot with an agreeable man who… told me of the strange accident by which he had married his wife – tho' he is a most ecstatic husband and father. He highly approves of birth control" (6-11 April, Friday-Wednesday, 1923, *The Lewis Family Papers (1850-1930)*, ed. W.H. Lewis, 11 vols, Leeborough Press (unpublished)).

it at once."[91] (1933 incidentally, also marks the first time Lewis publicly critiqued contraception.)[92] Elsewhere, he says that Gore's *Philosophy of the Good Life* "taught me a lot" and repeatedly recommends it (along with other Gore titles) to correspondents.[93] He quotes deferentially from Gore's *Sermon on the Mount* in a letter of 1952, a letter in which, interestingly, he also shows knowledge of the 1888 Lambeth Conference.[94] This brings us back to the decision of the 1930 Lambeth Conference, which Lewis certainly knew of, given his reference to the "almost unbroken" tradition of Christian teaching on the topic; clearly, he was aware that the tradition had been broken, and by his own church at that. The pamphlet Gore wrote to oppose the innovation is conceivably what put Lewis onto his other works. Perhaps the old pious clergyman, Canon Jewel, who makes a sincere but ineffective show of resistance to the sale of Bragdon Wood, is a nod in Bishop Gore's direction.

From outside the Church of England, opposition to the 1930 Lambeth decision came most notably from Pope Pius XI, who later that year re-emphasized tradi-

---

91. Letter to Arthur Greeves, September 12, 1933, *Collected Letters*, 2:125.

92. In *The Pilgrim's Regress*, through the mouth of the character of Mr. Sensible who praises the "beneficent contraceptive devices of our later times" (79). Mr. Sensible is a worldly-wise man whose urbanity and self-serving prudence are satirized.

93. Letter to Mary Neylan, March 26, 1940), *Collected Letters*, 2:375. He recommended books by Gore to Mr. H. Morland (August 19, 1942) and to Margaret Gray (May 9, 1961).

94. Letter to "Mrs. Lockley" (May 13, 1952), *Collected Letters*, 3:188–89.

tional Christian teaching on matrimony with his encyclical *Casti Connubii* (*Chaste Marriage*). The fact that the Roman Pontiff felt moved to restate the doctrine indicates how potent an issue contraception was at that time, as potent then as divorce, homosexuality, and abortion became in the 1960s, as same-sex marriage became in the 2010s, and as transgender matters are becoming today. Even though Lewis probably did not read *Casti Connubii*, he would have heard of it, and perhaps the devoutly Catholic Tolkien talked about it with his friend.

Be that as it may, in *That Hideous Strength* Lewis seems to be indicating that "the Church Catholic" (Gore's term for the church in its broadest sense, encompassing both Rome and traditional Anglicanism) had a clear view on this issue and was now coming under attack for it. This is suggested by the fact that the Fellows of Bracton once looked out onto Bragdon Wood through "the Henrietta Maria window." The window is mentioned three times in the story and it is worth asking why it is so named and so repeatedly referred to. Henrietta Maria (1609–1669) was the Catholic wife of the Anglican King Charles I; their marriage was famously a happy one, issuing in nine children, and Van Dyck immortalized their family in several portraits.[95] Within the story, the Henrietta Maria window is so called because, on a visit to Bracton, the Queen etched her name with a diamond on

---

95. Henrietta Maria was also the mother of Charles II, who was restored to British throne in 1660 after the Puritan Commonwealth. Her role as the preserver of a royal line thus has something in common with Jane Studdock's role as mother of the future Pendragon, ruler of Logres.

one of its panes.⁹⁶ The window is first shattered by bullets fired by operatives of the N.I.C.E., then reduced to "boarded blindness," and finally obscured altogether by a pile of heavy loads "flung down against the very walls of Bracton."⁹⁷ If we read these events symbolically, matrimony has not only been betrayed by its sale to "developers" (innovators who favor contraception), but the very vision of what matrimony is has been gradually destroyed and at last completely covered up.

This should put us in mind of the final sentences of *The Abolition of Man* where Lewis predicts the inevitable outcome of subjectivism:

> [Y]ou cannot go on "explaining away" for ever: you will find that you have explained explanation itself away. You cannot go on "seeing through" things for ever. The whole point of seeing through something is to see something through it. It is good that the window should be transparent, because the street or garden beyond it is opaque. How if you saw through the garden too? It is no use trying to "see through" first principles. If you see through everything, then everything is transparent. But a wholly transpar-

---

96. Lewis, *That Hideous Strength*, ch. 4, 117. In real life, Henrietta Maria visited Oxford, the Royalist capital during the Civil War, spending several months there in 1643 and lodging at Merton College.

97. Lewis, *That Hideous Strength*, ch. 6, 158–59.

ent world is an invisible world. To "see through" all things is the same as not to see.[98]

Subjectivism privileges the subject over the object. Subjectivists conceive of themselves as being (in Iris Murdoch's phrase) "an isolated principle of will,"[99] entitled to make everyone and everything in the world whatever they want it to be, regardless of its intrinsic nature. Each person thus becomes "a basilisk which kills what it sees and only sees by killing."[100]

But in Lewis's view "the facts of sex and sense on the natural level are opaque,"[101] resistant to analytical dissection. We observe that the human species propagates itself in the way that it does by means of male and female coupling, but we cannot discern why it should be so. We know that we apprehend the world through our five senses, but do not know why we have these sensory receptors and not other kinds. As embodied human creatures, these physiological facts are our data, our premises, which have to be accepted axiomatically; they are anthropologically basic. If we try to "see through" these facts of sex and sense in an attempt to find some deeper explanatory ground—such as might be provided by sheer willpower, our own minds making things thus and thus as we choose, rather than submitting to given reality—we will effectively be blinding ourselves. And blindness is what Lewis presents

---

98. Lewis, *Abolition of Man*, 81.

99. Quoted in *After Humanity*, 174, 176.

100. Lewis, *Abolition of Man*, 80.

101. Lewis, "Priestesses in the Church?," *God in the Dock*, 92.

in *That Hideous Strength* when Bragdon Wood, shrouded in fog, passes beyond human sight. The beautiful natural haven, the holy of holies, where the narrator had once enjoyed "the sound of running water and the cooing of wood pigeons," is transformed: all that can be heard is "clangings, thuddings, hootings, shouts, curses, and metallic screams in an invisible world."[102]

---

102. Lewis, *That Hideous Strength*, ch. 6, 157.

VIII

LEWIS'S APOCALYPSE AND OURS

Joseph Minich

INTRODUCTION: LEWIS AMONG THE SEERS

The dystopian novel is a fascinating cultural artifact of the twentieth century. Huxley's *Brave New World* (1932) and Orwell's *1984* (1949) are two of the more popular instances of a genre that has endured into the twenty-first century, retaining both critical acclaim (Cormac McCarthy's *The Road* won the Pulitzer Prize in 2007) and popular interest. C. S. Lewis's *That Hideous Strength*, first published in 1945, has arguably not been given the attention it warrants within this tradition. One might likewise compare *That Hideous Strength* with late twentieth-century Christian *apocalyptic* literature, such as Frank E. Peretti's *This Present Darkness* and Tim LaHaye's *Left Behind* novels. While these works of pop literature are unknown in some parts of Christendom, they were a staple of American evangelical literary consumption in the 1990s. Like many who came of age in that context, my own earliest memories of the apocalypse involve several moving parts: something about Israel; something about the Antichrist; probably a little bit of the United Nations; maybe some Russians. *Left Behind* was a late-in-the-making version of this tale. My own parents were (like many of their generation) either saved or discipled in the "Jesus Movement" so influential in the late '60s and early '70s. And so, as they passed on their own heritage, my earliest conscious encounter with the apocalypse was a childhood viewing of Donald Thompson's '70s horror camp films *A Thief in the Night* and *A Distant Thunder*.

While many evangelicals have begun, ironically, to leave *Left Behind*-style dispensationalism behind, its influence upon the evangelical imagination remains strong. As such, evangelicals who read *That Hideous Strength* today discern parallels between Lewis's apocalypse and their own reading of the times, even if they are much less likely than their parents' generation to see specific events, organizations, and figures as fulfilling specific End Time prophecies. And indeed, there are some parallels, though Lewis was not working within the typical End Times evangelical script so prevalent in America during the latter half of the twentieth century.

How, then, does Lewis's apocalyptic vision compare to our own? This essay is an attempt to understand Lewis's "apocalypse" on its own terms, and likewise to understand how this shaped his reading of the modern cultural situation and task. I will first situate the argument within a brief summary of the framework within which many evangelicals encounter Lewis on these questions. After naming our own vision of the apocalypse, I will then attempt to describe Lewis's apocalypse and his resultant reading of *his* culture wars. I will then briefly suggest what a twenty-first century parody of Lewis might emphasize, and conclude by assessing the role that gender plays in Lewis's reading of the times.

APOCALYPSE NOW

Twentieth-century evangelicalism drank deeply from the well of American dispensationalism.[1] This rendered the reading of various apocalyptic plot points into current events, if not inevitable, at least very likely. In the post-war period, this especially meant that the End Times would have something to do with supporting the new nation of Israel, and likewise with opposing anything that smelled of "one world government," even "one world bureaucracy." Already a people suspicious of too much domestic federal power, an enormous number of Americans were *especially* suspicious of the U.N. To many a "normie," such an apparatus simply looked like an underhand pitch to the coming Antichrist. This impression was not alleviated by the bureaucratic moral language in terms of which an increasing number of globalized institutions justified their own growing influence. Working class folks (who made

---

1. Dispensationalists are not monolithic in their emphases, but they remain committed to the notion that God works in historical "stages" (i.e. "dispensations") and that our contemporary age (the "church age") will terminate in an apocalyptic cataclysm ("the Tribulation") described in John's Revelation and in Christ's Olivet Discourse. A recent historical introduction to the movement can be found in Daniel Hummel's *The Rise and Fall of Dispensationalism: How the Evangelical Battle Over the End Times Shaped a Nation* (Grand Rapids: Eerdmans, 2023).

up a sizable chunk of twentieth century American evangelicalism) quite reflexively associate such language with obfuscation and ulterior motives (one might think of *That Hideous Strength*'s own Director Wither).[2]

Naturally, one's reading of the cosmic plot points is liable to impact one's approach to politics and culture. That said, the evangelical imagination on these questions was not as monolithic in the immediate post-war period as it became, for instance, in the Reagan years. Not that anything in the latter was (as such) *new*, but it was more consolidated and influential. For those like myself who grew up in the Reagan era, it is difficult to imagine an evangelical conversation unshaped by the kind of "culture wars" that had already *matured* by the '80s. The remarkable and trans-confessional broadening of American evangelicals into a voting block through the '70s and early '80s simultaneously remade the term "evangelical" (it now inevitably includes Catholics and Mormons) while consolidating its apocalyptic, cultural, and political instincts into a powerful interest group. My own generation's emergence into religious, cultural, and political consciousness happened in this context. And it was not solely mediated through our parents, but also through the vast proliferation of evangelical media (especially radio), homeschooling networks (a massively growing phenomenon by the early '90s), and the formal and informal instruction of church leaders. In this context, dispensational expectations were married to American anticommunism, and increasingly to the role

---

2. For an in-depth consideration of Lewis's portrayal of bureaucratic language in *That Hideous Strength*, see Jake Meador's essay in this volume.

that Islamic civilization might play in the apocalyptic plot. The Marxist-theory-influenced advisors of, for instance, Iran's Ayatollah Khomeini, did not escape the notice of evangelical commentators in the 1980s. Whatever the case, the battle between good and evil, between antichrist and church, between communism/Islam and the Christian West, were mythologically fused in many a head.

The fusion of dispensational apocalypse with a certain political and cultural reading of "cultural Marxism" helps to explain the peculiar relationship between supposedly "pessimistic" dispensationalists and the "optimistic" Reconstructionists.[3] Despite the dispensationalists' commitment to a premillennial eschatology (with its focus on impending cataclysm and a general "downward spiral" in human history before Christ's return) and the Reconstructionists' commitment to postmillennial eschatology (which foresees the near-total global spread of the gospel and an "upward trajectory" for Christianized humanity before Christ's return), the cultural analysis of Reconstructionists like Rousas Rushdoony was highly influential upon dispensationalists. Even if the Reconstructionists were *in principle* optimistic, they always noted that the success of the kingdom occurred alongside various sorts of cultural cataclysm. And so while they did not share the dispensa-

---

3. Christian Reconstructionism is a Protestant movement that largely centers around a belief in the reinstitution of Old Testament Mosaic law in civil society today ("theonomy") and the need to "reconstruct" contemporary society from the ground up. A key figure and text would be R. J. Rushdoony and his *Institutes of Biblical Law* (1973). A historical introduction to the movement can be found in Michael J. McVicar, *Christian Reconstruction: R. J. Rushdoony and American Religious Conservatism* (Chapel Hill: University of North Carolina Press, 2015).

tionalist reading of the end, they often shared its reading of the *present*, and indeed helped to shape it. And arguably, they have become one of the more enduring tribes of the extended evangelical family. While classical dispensationalist theory has significantly waned in influence, the concern about "cultural Marxism" has remained a stable and growing feature of the last forty years of American politics, and indeed has now become common parlance in the wider culture of the Anglophone world. Whatever the apocalypse might look like to a contemporary conservative evangelical, it probably involves something like a nefarious "long march through the institutions," and the consolidation of these underneath a centralized managerial power whose ultimate end is anti-human.

It would be easy to think that dispensational and Reconstructionist theory fully accounts for our culture's seemingly constant apocalyptic headspace. And yet, if we zoom out a bit, it would seem that "worrying that we're at the end" has been a fairly stable feature of our civilization for the last 150 years. As already noted, this is the era of the dystopian novel. Anthony Giddens' *The Consequences of Modernity*, written thirty years ago, can already draw upon enough apocalyptic stories to provide a taxonomy of them (relating various "end of the world" scenarios to various failed structures of the modern order).[4] Most obvious is the post-WW2 anxiety about nuclear weapons, poignantly captured in another campy film, *The Day After* (Edward Hume, 1983). One could go on to populate a list of films and novels—not to mention their real-world

---

4. Anthony Giddens, *The Consequences of Modernity* (Stanford: Stanford University Press, 1990).

"prophetic" counterparts—about an apocalypse of environment, an apocalypse of technology, an apocalypse of global dictatorship, an apocalypse of plague, an apocalypse of aliens, etc. And as in the case of dispensationalism above, many of these visions quite naturally cash out in a certain reading of our political and cultural situation. If nuclear war or environmental catastrophe are liable to be the end of humanity within a few generations, it isn't surprising that these become centralized political and cultural platforms for those who take this line. How, then, do a mid-century Oxford don's prognostications compare to our own (apparently quite variegated) dystopian visions?

THE APOCALYPSE OF LEWIS

Perhaps Lewis's own vision of the apocalypse is best summarized in the mouth of his famous tempter, Uncle Screwtape. In his seventh letter to the novice tempter, Wormwood, the master tempter writes,

> I wonder you should ask me whether it is essential to keep the patient in ignorance of your own existence. That question, at least for the present phase of the struggle, has been answered for us by the High Command. Our policy, for the moment, is to conceal ourselves. Of course this has not always been so. We are really faced with a cruel dilemma. When the humans disbelieve in our existence we lose all the pleasing results of direct terrorism and we make no magicians. On the other hand, when they believe in us, we cannot make them materialists and sceptics. At least, not yet. I have great hopes that we shall

learn in due time how to emotionalise and mythologise their science to such an extent that what is, in effect, belief in us, (though not under that name) will creep in while the human mind remains closed to belief in the Enemy. The "Life Force," the worship of sex, and some aspects of Psychoanalysis, may here prove useful. If once we can produce our perfect work—the Materialist Magician, the man, not using, but veritably worshipping, what he vaguely calls "Forces" while denying the existence of "spirits"—*then the end of the war will be in sight.*[5]

That Hideous Strength parallels this vision of the end. Writing decades before our contemporary interest in transhumanism, Lewis tells the story of an institution (the National Institute of Coordinated Experiments) whose public face masks the real goal of its Inner Ring. What sells itself as an institution of public progress is really run by a coterie of servants to a literal severed "Head" who is understood by various members to be "kept alive" by a machine, and by the innermost Inner Ring to be a medium of some consciousness from another dimension. The goal of this "group within the group" is precisely to throw off the limitations of the body so that "The individual is to become all head. The human race is to become all Technocracy."[6] Indeed, "here surely at last … was the true inner

---

5. C. S. Lewis, *The Screwtape Letters* (New York: HarperOne, 2015), 31–32. Emphasis added.

6. C. S. Lewis, *That Hideous Strength* (London: Harper Collins, 2003), ch. 12, 355.

circle of all, the circle whose centre was outside the human race—the ultimate secret, the supreme power."[7] It is this peculiar fusion of materialist and pagan magics (whether explicitly understood or not) that constitutes Lewis's apocalypse. As Lewis narrates,

> Dreams of the far future destiny of man were dragging up from its shallow and unquiet grave the old dream of Man as God.... You could not have done it with Nineteenth-Century scientists.... It was different now. Perhaps few or none of the people at Belbury knew what was happening; but once it happened, they would be like straw in a fire. What should they find incredible, since they believed no longer in a rational universe? What should they regard as too obscene, since they held that all morality was a mere subjective by-product of the physical and economic situation of men? The time was ripe. From the point of view which is accepted in Hell, the whole history of our earth had led up to this moment. There was now at last a real chance for fallen Man to shake off that limitation of his powers which mercy had imposed upon him as a protection from the full results of his fall. If this succeeded, Hell would be at last incarnate.[8]

---

7. Lewis, *That Hideous Strength*, ch. 12, 356.

8. Lewis, *That Hideous Strength*, ch. 9, 276–77.

Ransom likewise elaborates,

> If this technique is really successful, the Belbury people have for all practical purposes discovered a way of making themselves immortal.... It is the beginning of what is really a new species—the Chosen Heads who will never die. They will call it the next step in evolution. And henceforward, all the creatures that you and I call human are mere candidates for admission to the new species or else its slaves—perhaps its food.[9]

The consciousness of the NICE's Director, Wither, is already given over profoundly to the consciousness from another dimension as he seeks total fusion with it. The distance of his face and eyes from each of his conversations is frequently mentioned in the book. And tellingly, Lewis's Heiser-esque take on Genesis 6 is hinted at when he speaks of Wither's "antediluvian tone"[10] and the "pre-glacial"[11] nature of the power to which the NICE seeks access.[12] And it is in the image of these other-dimensional minds that they seek to make themselves. A mode of mind

---

9. Lewis, *That Hideous Strength*, ch. 9, 267.

10. Lewis, *That Hideous Strength*, ch. 10, 282.

11. Lewis, *That Hideous Strength*, ch. 12, 364.

12. Michael Heiser argues that the first century Jewish reading of Genesis 6 (heavily dependent on the influence of 1 Enoch and reflected in the New Testament) interpreted the famed "sons of God" to be sinister angels. See his *Reversing Hermon: Enoch, the Watchers, and the Forgotten Mission of Jesus Christ* (Bellingham: Lexham, 2017).

free from the organic, fitted to the metallic trees about which the NICE fantasize, they seek to "learn to make our brains live with less and less body: learn to build our bodies directly with chemicals, no longer have to stuff them full of dead brutes and weeds. Learn how to reproduce ourselves without copulation."[13] Indeed, true civilization is only possible after the force of human sexuality is suspended altogether.[14]

Of course, as Lewis constantly emphasizes, very few members of the NICE fully understand this program, but crucially, it is no small part of Mark's own conversion in the story to realize that the logic of his own philosophical and social views leads inevitably to such a program when worked out consistently. "When you have attained real objectivity," Frost tells him, "you will recognize, not some motives, but all motives as merely animal, subjective epiphenomena. You will then have no motives and you will find that you do not need them."[15] Mark's response to seeing the end of his own project is described,

> The philosophy which Frost was expounding was by no means unfamiliar to him. He recognized it at once as the logical conclusion of thoughts which he had always hitherto accepted and which at this moment he found himself

---

13. Lewis, *That Hideous Strength*, ch. 8, 232–33.

14. In this latter point in particular, Lewis's apocalypse shares something with the post-sexual transhumanism depicted in Michael Houellebecq's 1998 novel *The Elementary Particles* and his 2005 novel *The Possibility of an Island*.

15. Lewis, *That Hideous Strength*, ch. 14, 408–9.

> irrevocably rejecting. The knowledge that his own assumptions led to Frost's position combined with what he saw in Frost's face and what he had experienced in this very cell, affected a complete conversion. All the philosophers and evangelists in the world might not have done the job so neatly.[16]

Of course, for most of the NICE, things are not spelled out so explicitly, and Mark is brought to the realization of the program in ascending steps toward the innermost ring. As already implied, part of the apocalyptic nature of this project is that—under the subterfuge of equality, progress, and democracy—it represents the least democratic force in history. *That Hideous Strength* contains the very claim that we find didactically expressed in *The Abolition of Man*: "Man's power over Nature means the power of some men over other men with Nature as the instrument."[17] But how is it possible that the mass of human beings could be shaped to endorse such an anti-human program? It is here that Lewis is especially insightful.

THE "CULTURE WARS" OF LEWIS

It would, of course, be anachronistic to project all the contours of what we have come to call "the culture wars" onto Lewis's novel. 1980s America—let alone 2020s America—is not Oxford in the 1940s. And yet Lewis is explicitly speculating about the future direction of West-

---

16. Lewis, *That Hideous Strength*, ch. 14, 409.

17. Lewis, *That Hideous Strength*, ch. 8, 240.

ern civilization—a future in which we now find ourselves. Despite the decades separating us, we are more like him than unlike, and there is some overlap (we shall point out differences below) between his reading of the times and our own anxieties.

To get at this, it is important to understand precisely how the NICE publicly justifies its existence. It said that the NICE is "the first-fruits of that constructive fusion between the state and the laboratory on which so many thoughtful people base their hopes of a better world. It was to be free from almost all the tiresome restraints—'red tape' was the word its supporters used—which have hitherto hampered research in this country."[18] It is later stated that "It's the first attempt to take applied science seriously from the national point of view."[19] In short,

> The N.I.C.E. marks the beginning of a new era—the *really* scientific era. Up to now, everything has been haphazard. This is going to put science itself on a scientific basis. There are to be forty interlocking committees sitting every day and they've got a wonderful gadget—I was shown the model last time I was in town—by which the findings of each committee print themselves off in their own little compartment on the Analytical Notice-Board every half hour. Then, that report slides itself into the right position where it's connected up by little arrows

---

18. Lewis, *That Hideous Strength*, ch. 1, 15.

19. Lewis, *That Hideous Strength*, ch. 2, 37.

> with all the relevant parts of the other reports. A glance at the Board shows you the policy of the whole Institute actually take shape under your own eyes.... They call it a Pragmatometer.[20]

The parallel to contemporary "algorithmic governance," so much a part of contemporary political infrastructure, is uncanny. And of course, not everyone can manage the algorithms. "Man has got to take charge of Man. That means, remember, that some men have got to take charge of the rest."[21] As Lord Feverstone exegetes the program, "Of course, it'll have to be mainly psychological at first. But we'll get on to biochemical conditioning in the end and the direct manipulation of the brain."[22] Of course, this entire program is justified in publicly humanitarian terms. Lewis is highly prescient about the manner in which language can be used to groom the public imagination into pathological visions of "progress." Commenting on how the magistrate outsources the management of criminals to this private entity, Feverstone states:

> If it were even whispered that the N.I.C.E. wanted powers to experiment on criminals, you'd have all the old women of both sexes up in arms and yapping about humanity. Call it re-education of the mal-adjusted, and you have them all slobber-

---

20. Lewis, *That Hideous Strength*, ch. 2, 38.

21. Lewis, *That Hideous Strength*, ch. 22, 44.

22. Lewis, *That Hideous Strength*, ch. 2, 44.

ing with delight that the brutal era of retributive punishment has at last come to an end.[23]

But, of course, "Remedial treatment ... need have no fixed limit: it could go on till it had effected a cure, and those who were carrying it out would decide what *that* was."[24] Most hauntingly, "There's no distinction in the long run between police work and sociology."[25]

Crucially, however, while the NICE remains "in bed" with the state (or rather the state is "in bed" with the NICE), it is not a truly political institution, and it does not really represent the interests of either the Left or Right. As Fairy Hardcastle notes, asking Mark to write propaganda for *both* sorts of newspapers, "*Of course* we're nonpolitical. The real power always is."[26]

Fairy Hardcastle's rebuke to Mark's worry that he won't be able to persuade an educated audience is often quoted:

> Why you fool, it's the educated reader who *can* be gulled. All our difficulty comes with the others. When did you meet a workman who believes the papers? He takes it for granted that they're all propaganda and skips the leading articles. He buys his paper for the football results and the little paragraphs about girls falling out of windows

---

23. Lewis, *That Hideous Strength*, ch. 2, 45.

24. Lewis, *That Hideous Strength*, ch. 3, 83–84.

25. Lewis, *That Hideous Strength*, ch. 3, 84.

26. Lewis, *That Hideous Strength*, ch. 5, 126.

and corpses found in Mayfair flats. He is our problem. We have to recondition him. But the educated public, the people who read the highbrow weeklies, don't need reconditioning. They're all right already. They'll believe anything.[27]

What is often missed is Mark's realization (soon thereafter) that "Miss Hardcastle had rated too high the resistance of the working classes to propaganda,"[28] achieved when he overhears men in a local pub credulously discussing misleading newspaper articles about the NICE that he himself had written. And indeed, the capacity of the NICE to play across the ideological spectrum (including the instrumentalization of antisemitism) is matched by its capacity to play across the national one. As Mark's thoughts are narrated, "Even the vague idea of escaping to America which, in a simpler age, comforted so many a fugitive, was denied him. He had already read in the papers the warm approval of the N.I.C.E. and all its works which came from the United States and from Russia."[29] Indeed, it takes a fairly long conversation for Ransom to convince the resuscitated Merlin that there is no appeal to other nations to fight "that hideous strength," for its reach is global.[30] One is reminded of Arthur Jensen's remarkable speech in the 1976 Sidney Lumet film *Network*: "There are no nations. There are no peoples. There are no Russians.

---

27. Lewis, *That Hideous Strength*, ch. 5, 126.

28. Lewis, *That Hideous Strength*, ch. 10, 293.

29. Lewis, *That Hideous Strength*, ch. 10, 289.

30. Lewis, *That Hideous Strength*, ch. 13, 404–5.

There are no Arabs. There are no third worlds. There is no West." As for Uncle Screwtape, materialism and communism are but useful pawns for something else.

This trans-political and trans-cultural reading of the enemy of humankind seems to provide Lewis an opportunity to contrast the communities of Belbury and the community of St. Anne's in some remarkable ways. While each of them notes the impossibility of ultimate neutrality, this cashes out quite differently in each community. The NICE are portrayed as dispensing quite easily with others, whereas St. Anne's contains a token skeptic, MacPhee, among its members. Indeed, Ransom notes that his skepticism is a "very important office" for them![31] Moreover, a good portion of the novel is about the attempt of St. Anne's company to gain the loyalty of both a modern "liberal" female and a man who is as close to the heart of the enemy's territory as one can conceive. The NICE, by contrast, have no real desire to "win" Jane—bringing her to Belbury is merely a means to manipulate Mark (and to exploit Jane's gift). And indeed, after Dr. Dimble confronts Mark with anger, he immediately spends time concerned about whether or not his anger was fully righteous. He goes on to say, "Good is always getting better and bad is always getting worse: the possibilities of even apparent neutrality are always diminishing."[32] One might say that the NICE's anti-neutrality was absolute in character, whereas St. Anne's is "eschatological" in character, open to preparing souls for that encounter with God when

---

31. Lewis, *That Hideous Strength*, ch. 9, 248.

32. Lewis, *That Hideous Strength*, ch. 13, 391.

all must come to a reckoning. Indeed, before Jane is fully converted, Ransom tells her that her provisional commitment "will not be enough for always. He is very jealous. He will have you for no one but Himself in the end. But for tonight, it is enough."[33]

It is likewise fascinating to note the *theoretical* progressivism of the NICE versus the *actual* equality of St. Anne's. While Ransom elsewhere tells Jane that she emphasizes equality precisely where it does not belong, Jane is struck by the fact that Miss Maggs, a working class woman, is treated as an equal member of this profoundly important community.[34] Indeed, Ransom at one point reiterates that the whole community of St. Anne's is not a matter of his choosing, but rather of divine providence. This is in stark contrast to "those who are selected for eternal life" by social engineers at the NICE.[35] Notably, Jane "was theoretically an extreme democrat, no social class save her own had yet become a reality to her in any place except the printed page."[36] Similarly, when Mark is tasked with "studying" the humans at a nearby town,

> his education had had the curious effect of making things that he read and wrote more real to him than things he saw. Statistics about agricultural labourers were the substance: any real ditcher, ploughman, or farmer's boy, was the

---

33. Lewis, *That Hideous Strength*, ch. 10, 314.

34. Lewis, *That Hideous Strength*, ch. 3, 224.

35. Lewis, *That Hideous Strength*, ch. 8, 240.

36. Lewis, *That Hideous Strength*, ch. 2, 56.

shadow. Though he had never noticed it himself, he had a great reluctance, in his work, ever to use such words as "man" or "woman." He preferred to write about "vocational groups," "elements," "classes," and "populations": for, in his own way, he believed as firmly as any mystic in the superior reality of the things that are not seen.[37]

Moved by divine providence instead of the cosmic instrumentalization of the planners, St. Anne's likewise is limited by the boundaries of basic morality. As Ransom states, "I am not allowed to be too prudent. I am not allowed to use desperate remedies until desperate diseases are really apparent. Otherwise we become just like our enemies—breaking all the rules whenever we imagine that it might possibly do some vague good to humanity in the remote future."[38] In one fascinating instance, Dimble escapes the suspicion and capture of Fairy Hardcastle because he is judged to "be too full of scruples to be much use to them."[39]

LEWIS'S CULTURE WAR AND OURS

It is worth trying to imagine what Lewis's apocalypse might look like in updated fashion. If *That Hideous Strength* were written in the twenty-first century, it is plausibly the case that "the Head" would be portrayed as a form of artificial intelligence and that the transhuman-

---

37. Lewis, *That Hideous Strength*, ch. 4, 108–9.

38. Lewis, *That Hideous Strength*, ch. 7, 192.

39. Lewis, *That Hideous Strength*, ch. 11, 324.

ist element of the narrative would include reference to the many developments going on in Silicon Valley—including visions of "uploading" our consciousness to various sorts of "cloud." Moreover, it is likely that the apocalypse would have a less exclusively "male" quality. The symbol of the NICE is a "muscular male nude grasping a thunderbolt."[40] However, a plausible twenty-first century apocalypse would likewise have to reckon with "witchier" versions of totalitarian power in which transcending the limits of the body is more tied to identity and agency than to technological transformation as such.[41] Arguably, of course, there is a link between "treating of the body" as a canvas for self-expression and openness to upgrading human hardware altogether.

Most crucial here, however: what would the ballad of Mark and Jane sound like if played in a twenty-first century key? And does that tell us anything about Lewis's vision of "culture wars?" The hero and heroine of his novel—destined (in fact) to produce the eightieth Pendragon—are precisely *not* who many evangelical culture warriors might tend to write as their heroes. If 1940s Jane were tuned to a twenty-first century character, she would likely be written as a "Woke white woman," even more offended by masculinity than Jane is. Mark, likewise, would likely be written as a weak-willed ladder-climbing bureaucrat in some gray area between Silicon Valley and the state. In short, the book would be about people whom many contem-

---

40. Lewis, *That Hideous Strength*, ch. 10, 293.

41. One might likewise point out the quasi-totalitarian weaponization of empathy on this score.

porary evangelicals *reduce* to enemies. One can imagine many twenty-first evangelicals regarding contemporary Marks and Janes with enough contempt to be able to write a biting fake satirical news story about them, but not with enough depth and compassion to be able to make them compelling and believable protagonists in a novel.

And yet it is the Christian imagination of Lewis to make precisely these the *key* to his imagined future. This is partly because they are not as disconnected from their roots as their education and habits suggest. Lewis writes that "the virtues he had almost succeeded in banishing from his mind still lived, if only negatively and as weaknesses, in his body."[42] More poignantly, "Ancestral impulses lodged in his body—that body which was in so many ways wiser than his mind—directed the blow which he aimed at the head of his senile obstructor."[43] It is *this* weak man who undergoes an atavistic re-connection to himself. It is questionable whether such a type would be taken seriously by contemporary movements that seek to reconnect with the primal energies of maleness. At the climax of his "re-education" at the NICE, Lewis describes Mark's discovery of reality:

> The built and painted perversity of this room had the effect of making him aware, as he had never been aware before, of this room's opposite. As the desert first teaches men to love water, or an absence first reveals affection, there

---

42. Lewis, *That Hideous Strength*, ch. 9, 249.

43. Lewis, *That Hideous Strength*, ch. 10, 290.

rose up against this background of the sour and the crooked some kind of vision and sweet and straight. Something else—something he vaguely called the "Normal"—apparently existed.... It was all mixed up with Jane and fried eggs and soap and sunlight and the rooks cawing at Cure Hardy and the thought that, somewhere outside, daylight was going on at that moment. He was not thinking in moral terms at all; or else (what is much the same thing) he was having his first deeply moral experience.[44]

He realizes that the sequence of inner rings that he so craved access to all of his life were in the end only so many concentric circles of losing his own humanity. "When had he ever done what he wanted?"[45] Uncle Screwtape's thirteenth letter likewise notes the manner in which unbelief often avoids the "simple pleasures" for instrumentalized ones that are about something other than themselves (i.e. reading a book because you want to be able to tell someone else you read it, rather than reading a book that *you* want to read *simpliciter*). Mark's new awareness of his own stubborn humanity quickly takes firm root in his soul.

If Mark seeks an antihuman "inner ring" that he should never have sought, Jane's relationship to moving "in" is the opposite. Jane is frequently portrayed as refusing to be "taken in" by anything—including the fullness of her own humanity and vocation. She is portrayed as

---

44. Lewis, *That Hideous Strength*, ch. 14, 413.

45. Lewis, *That Hideous Strength*, ch. 11, 338.

frequently fretting about the possibility of getting too consumed by marriage, and is likewise slow to take up with St. Anne's. "The bright, narrow little life which she had proposed to live was being irremediably broken into.... She didn't want to get drawn in."[46] But "taken in" she is. And indeed, as she moves closer and closer to her own conversion, she (like Mark) experiences the firing of something dormant in her nature as well. She is described as "moved by a kind of impulse which was rare to her experience."[47] And indeed after her conversion, she is quickly leading the conversation about what it means to be a woman among the women at St. Anne's.[48] The very last line in the book, when Jane approaches the bedroom in which Mark awaits her, reads, "Obviously it was high time that she went in."[49]

But what does all this amount to? Is Lewis saying anything about the world of men and women that means something concrete for modern readers? Whatever the answer to this, it is clear that Lewis believed that the world of gender represented a "ground zero" for civilization—the site of both its fracture and its healing. Indeed, *That Hideous Strength*, as many have noted, is set up by novels concerning the "masculine" Mars and the "feminine" Venus, where Earth (between these planets) represents a site of their mutuality. Nevertheless, unlike the "merely imperfect" Mars and the unfallen Venus, our own "silent planet" is a place of fracture and war between men and women.

---

46. Lewis, *That Hideous Strength*, ch. 4, 103.

47. Lewis, *That Hideous Strength*, ch. 9, 263.

48. Lewis, *That Hideous Strength*, ch. 17, 502–8.

49. Lewis, *That Hideous Strength*, ch. 17, 534.

But, one might riff on the Apostle, what will their reconciliation be but the resurrection of the dead?

CONCLUSION

For all the principles one might seek to elicit from *That Hideous Strength*, it is the fascinating way that Lewis writes of modern gender that most strikes this reader. We began by speaking about dystopia and apocalypse, and at the root of Lewis's dystopian vision lies a world in which the tensions between the sexes have been obliterated by a sexless, posthuman regime. In a civilizational moment dominated by extreme tension between the sexes (the Woke and Red Pill movements *strongly* reflect these tensions), Lewis's world is not wholly unlike our own. But his narrative thought-experiments are fascinating. Space forbids me to answer anticipated objections to Lewis's vision and so I will simply express three thoughts as principally as I can.

First, the healing of the conflict between the sexes is not portrayed as a frontal negotiation between Mark and Jane, but occurs in the individual engagement of each soul with God. Separated for most of the novel, it is *apart* that Mark and Jane come to themselves, and they are brought together having chosen to take on their manly and womanly vocation *whether or not the other does*. Said differently, they each come to *independently choose* service to one another as a regal act of dominion and self-possession. And yet this does not quite say it right. For Lewis, such choices are always portrayed as events of being caught up in forces (or perhaps, wary of Screwtape, we should say "spirits"), designs, and myths whose demand upon us is more dignifying and vivifying than our own supposedly sovereign self-crafting. In fact, it is food and drink for the human soul to do the will of the Father. Lewis's emphasis in this respect is less about "roles" and "rules" than it is about a more basic spiritual orientation that is beneath and beyond obsession with these. It is the life that is already given away that is of the Spirit and beyond the law. Mark and Jane do not take up a set of rules or begin to perform assigned roles that sit outside of themselves, but give themselves over to the rhythm and melody of reality.[50]

Second, Ransom comments on the sexes that "it ought never to have been a cause of war. But you see that obedience and rule are more like a dance than a drill—specially between man and woman where the roles are always changing."[51] Crucially, Mark and Jane remain a *modern* man and a *modern* woman—the roles are always changing. They do not morph into Dr. and Mrs. Dimble, who remain of a different generation than themselves. While certain basic "natural law" frequencies between men and women remain orienting and crucial for understanding ourselves, Lewis is aware that natural law is always inflect-

---

50. This seems consonant with Lewis's depiction of gender at the climax of Perelandra, when Ransom meets the Oyéresu of Malacandra and Perelandra. "He has said that Malacandra was like rhythm and Perelandra like melody. He has said that Malacandra affected him like a quantitative, Perelandra like an accentual, meter. He thinks that the first held in his hand something like a spear, but the hands of the other were open, with the palms towards him" (C.S. Lewis, *Perelandra* [London: HarperCollins, 2005], ch. 16, 253).

51. Lewis, *That Hideous Strength*, ch. 7, 198.

ed through custom and tradition.[52] He is likewise aware that custom changes, especially—even inevitably—in the modern world. Elsewhere, I have characterized *the* defining feature of modernity as this: the simultaneous global renegotiation of all human custom.[53] Although the basic principles of natural law don't change, the "living dance" that particularizes these principles does. The *independent* conversions of Mark and Jane are perhaps a commentary on what Lewis expects will become increasingly normative in contemporary civilization.[54] Putting these two points together, then, whatever it means for modern people to inflect the old patterns is liable to be rooted more in individual internalization of God's way than "peer pressure" to behave in certain ways that modernity often renders practically impossible. As much as some conservatives may desire it, there is not likely to be a large scale "RETVRN!" to the gender economy of past ages any time soon. While pushing for broad social change that enables the mutual flourishing of men and women *as* men and women is desirable, Lewis anticipated that we have entered a time in which *individual* men and

---

52. Note Lewis's comments on the modification of the *Tao*: "Those who understand the spirit of the *Tao* and who have been led by that spirit can modify it in directions which that spirit itself demands." *The Abolition of Man* (New York: Macmillan, 1947), 30.

53. See my forthcoming book with Davenant Press, *A Faith Observed* (2025), which extends reflections on this matter that I began in *Bulwarks of Unbelief: Atheism and Divine Absence in a Secular Age* (Bellingham: Lexham, 2023).

54. Compare with Lewis's comments on the trial of modernity and the possible emergence of a "civilization of sages" in *Miracles* (New York: HarperOne, 2015), 65–67.

women who are attuned to their gender vocations must *personally* take up the task of working out what this looks like in our increasingly sexless world. But what does this really amount to?

Third, and most fundamentally, it seems to this reader that Lewis captures a paradox: we live in a world in which gender is deeply inflected through choice and commitment, and yet he seems to narratively suggest that orientation is not simply a matter of well-chosen performance. Jane's refusal to be taken in is not ultimately a matter of "refusing some duty," but rather a matter of self-framing altogether. Said differently, she does not "imagine herself" as living in a story where her very self and dignity are discovered through being "taken in" by relationships and events that she does not ultimately manage, and that *call* her in her depths. In short, the very meaning of manhood and womanhood is co-relative. Even if we discover the meaning of our gender in the peculiar and distinctive "worlds" of men and women, it remains the case that *mankind* is for womankind, and *womankind* is for mankind. At the very roots of human civilization is an interdependence whose full flowering is interrupted by sin, and that (in our civilization) threatens to be forgotten. Even if individuality and choice take on a greater degree of prominence in the modern experience of our gendered selves, this can *result* in either curse or blessing. It will be a curse to the extent that our own radically peculiar (by historical standards) freedoms come to seem *more basic* in our vision than the self-giving patterns of interdependence that are stamped into our very bodies and natures. It will be a blessing to the extent that the individualism of modern civilization catalyzes a greater depth of engagement with the basic principles themselves. Indeed, perhaps the healing of our civilization will be to discover that "freely" giving ourselves away is to be given our life back again, because this is when our dominion is most like that of our Father.

IX

THE UNTABLED LAW OF NATURE

Colin Redemer

"The pen is mightier than the sword," say the aphorists.[1] And yet the aphorists also teach us to "never bring a [pen] knife to a gunfight." Immediately upon our reflection, strange tensions arise: is there any reconciliation between man's capacity for reason or language and our insistence on competition that, if not kept in check, leads to violence? In the 1983 film *Scarface*, the main character, Tony Montana, played by Al Pacino, is a rising gangster with a prominent scar who responds to every challenge he faces by upping the ante. At one point, as he is trying to take his former boss's girlfriend, his boss looks at him and says, "I'm giving you orders. Blow!" Tony stares back at his former boss and replies in a measured tone, "You're giving

---

1. First expressed in this form by Edward George Earle Lytton Bulwer-Lytton, 1st Baron Lytton (1803–1873).

me orders?" and he slows down his cadence even further. "Amigo," Tony continues, "the only thing in this world that gives orders is *balls*." It is a confrontation loaded with tension—a tension that explodes by the end of the film.

It might be odd to compare *Scarface* to an Oxford don's science fiction novel, but in fact in *That Hideous Strength* C. S. Lewis says something very similar to Tony Montana's icy response to his old boss. How can this be? Lewis was a pious man and a Christian. He would surely never stoop to write something so crass, nor would he approve of a film that ends with such gratuitous bloodshed. Yet I would not be the first to point out that, in reality, such bawdy humor was not uncommon in Lewis's life, and even in his serious argumentative work.[2] And as for blood, well, one simply has to finish the novel to see the orgy of violence that ensues. *That Hideous Strength*, like *Scarface*, stages for its audience a confrontation between two men, or types of men. And the question that sits just beneath the surface throughout is: for men to be men, must they engage in violent—bloody—confrontation? Does a man who refuses this confrontation expose an underlying natural tendency toward impotence and effeminacy? The answer to this question, of whether violence makes the man, lies further afield from the text under immediate consideration, in Lewis's short book *The Abolition of Man*.

---

2. The prime example of this is when he wrote "Priestesses in the Church," an essay opposing women's ordination. For an excellent analysis of that essay and Lewis's humor see a short article from this volume's editor, Rhys Laverty, "A Bawdy Theological Joke from C. S. Lewis?," *Ad Fontes*, November 25, 2022, https://adfontesjournal.com/pulpit-and-pew/a-bawdy-theological-joke-from-c-s-lewis/.

The Untabled Law of Nature

It should not come as a surprise that keys to understanding one text lay hidden in the other. In the preface to *That Hideous Strength*, Lewis writes that the novel "has behind it a serious 'point' that I have tried to make in my *Abolition of Man*."[3] But the two works—one a novel, the other a lecture series—are fraternal twins not just in theme, but in time. *The Abolition of Man*, as we now know it, is the collection of the three Riddell Memorial Lectures that Lewis delivered at Durham University in 1943 at the height of the Second World War. The preface to *That Hideous Strength* was also written in 1943. Lewis, Oxford-trained philosopher that he was, looked at the maladies of the Nazis and the Bolsheviks and at the soul-sucking reality of life in western liberal democracies, and he recognized a real spiritual pathogen infecting all of modernity. These two works on natural law were his attempt to identify and neutralize this pathogen common to every regime on every side of the war. This medical intervention on the spirit is, in large part, a confrontation with reconceptualizations of man and his place in the cosmic order offered by modernity. I am not the first reader of *Abolition of Man* to read it as a response in this way. However, this essay will show how those themes carry through into *That Hideous Strength* and how Lewis grounds morality not just in nature, but in *our* nature as it is in our embodied and sexed existence—and he shows us the importance of men.

You see, our times are not so dissimilar to Lewis's. And I take this to be part of why his legacy is so enduring. We are living through concerns of an imminent World War

---

3. C. S. Lewis, *That Hideous Strength* (London: HarperCollins, 2003), "Preface," ix.

Three, claims of dangerous neo-Nazis marching through the streets, Communists worming their way into power, and national churches that are by turns ready to meekly close up shop or submit to base desires. Reading Lewis allows us to take heart, knowing that we are not the first people in history to live through trouble.

In the life of C. S. Lewis, actual world war happened, twice; actual Nazis were just an ocean channel away from marching through the streets of England; Communists had staged bloody revolutions across Europe; the church was roughly as feckless as it had ever been. Oh, and the atomic bomb was developed and deployed on civilians and fellow Christians no less.[4]

In the Olympics of troubled times, Lewis has us beat. And it was in the middle of all that trouble that Lewis chose to spend his time writing science fiction and a trilogy of essays on moral law. An odd choice, it seems. But looking more closely at his oeuvre, it becomes clear that Lewis's mind was relatively unconcerned with these immediate dangers. Bombings are bad, and should be dealt with, but as an epidemiologist leaves the care of patients to doctors and nurses in order to find the origin of the pathogen and its vectors of transmission, Lewis was searching for where modernity's malady came from—and how it might be stopped.

That origin point is an abandonment of all values. Or, rather, not an abandonment of values but a turn away from *nature* and *essences*, and the embrace of "values" in their place. No thinker has more clearly articulated how

---

4. Look up the history of the bombing of Nagasaki and the Catholic community it once held.

this happens and what it might mean than Lewis and, perhaps, the philosopher Friedrich Nietzsche.

In Nietzsche's short life he produced a body of work and of arguments that have had an outsized impact on Western philosophy, unequaled by any thinker since, perhaps, ancient Athens. His arguments are pointed, his prose is terse, and he had the intelligence and wit to write in such a way that both the learned and the masses could absorb his thought. Often his arguments are couched in thinly veiled stories, as in *Thus Spake Zarathustra*. He is, in many ways, rather similar to Lewis.

And while, as is commonly known, some very bad people have been self-confessed believers in Nietzsche, this has become something of a smoke screen for contemporary people to ignore the philosopher's arguments instead of reading them.[5] Nor have they read Max Weber, who in 1917, expressed a consensus position that after Nietzsche *no one* can believe in objectivity of the fundamental truths, or believe that reason could ever establish a firm basis for values.[6] In saying this, Weber was not blaming modernity on Nietzsche, but rather saying that Nietzsche's critique of our modern world destroyed any hope of reconstructing our political or moral world on pure Enlightenment reason.

While Weber was expressing his understanding of the consensus of the German intellectuals in the early 1900s,

---

5. I have in mind here the popular depictions of Nietzsche as the thinker behind Nazism or the misdeeds of Leopold and Loeb.

6. Max Weber, "Science as a Vocation," in *The Vocation Lectures*, ed. David Owen and Tracy B. Strong, trans. Rodney Livingstone (Indianapolis: Hackett, 2004), 16–20.

the impact of Nietzsche and the inevitable reassessment of moral vocabulary in light of his critique did not come to America until a half century later. Alan Bloom, in his *Closing of the American Mind*, follows Weber and claims that the implications of Nietzsche's critique are still being digested in Anglo-American culture. This can be seen in what Bloom calls a "new language" of values.[7] Bloom says this new language, "constitutes a change in our view of things moral and political as great as the one that took place when Christianity replaced Greek and Roman paganism. A new language always reflects a new point of view, and the gradual, unconscious popularization of new words, or of old words used in new ways, is a sure sign of a profound change in people's articulation of the world."[8] Indeed, the concept of a new language that is actually a reduction of language's true potential is a concern throughout Lewis's work, notably in the Babel-like end of

---

7. Bloom himself was a student of Leo Strauss. Strauss commended *Abolition of Man* to his students at least as early as 1962: "We don't have time to read it here: there is a book, or rather a series of lectures by C. S. Lewis, the English author, *The Abolition of Man*, which is worth reading from every point of view" ("Seminar in Political Philosophy: Rousseau. A course offered in the autumn quarter, 1962," ed. Jonathan Marks, University of Chicago, https://wslamp70.s3.amazonaws.com/leostrauss/pdf/Rousseau_1962_1.pdf, 125). However, Strauss is also supposed to have used it in class from his earliest time teaching in the USA (see Geoffrey M. Vaughan, "Strauss as Teacher," *Law & Liberty*, May 15, 2020, https://lawliberty.org/book-review/strauss-as-teacher/).

8. Allan Bloom, *The Closing of the American Mind: How Higher Education Has Failed Democracy and Impoverished the Souls of Today's Students* (New York: Simon & Schuster, 2012), 141

*That Hideous Strength.*⁹ In the refutation of the NICE, we hear Lewis echo Weber, who claims that science cannot provide an answer to the question "How shall we live?" or "What shall we do?" "The fact that science cannot give us an answer is indisputable."[10] Lacking the firm rational basis for our convictions and actions, we are tempted to turn to "values."

Bloom notes a cultural arrogance, perhaps even chauvinism, inherent in the words "good" and "evil" that the term "values" allows us to wiggle out of. "Values" is so much more tolerant: I value family life, you value professional life, and Bob down the street values his pet cockroach. But baked into the presumption that someone might know what is *good*, Bloom says, there is a "closedness to the dignity of other ways of life; its implicit contempt for those who do not share our ways." If instead of telling Bob "I value family life," I instead tell him "It is good to have kids," then he might conclude that I consider his childless cockroach-life to be bad—perhaps even evil! The consequences of such a statement to Bob might not matter much, but on a bigger scale, they do. As Bloom says of the man who insists on "good" and "evil" instead of "values":

---

9. In particular, see his use of the term "verbicide" in *Studies in Words* (repr., Cambridge: Cambridge University Press, 2013). See also here (and throughout) T. A. Shippey's excellent chapter on "The Ransom Trilogy" in *The Cambridge Companion to C. S. Lewis*, ed. Robert MacSwain and Michael Ward (Cambridge: Cambridge University Press, 2010), 237–50.

10. Weber, "Science as a Vocation," 17.

The political corollary is that he is not open to negotiation. The opposition between good and evil is not negotiable and is a cause of war. Those who are interested in "conflict resolution" find it much easier to reduce the tension between values than the tension between good and evil. Values are insubstantial stuff, existing primarily in the imagination, while death is real. The term "value," meaning the radical subjectivity of all belief about good and evil, serves the easygoing quest for comfortable self-preservation.[11]

We know that Bloom was hunting in the same hills as Lewis, for this "comfortable self-preservation" can be seen in Mark Studdock and his "easygoing quest" for comfort and acceptance within "the inner ring." His moral lassitude is based on a detached view of ethics that devolves into value relativism. "'My wife' or 'those friends' wouldn't really understand these sorts of things that 'we' and 'our sort' of urbane thinking can see through." Lewis and Bloom understand the psychological appeal of value relativism in a similar way. Values, Bloom says,

> can be taken to be a great release from the perpetual tyranny of good and evil, with their cargo of shame and guilt, and the endless efforts that the pursuit of the one and the avoidance of the other enjoin. Intractable good and evil cause infinite distress—like war and sexual repression—which is almost instantly relieved when more

---

11. Bloom, *Closing of the American Mind*, 142

flexible values are introduced. One need not feel bad about or uncomfortable with oneself when just a little value adjustment is necessary. And this longing to shuck off constraints and have one peaceful, happy world is the first of the affinities between our real American world and that of German philosophy in its most advanced form.[12]

The therapeutic is implicit in favoring *values* over essentialist morality; we can always adjust our values since they are up to us and not grounded in any solid reality beyond our orientation to the world around us.[13] Similarly, if others disagree with us, it can be chalked up to merely a difference of values—not the possibility that one of us might be right and the other wrong, or that one might be good and the other evil.

When, upon first reading Nietzsche's *The Gay Science*, you encounter a madman who shouts, "What were we doing when we unchained the earth from its sun?"[14] you are likely to sit with the same puzzled look that you see on

---

12. Bloom, *Closing of the American Mind*, 142

13. See Freud's *Civilization and Its Discontents* for more on this. In that work Freud makes basically the same point: if we just loosen up about our "moral" and "religious" concerns over sex, then we will enjoy ourselves a lot more and fight a lot less. Bloom is, of course, more realistic about the possible dangers of this and less utopian than Freud, but the arguments are strikingly similar.

14. Friedrich Nietzsche, *The Gay Science*, ed. Bernard Williams, trans. Josefine Nauckhoff (Cambridge: Cambridge University Press, 2001), 120.

cows in a feeding lot, just a few months away from slaughter. Who couldn't care less, Nietzsche?! And it is puzzling, thinking about what this and the other passages where he says we have "unchained" ourselves from the sun mean.[15] More puzzling still, these rarely contemplated passages are a mere few sentences before his *most* quoted line: "God is dead! God remains dead! And we have killed him!"

To Nietzsche, the progress that man has made in his rational capacity has far outstripped his development in religious practice, as well as moral attitude. Worse yet, the human "turn to science" is an inevitable failure when it comes to what humans ought to *do* with themselves. It cannot offer inner direction.[16] Nietzsche intends his work to be an effort at overcoming our predicament. Nietzsche is often cast in the role of the great evil relativist, an anti-religion thinker, or even a nihilist. On a closer inspection, it is less obvious that this is a fair reading. The death of God, to him, is tragic. Nietzsche's point is that modernity, and relativism, is the end point of rationalism divorced from God. Relativism, nihilism, is where we currently *are*. His philosophical works are an attempted battle against a civilization-ending nihilism.[17] It might even be fair to say that he is a deeply religious writer working to articulate the "religion" that can answer modernity. "You know," Nietzsche whispers to us, "that you're not bound by all this modern

---

15. I have in mind here a series of questions Nietzsche asks about the relationship between humans and nature.

16. This is explored by Lewis in *That Hideous Strength* too, see the (rather silly) discussion of "pragmatomatry," ch. 2, 38–41.

17. Cf. Lisa van Boxel, *Warspeak* (Chicago: Political Animal, 2020).

stuff. The truth is that whatever man is, he is free; he must overcome the current state of the world."

Lewis is aware of this alienation between modern man and our nature, and of the temptation that it offers us, but his approach is quite different. He begins *The Abolition of Man* by directly confronting this idea, in a surprising way: by examining an English textbook for schoolboys. The authors, two teachers codenamed Gaius and Titius, have us consider a waterfall, presenting us with a tourist who, looking at the waterfall, says, "This waterfall is Sublime." The teachers, stand-ins for modern sensibility, respond just as Nietzsche's "rational" boyhood teachers would have and correct the boy, "No, silly, the waterfall is not sublime. It is just 15,000 gallons of water falling from fifty feet up. You merely *feel* sublime." A subtle shift, but it is the same shift we saw Bloom articulate above: your inner response is closed off from the outer world; it is yours and private. A *value* is not something essential; it cannot be said to *fit* with the nature of reality.

Lewis argues fervently that, no, in fact a waterfall *can* be sublime. In fact, to crib from William Carlos Williams, so much depends upon the sublimity of the waterfall—more than we can imagine. Whatever it has meant, traditionally, for humans to be *human*, whatever aspect of our being that is, it is the aspect that would *feel awe* by looking at a sublime waterfall. If we unchain sublimity from the waterfall, then we end up with merely so many gallons of water over there and so much of whatever feeling in here. If we decide to go about decoupling these two, there is little preventing us from recoupling our sentiments to other things. Why feel any more awe at your ability to beget a child than at the fact that you can tie your shoes?[18] Lewis argues, in *Abolition of Man*, that the English composition textbook authors are reprogramming their students—whether they know it or not—in just this way.

What is at stake, Lewis and Nietzsche both know, is far bigger than a waterfall, or even a schoolboy. What is at stake is God, humans, and *nature*. Is there such a thing as sublimity? Is the earth related to the sun? Are we related to God? If you answer "yes," you're with Lewis; "no" and you're with Gaius and Titius and modernity. But behold the nefarious consequences of saying "no": if the waterfall is truly sublime, you have an obligation toward it; it requires something of you. Modernity knows this and resents it, and wants you to resent it too. Lewis is helping you to see: the waterfall is your husband, your wife, your church, and your God. You cannot worship God if your inner response to him is *chosen* and humans who choose their God or their nature are not humans. As Nietzsche says that in our strange new world "there are no moral phenomena at all, only a moral interpretation of phenomena."[19] It is precisely at this point that Lewis contests. He tells us that children are delightful and old people are venerable, for example. If a given person doesn't experience them this way there is something wrong with that person. This is why Lewis is working to recover the objective meaning of "values" to articulate situations and essences that make demands on us. He does not want us to throw

---

18. Many potheads would beg to disagree here. I refute them thus.

19. Nietzsche, *Beyond Good and Evil*, trans. R.J. Hollingdale, (London: Penguin, 2003), 96.

the baby of the word "values" out with the bathwater of its accrued, modern meaning. We must recover the old ways.

Lewis, having begun with the waterfall, continues on to show the clear moral implications of what he calls the *Tao*, or "the doctrine of objective value, the belief that certain attitudes are really true, and others really false, to the kind of thing the universe is and the kind things we are."[20] But this, we will note again, is not really about values at all; rather, it is about being objective about natures or essences and recognizing that these essences elicit from humans a fitting response.

The thing required of humans, to Lewis, is to directly and rationally work through what the thing in front of us *is* and to learn to orient our subjective experience of that objective reality accordingly. The human animal must be trained. A puppy, to Lewis, is a thing that we can indeed measure. But we also need to *feel* a certain way about it. We must put it in front of our children and ask, "How does this make you feel?" What kind of responses does the puppy draw up to the surface? Cuddle, feed, and care, yes. But also: kill. Everyone who has held something small and vulnerable for long enough has felt the momentary, but insane, sense of the potential to *injure*. This is similar to the sense, on the edge of a cliff or a train platform, that one should just *jump*. How do we determine what a human should do with this ball of playful fur?

Lewis makes a radical break from all contemporary ethical thinkers here: you must consult the unbroken tradition of received ethical wisdom. Your parents told you to care for vulnerable things when you were small. They

---

20. C. S. Lewis, *The Abolition of Man* (New York: Macmillan, 1947), 12.

heard it from their parents, or their pastor. They in turn received it from their book of wisdom, and on and on.

Far from being arbitrary, human wisdom is powerful and basically correct. It is the wisdom received by our first parents from God at the creation. The person who gives in to the instinct to crush the puppy is doing wrong and is in some way leaving the realm of humanity and becoming a monster. The person who cuddles and cares for it is doing right and becoming more fully human. And moral formation is a sort of pruning of the soul, leading to healthful growth and flourishing. This is what education means, and why bad education is so desperately wicked. You can accept this reality or reject it, but to reject it is to reject ethics itself.

Nietzsche would tell us that we have developed in our moral thinking from consequence to origin to intention because we are gradually becoming aware that *the phenomena itself* is amoral, neither good nor evil, and all "moralities" are attempts to justify the existence of morality itself. Lewis responds by saying clearly: to move beyond morality is to check your humanity at the door. While Nietzsche's attempt to reconstitute our morality is in fact noble, it must be rejected since it is doomed to fail at the start in its rejection of the true God. But Nietzsche is right, and Lewis agrees, that *contra* the modern claim, the turn to modern relativism does not in fact reduce conflict or the shedding of blood. The baseline acceptance of moral systems that will judge our capacity for humanity, and even for human greatness, is as fundamental to the essence of humanity as the law of non-contradiction is to the essence of logic. Nietzsche simply thinks we need to invent these afresh since the way back to a Christianity that could hold

The Untabled Law of Nature

mastery is blocked like the gates of Eden.[21] This desire for a greatness that fits our nature is what drives both him and Lewis.[22] This desire can be fulfilled and it is not opposed to reason, though it cannot be deduced from reason. It must simply be accepted.

Bloom notes that "values are not discovered by reason, and it is fruitless to seek them, to find the truth or the good life."[23] We are free to continue to seek those things, but in the end we will realize that there is nothing to seek. This is what Nietzsche meant when he said, "God is dead."

---

21. In accepting the need for human greatness, they stand beside thinkers from Manu to Confucius, who said: "There are three things which the superior man guards against. In youth, when the physical powers are not yet settled, he guards against lust. When he is strong and the physical powers are full of vigor, he guards against quarrelsomeness. When he is old, and the animal powers are decayed, he guards against covetousness. There are three things of which the superior man stands in awe. He stands in awe of the ordinances of Heaven. He stands in awe of great men. He stands in awe of the words of sages. The mean man does not know the ordinances of Heaven, and consequently does not stand in awe of them. He is disrespectful to great men. He makes sport of the words of sages." Confucius, *The Analects*, 4.16, https://classics.mit.edu/Confucius/analects.4.4.html.

22. In a commentary on the Laws of Manu, Nietzsche writes: "The most intelligent men, like the strongest, find their happiness where others would find only disaster: in the labyrinth, in being hard with themselves and with others, in effort; their delight is in self-mastery; in them asceticism becomes second nature, a necessity, an instinct. They regard a difficult task as a privilege; it is to them a recreation to play with burdens that would crush all others." *The Antichrist*, trans. H. L. Mencken (New York: Alfred A. Knopf, 1931), 165. More work needs to be done considering Lewis's and Nietzsche's thought in relation to one another.

23. Bloom, *Closing of the American Mind*, 143.

At this point in modernity, good and evil themselves have disappeared from the stage because they have become subsumed in "values." Each of us has his own preferred flavors of "the good." But

> for Nietzsche this was an unparalleled catastrophe; it meant the decomposition of culture and the loss of human aspiration. The Socratic "examined" life was no longer possible or desirable. It was itself unexamined, and if there was any possibility of a human life in the future it must begin from the naive capacity to live an unexamined life. The philosophic way of life had become simply poisonous. In short, Nietzsche with the utmost gravity told modern man that he was free-falling in the abyss of nihilism. Perhaps after having lived through this terrible experience, drunk it to the dregs, people might hope for a fresh era of value creation, the emergence of new gods.
>
> Modern democracy was, of course, the target of Nietzsche's criticism. Its rationalism and its egalitarianism are the contrary of creativity. Its daily life is for him the civilized reanimalization of man. Nobody really believes in anything anymore, and everyone spends his life in frenzied work and frenzied play so as not to face the fact, not to look into the abyss. Nietzsche's call to revolt against liberal democracy is more powerful and more radical than is Marx's. And Nietzsche adds that the Left, socialism, is not the opposite of the special kind of Right that is

capitalism, but is its fulfillment. The Left means equality, the Right inequality. Nietzsche's call is from the Right, but a new Right transcending capitalism and socialism, which are the powers moving in the world.[24]

Here we will return to *That Hideous Strength*. Mark Studdock is a Fabian, a fashionable type of champagne socialist native to England. He is also, still, a human. But he is a human who has a particularly weak understanding of his own humanity. He doesn't know what drives him, and he lacks any inner conviction that would cause him to endure pain. He longs for comfort, for status, but he seeks those things forever outside himself. "Maybe this man can give me status? Perhaps this job title will satisfy the desire for meaning. If I only had a little more cash I would finally be *happy*." He is, at the outset, a genuinely pathetic character, and the stakes for him throughout the novel are *manliness* and *potency*.

The first word of the book is "matrimony," as many have pointed out—that is, the state of mother-making, something only achievable with the aid of male potency.[25] The final scene of the novel is one of reconciliation in the consummation of the marriage bed.[26]

But to focus on the marriage relation is to miss the overwhelming concern that the novel has with gender beyond their relationship. Jane spends much of the novel

---

24. Bloom, *Closing of the American Mind*, 143.

25. Lewis, *That Hideous Strength*, ch. 1, 1.

26. Lewis, *That Hideous Strength*, ch. 17, 534.

learning to be a woman, observing healthy married couples, and discovering how to submit to her husband as she does to Ransom, the true, but hidden, king. And no doubt more could be said of Jane and her discovery and embrace of her half of the sexed body that is humanity. Her part, however, is responsive and requires the encounter with the masculine to bring it to its fullest expression in reality. Her husband, Mark, descends into a world where there is no authority, men and women are interchangeable, and morality and lawfulness is a laughing matter. Yet what drives them into these very different communities is sex itself. Jane is nervous about her trip to St Anne's initially, and at every step of the way she is hesitant and a bit diffident about the frowsty traditionalism on display. Mark, meanwhile, is lured by the sense of being inside a group of serious men. They are influential and potent. One of their leaders, a man nicknamed "Dick," is described as having an "extremely virile and infectious laugh."[27] He makes jokes about how inflammatory it would be for the British public to know what the government is really up to because if they found out "you'd have all the old women of both sexes up in arms."[28] Mark is lured into Belbury by a "fine male energy."[29] However, like a man who buys a car for its paint job only to realize he's been sold a lemon upon leaving the lot, he soon realizes that the masculine energy here is a mirage, as most people are doing little more than gossiping and backbiting. Meanwhile we, the

---

27. Lewis, *That Hideous Strength*, ch. 2, 34.

28. Lewis, *That Hideous Strength*, ch. 2, 45.

29. Lewis, *That Hideous Strength*, ch. 2, 54.

reader, witness deep fascination with sterility and, at the innermost center of the inner circle, a homoerotic lust for power seen most clearly in the embrace between Wither and Frost who attempt to "interpenetrate" one another in an attempt to bring about a union that is clearly a mockery of the union that Christians find in God.[30]

The appearance of the masculine without its potency is also evident in *Abolition of Man*. Lewis famously ends his first chapter of that work with the lines:

> You can hardly open a periodical without coming across the statement that what our civilization needs is more "drive," or dynamism, or self-sacrifice, or "creativity." In a sort of ghastly simplicity we remove the organ and demand the function. We make men without chests and expect of them virtue and enterprise. We laugh at honour and are shocked to find traitors in our midst. We castrate and bid the geldings be fruitful.[31]

To castrate is, of course, to make something infertile—infertile like the Studdocks' marriage, infertile like Frost and Wither's embrace, infertile like the NICE would have all biological life. Which is more tragic is hard to say. The image of a castrated horse is, of course, calling the reader back to Lewis's earlier discussion of θυμός (*thymos*).[32] *Thymos* is a word in ancient Greek that is often translated as

---

30. Lewis, *That Hideous Strength*, ch. 11, 332–33.

31. Lewis, *Abolition of Man*, 16.

32. Pronounced "thoo-moss."

"spiritedness." It is the spirited aspect of man. In Plato's analysis of the human soul there are three powers: the lowest is the ἐπιθυμία (*epithymia*) or desiring power, the middle is the *thymos* or competing power, and the highest is the λόγος (*logos*) or reasoning power. Lewis likens these to the belly, the chest, and the head respectively, and it is the chest, he says, that modernity misses in its overemphasis on the rational. Aristotle claims that the higher forms of animals have *thymos*.[33] And who, coming across a family of bears playing in an alpine lake, or a young deer leaping in a pinewood clearing, or an eagle diving from the sky to snatch a fish from a river, can deny it? Yet animals have this capacity in an ungoverned way; they lack the *logos* to keep their *thymos* well ordered. It is precisely the right ordering of the three that makes man man. Animals desire and breed and compete, angels have rationality, but man alone possesses all of these potencies. While Lewis calls it the "chest" in *The Abolition of Man*, given the final line's reference to *gelding* in that chapter and given *That Hideous Strength*'s emphasis on manliness, we may wonder if it is in fact more accurate to say that what is missing from the modern world is actually *balls*, the clearest source of our potency—not simply right sentiments, but "*stable* sentiments," as Lewis says, maintained in the face of those who would tell us that such sentiments are bogus. The balls may be associated in our minds with lust and the epithymotic desires of the belly, and for that reason Lewis perhaps wisely used the image of the chest, but the balls are more than mere lust; they're also a source of stability in the

---

33. Aristotle, *History of Animals*, Book IX. Let this stand as one example among several others.

The Untabled Law of Nature

face of an uncertain world when challenge must be met. Imagine Gaius and Titius's students standing up and telling them, "No, sir, the waterfall *is* sublime." That would take a strong chest—or as we would colloquially say, balls. Cormac McCarthy, in *All The Pretty Horses*, writes of a cowboy who was breeding a stallion. In the mornings, before it was time to breed,

> He'd ride sometimes clear to the upper end of the laguna before the horse would even stop trembling and he spoke constantly to it in spanish in phrases almost biblical repeating again and again the strictures of a yet untabled law. Soy comandante de las yeguas, he would say, yo y yo sólo. Sin la caridad de estas manos no tengas nada. Ni comida ni agua ni hijos. Soy yo que traigo las yeguas de las montañas, las yeguas jóvenes, las yeguas salvajes y ardientes. While inside the vaulting of the ribs between his knees the darkly meated heart pumped of who's will and the blood pulsed and the bowels shifted in their massive blue convolutions of who's will and the stout thighbones and knee and cannon and the tendons like flaxen hawsers that drew and flexed and drew and flexed at their articulations and of who's will all sheathed and muffled in the flesh and the hooves that stove wells in the morning groundmist and the head turning side to side and the great slavering keyboard of

his teeth and the hot globes of his eyes where the world burned.[34]

McCarthy's words are worth quoting as a stirring bit of prose that gives us the sense of what *thymos* is. And the relationship of the horse and the man shows the relation *logos* and *thymos* can have in right order. The horse gets what it gets by the hand of man but through, and because of, the balls. This is the "untabled law" referenced—the untabled law of nature, of balls. And while by the man the horse is tamed and directed justly, without the testicles the rational faculty will fail to live up to its determined judgements—it will lose the capacity to govern. Testicles are not just the source of fertile potency in men, they are also essential for the production of vastly greater quantities of testosterone in the male of the species, as well as maintaining other hormone modulation. Testosterone causes muscle development and greater bone density, but it also spurs a desire to compete and dampens stress responses, enabling cool and rational decision-making under pressure. Without the balls, the male cannot contribute to the propagation of the species, but without the testosterone they provide he might not be able to win a female mate in the first place. And while the virtue (or excellence) related to the "belly" is moderation and the excellence of the "head" is wisdom or prudence, what is the virtue of the balls?

That virtue would be none other than courage, the ability to face the right quantity of pain and suffering for the right reason. Lewis speculates that perhaps the reason

---

34. Cormac McCarthy, *All the Pretty Horses* (London: Picador, 1992), 131–32.

God created a dangerous world was so that there would be natural reasons for moral issues to come to the point. As he says in *The Screwtape Letters*, "courage is not simply *one* of the virtues, but the form of every virtue at the testing point."[35] And it is precisely courage, willingness to face pain, that Mark must develop if he is to grow a pair and become a real man. Both men and women can, of course, be courageous, but courage has always been understood as a "male coded" virtue. The NIV translates Paul's command to the Corinthian church, in 1 Corinthians 16:13, ἀνδρίζεσθε (*andrizesthe*), as "be courageous." The King James, however, reads "quit you like men," a more accurate translation of the Greek verb ἀνδρίζω (*andrizo*), which comes from the word ἀνήρ (*aner*), the Greek term not merely for a human male as opposed to a female, but for a grown man, one in the prime of his powers, especially a warrior.[36] If the KJV's "quit you like men" is a bit obscure and the NIV's "be courageous" is castrated, you could try translating Paul's command as, "Act like men!"[37]

---

35. C. S. Lewis, *The Screwtape Letters* (London: HarperCollins, 2001), 161

36. For a particularly illustrative use of the word ἀνήρ (*aner*) to mean a brave and powerful man, see Herodotus's disdainful assessment of Xerxes' massive forces who were repeatedly repulsed by a tiny band of well-armed Spartans in the Battle of Thermopylae: πολλοὶ μὲν ἄνθρωποι εἶεν, ὀλίγοι δὲ ἄνδρες ("There were many people, but few men."). *Histories*, book VII.

37. Paul's command to the Corinthians isn't the only call we find in the early church for Christians to man up. Before his martyrdom, Polycarp hears a voice telling him first to be strong, and then it commands him with the same verb Paul had used: ἀνδρίζου (*andrizou*). As one famous translation has it: "Play the man!" In the minds of the early Christians, insofar as a woman acts courageously, she becomes a

Meanwhile, someone following Aristotle would also conclude that courage is most clearly seen in men. But if we follow his reasoning it isn't men qua their biological difference that show us courage. Rather we must look at men where they shed blood, in war. War, outside the city gates, is where they willingly shed their blood—putting their life at risk—for the common good. While for men that happens on the battlefield, for women it happens in the marriage bed.[38] In childbirth, the female expression of fertility, blood is shed and life is risked for the sake of the common good.

In the climactic scene of *That Hideous Strength*, Mark, not a Christian, is asked to trample on a crucifix. The demonic forces at the NICE are hoping to inculcate in him a radical belief in the subjectivity of values, the absence of essences, and finally Mark has had enough of being pushed around. "It's all bloody nonsense, and I'm damned if I do any such thing," he says to them. But the narrator continues, "When he said this he had no idea what might happen next. He did not know whether Frost would ring

---

man. This is borne out not only by the sexed calls to courage in Paul and Polycarp, but also in a shocking passage from the first-person account of the early female martyr-saint Perpetua. In her last of three visions leading up to her execution, the young mother recounts being led out into the arena, and before—in the customary fashion—being rubbed down with oil to fight, she says, "I was stripped nude and *became a man*" (ἐγενήθην ἄρρην). For the early Christians, increasingly accustomed to seeing their co-religionists spilling their blood in the arena like gladiators, courage—the refusal to back down in the face of pain, fear, and mockery—was manliness epitomized.

38. Aristotle, *Nicomachean Ethics*, Book III, and *Rhetoric*, Book I.

a bell or produce a revolver or renew his demands. In fact, Frost simply went on staring at him and he stared back."³⁹

This moment, facing possible death, the extremity of pain and the shedding of his own blood, is the moment of courage. Mark has grown a pair—or, to return to Lewis's language, grown a chest, and it is puffed out, consequences be damned. Joseph Pieper counsels that courage is not the absence of fear. In fact such absence is, as Aristotle long ago knew, recklessness that sits opposite cowardice as the vices between which courage sits. So courage does not negate fear but also doesn't give into it. Rather it is a right relationship to fear. Pieper proposes an *ordo timoris* (playing on the Augustinian *ordo amoris*) in which we learn not to fear "things that are not truly and ultimately fearful, and to fear things that are. The ultimate fearful reality ... is none other than the possibility that we may sever ourselves, willingly and culpably, from the very source of our being."⁴⁰

It is by the balls that man rules and exerts dominion on the earth—or dies trying. If young boys are not trained to believe that some things are worthy of competing, even dying, for and instead follow Gaius and Titius, they will be spiritually and mentally (perhaps even physically) castrated.⁴¹ If legitimate authority abdicates or abuses that governing authority, the fundamental (if untabled) law

---

39. Lewis, *That Hideous Strength*, ch. 15, 468.

40. Joseph Pieper, "Courage Does Not Exclude Fear," *An Anthology* (San Francisco: Ignatius, 1982), 72.

41. As Lewis says in *Abolition*: "A boy ... thinks he is 'doing' his 'English prep' and has no notion that ethics, theology, and politics are all at stake" (Lewis, *Abolition of Man*, 3).

will reassert itself and another will rise in its place. Nature always reasserts itself. "Values" never can. While in the body there is work to do, and confronting that work and its pain requires courage. The question is not whether our virtue can transcend politics, escaping the world we live in as if we were angels, but whether our virtue can descend into the political world of confrontation and competition so that it may order it justly.[42]

The powerful man must strive to ensure there is good rule. And this means there will be confrontation and, ultimately, blood. God, through Ransom and Merlin, executes just judgment on the evil and bloody but castrated leaders of the NICE. Mark faces his possible death with excellence and lives to know his own potency. And the orgy of blood that follows is gruesome and deadly serious, but also an ultimately just act that allows for the perfection of all virtue. While Mark does not himself take up arms, it cannot be contested that the conclusion of the book is violence instigated by the band of saints at St Anne's. Merlin is violently possessed by the *eldila* at the behest of Ransom who, in *Perelandra*, has violently beaten a man to death with his hands. Merlin is the conduit for the violence of human and animal chaos at the final dinner. Humans who abdicate their governing authority, or who attempt to transcend it, invite the reassertion of nature in which man is a beast to man and the zoo of the soul is opened, unleashing predators who know no law. Natural law, the untabled law, reasserts itself and blood will flow.

---

42. Just as Tony Montana knew, albeit in a tragic, bent, and perverted way, there will be ruler and ruled while we live on this earth

The Untabled Law of Nature

Follow the blood. In our lives the trail leads to our bloody and painful birth and then in the other direction to our death. In Scripture we see its trail, drip by drip, leading off in one direction where it goes all the way back to Cain's bloody hand hovering over the body of his dead brother. In the other direction we see it trailing off to the last judgment and the winepress of God's wrath.

However, Lewis is asking us, can we look farther than this? There beyond Cain is the hand of God cutting the first animals open to use their skins to cover over the sin of our first parents. And there at the end we see the trail leading right to the foot of Golgotha. The crucifixion of Jesus is the end of the blood. The manliest act of the most omni-potent law giver. The makrothymotic suffering of Jesus as he finishes the job set before him is itself the meaning of manliness and the unitive act of the untabled law of nature with the tabled law of revelation. His blood is fertile and potent and flows to heal and to win children to his family.

It is only in our efforts to humbly live up to the excellence laid down for us by this Law Giver in His law that we can fully embody the excellences of our essential nature as humans. We must accustom ourselves to embrace and be embraced by this reality. This sexed and embodied way requires courage, for there is still much pain to endure along the way, but it is the way laid out for us, and the way that Lewis is pointing us toward. There are certain sexed necessities that, Lewis thinks, are clues to the nature of reality.[43]

---

43. Gilbert Meilander, *The Taste for the Other: The Social and Ethical Thought of C. S. Lewis* (Grand Rapids: Eerdmans, 1998), 155.

It is us locating ourselves rightly within that reality that allows us to escape the hall of mirrors that the radically subjective "values" language drives us toward. We must embrace ourselves as desperately human, created in a world filled with wonders and terrors to be discovered. Beyond the sublime waterfalls, and the fertile loins of our humanity that enable us to fully embrace them with fitting awe, is nothingness. As Lewis says at the end of *The Abolition of Man* "It is no use trying to 'see through' first principles. If you see through everything, then everything is transparent. But a wholly transparent world is an invisible world. To 'see through' all things is the same as not to see."

We must embrace reality, including the reality of our bodies (and get God thrown in with it) or reject it all. God's grace does not destroy or replace our nature; it perfects it. We must learn to love the Law revealed in Scripture without neglecting to learn the as yet untabled law.

X

ARTHUR IN EDGESTOW

Holly Ordway

C. S. Lewis's science fiction novels are known as the Ransom Trilogy because their protagonist is a man called Elwin Ransom. Yet in the third tale, *That Hideous Strength*, Ransom has changed his name to Mr. Fisher-King, an odd turn of events in a book full of odd things. In the preface, Lewis himself draws attention to the novel's heterogeneous elements: "magicians, devils, pantomime animals, and planetary angels."[1] It is interesting that he mentions "magicians" first, for the only true magician in the book, Merlin, derives from Arthurian legend, as does the "Fisher-King."[2] These two elements indicate how important it is

---

1. C. S. Lewis, *That Hideous Strength* (London: HarperCollins, 2003), "Preface," ix.

2. Merlin is a true magician because he deals in *magia*, relating to the natural world and its spiritual beings as "a kind of personal contact," whereas the other "magicians" (the NICE technicians) deal in *goeteia*: they treat nature as a machine to be manipulated and "simply want to

to understand Arthuriana if we wish to understand *That Hideous Strength*. This essay will survey Lewis's lifelong familiarity with all things "Arthur" and show how "the Matter of Britain" plays an important role in the story that heightens the relevance of the novel's themes and ideas for the Christian life.

CONTEXT

By the early twentieth century, the story of King Arthur was fully absorbed into the modern imagination, due in large part to the "Arthurian revival" facilitated by new editions of Thomas Malory's *Morte d'Arthur*, as well as Tennyson's *Idylls of the King* and the art of the Pre-Raphaelites. The presence of several recognizably Arthurian features in *That Hideous Strength* makes it easy to assume that Lewis is working with a story that is very familiar to us—and therein lies a major pitfall to avoid as we engage with his use of these materials. We will be better able to appreciate Lewis's use of the legendarium if we first take a brief survey of his familiarity with the source materials.

What we call "Arthurian legend" comprises what the medieval authors called "the Matter of Britain." It was not a single story, but a complex web of narratives that developed over the course of several centuries; particular characters appear in different, sometimes contradictory, ways in different texts.[3] As a literary scholar, Lewis was

---

increase their power by tacking onto it the aid of spirits—extra-natural, anti-natural spirits" (Lewis, *That Hideous Strength*, ch. 14, 394).

3. The popular idea of a general "Arthurian" story can lead us into mistakes. For instance, Janina P. Traxler argues that Lewis's use of Arthurian materials partakes of a "nostalgic view" found in "much of

well aware of these variants; in fact, his awareness of this textual diversity is apparent as early as 1916, when he challenged Arthur Greeves's simplistic view of Malory's *Morte d'Arthur*: "What do you mean by saying 'It' is 'an old French legend': the 'Morte' includes a hundred different Arthurian legends & as you know the Arthur myth is Welsh."[4] As an imaginative writer Lewis was willing to assess the stories for their literary merits, as in his remark to a correspondent in 1963 that "The prophecies of Merlin are much the least interesting thing about him"—referring probably to Geoffrey of Monmouth's *Prophecies of Merlin* (ca. 1130)—and adding, "The fullest source for the Merlin story is the prose *Merlin*"—that is, the

---

modern fantasy literature, especially Arthurian fantasy": that in medieval or pre-industrial times "Men were braver and more courteous ... right and wrong were clearer" ("Pendragon, Merlin, and Logos: The Undoing of Babel in *That Hideous Strength*," *Arthurian Literature* vol. 20. 2003), 192). As for greater courtesy, it is worth observing that the newly awakened Merlin expresses an inclination, on seeing Jane, that "her head should be cut from her shoulders; for it is a weariness to look at her." (Lewis, *That Hideous Strength*, ch. 13, 384). More strikingly, the idea that "right and wrong were clearer" in the past is precisely the opposite of what Lewis suggests. Dimble says that the key characteristic of the working of history is that "Good is always getting better and bad is always getting worse: the possibilities of even apparent neutrality are always diminishing." (Lewis, *That Hideous Strength*, ch. 13, 391). It is for this reason that the kind of magic Merlin did was permissible in his day, but not in the modern day. Whatever else Lewis is doing, he is not indulging in nostalgia.

4. C. S. Lewis, Letter 48, in *They Stand Together: The Letters of C. S. Lewis to Arthur Greeves: 1914–1963*, ed. Walter Hooper (London: Collins, 1979), 148.

French prose romance that composes part of the Vulgate Grail cycle.[5]

His first academic work, *The Allegory of Love* (1936), draws extensively on Chrétien de Troyes' Arthurian romances, and his magnum opus, *English Literature in the Sixteenth Century (Excluding Drama)*, shows a deep knowledge of Arthuriana.[6] Malory's *Morte* was a favorite work of lifelong significance to Lewis: he first read it in 1915, announcing that "it has opened up a new world to me."[7] When, in 1934, an early manuscript copy of Malory's *Morte* was discovered, Lewis described it as "the most startling literary discovery of the century."[8] Matters Arthurian also made an early appearance in Lewis's imaginative writings, including "The Quest of Bleheris," an Arthurian anti-hero story, the darkly pessimistic poem "Lancelot," and a poem about Merlin and Nimue (to which we will return below).

The key point from this overview is that Lewis did not conceive of "Arthurian legend" in a generalized sense, but in terms of particular texts and authors. We can also see that Lewis's familiarity with the Arthurian corpus long

---

5. C. S. Lewis, *The Collected Letters of C. S. Lewis*, vol. 3, *Narnia, Cambridge, and Joy 1950–1963*, ed. Walter Hooper (London: HarperCollins, 2006), 1074.

6. He is able to state definitively that in the *Faerie Queene* Spenser invents a childhood for Arthur "which had no precedent either in Tudor or in medieval tradition." (*English Literature in the Sixteenth Century (Excluding Drama)* (Oxford: Clarendon Press, 1954), 382).

7. Lewis, Letter 10, *They Stand Together*, 63.

8. C. S. Lewis, *Studies in Medieval and Renaissance Literature* (Cambridge: Cambridge University Press, 1966), 103.

predates his encounter in 1936 with the work of Charles Williams, whose possible influence on *That Hideous Strength* provides our next point of discussion.

THE EXTENT OF WILLIAMS'S INFLUENCE

Known today mainly for his membership in the Inklings and his "spiritual thrillers," Charles Williams also produced two volumes of an Arthurian poetic cycle, *Taliessin through Logres* and *The Region of the Summer Stars*. Lewis thought highly of these volumes, which, in a rare lapse of literary judgment, he believed would be recognized as important poetic works. After Williams's unexpected death in 1945, Lewis attempted to further that recognition by writing an extended commentary on these poems, published as *Arthurian Torso*.

In their biography of Lewis, Roger Lancelyn Green and Walter Hooper observe that *That Hideous Strength* has been called "a Charles Williams novel written by C. S. Lewis." This catchy statement has unfortunately been too often taken as a sober statement of Williams's influence on the book, without taking into account Green and Hooper's caution that this description is "a wild exaggeration."[9] It is helpful here to consider that J. R. R. Tolkien, who knew Williams's work nearly as well as Lewis did,[10] held that "The 'space-travel' trilogy ascribed to the influ-

---

9. Roger Lancelyn Green and Walter Hooper, *C. S. Lewis: A Biography* (New York: Harcourt, Brace, Jovanovich, 1974), 174.

10. For instance, it was to Tolkien and Lewis together that Williams read the first chapters of his Arthurian study, *The Figure of Arthur* (C. S. Lewis, *Arthurian Torso* [Oxford: Oxford University Press, 1948], 2)

ence of Williams was basically foreign to Williams's kind of imagination."[11]

In the course of the novel, Lewis gives a nod to Williams's Arthuriana when Camilla Denniston remarks that a poem she is reading, *Taliessin through Logres*, expresses her difficulty with waiting patiently. But in much the same way, Lewis also acknowledges George MacDonald's Curdie books and the writings of Owen Barfield; we should not attach undue importance to the allusion.

With regard to the Arthurian elements in *That Hideous Strength*, it is more accurate to refer to areas of overlap, as each reached for characters and symbols that had shared literary resonances, rather than a definite or deep influence from Williams upon Lewis. Not only had Lewis known and loved the stories of Arthur long before he met Williams or read any of his work, but he knew the source material far better, even remarking in a letter that "[Williams'] knowledge of the earlier Arthurian documents was not that of a real scholar: he knew none of the relevant languages except (a little) Latin."[12]

---

11. J.R.R Tolkien, Letter 252, in *The Letters of J. R. R. Tolkien: Revised and Expanded Edition*, ed. Humphrey Carpenter (London: HarperCollins, 2023), 479. This is not to say that Tolkien saw no influence from Williams on *That Hideous Strength*. He felt that Lewis's cosmic mythology had been "broken to bits before it became coherent by contact with [Charles] Williams and his 'Arthurian' stuff" (Letter 276, *Letters*, 505). Tolkien disliked Williams's Arthurian poetry so intensely that he may well have found parts of *That Hideous Strength* "guilty by association" merely for using the Arthurian elements at all.

12. See Lewis, *Collected Letters*, 3:232.

THE ARTHURIAN LEGENDARIUM

When Lewis decided to integrate certain Arthurian elements into the third volume of his Ransom Trilogy, he had behind him decades of both personal enjoyment and academic study of the original sources and had already tried his hand at adaptations. He knew that he would have to reckon with the variations and contradictions in the Arthuriad, most notably that the martial world of works like Gildas's *On the Downfall and Conquest of Britain* (ca. 547), Bede's *Ecclesiastical History of the English People* (731), and Geoffrey of Monmouth's *The History of the Kings of Britain* (1138) is very different from the elegant, courtly setting of Chrétien de Troyes' twelfth-century French romances and the spiritual themes of the thirteenth-century Vulgate Grail cycle.

Lewis makes the choice to ground his Arthurian material in the setting of the earliest tales, the only ones with any historical plausibility, in which Arthur was a military leader fighting the Angles and Saxons who invaded at the same time that the Romans were retreating from Britain to defend Rome. In *That Hideous Strength*, Dimble sketches out a picture of "Britain as it must have been on the eve of the invasion" and envisions Arthur as "a man of the old British line, but also a Christian and a fully-trained general with Roman technique, trying to pull this whole society together and almost succeeding."[13]

Here Lewis makes a very interesting literary move. As Dimble puts it:

---

13. Lewis, *That Hideous Strength*, ch. 1, 27–28.

> You've noticed how there are two sets of characters? There's Guinevere and Launcelot and all those people in the center: all very courtly and nothing particularly British about them. But then in the background—on the other side of Arthur, so to speak—there are all those dark people like Morgan and Morgawse, who are very British indeed and usually more or less hostile though they are his own relatives.... Merlin too, of course, is British, though not hostile.[14]

Rather than simply choosing the Gildas-Bede-Geoffrey thread of the tradition over against the post-Norman Conquest French developments of the legendarium, Lewis retroactively assimilates the two, finding a way to integrate the French characters (invented centuries later) into the British context. Lewis manages, in effect, to have his cake and eat it too. He is freed to use any thematic elements of the Arthurian legendarium that he likes, whether from the earlier Welsh and British stories or from later French romances, while keeping it all rooted in the historical setting of a Britain that not only predates the Norman Conquest, but also predates the Anglo-Saxon invasion: Britain before it became Angle-land, England. In this way, Lewis suggests that the story unfolding in *That Hideous Strength* is of particular relevance to the British people.

ARTHUR

One interesting aspect of Lewis's use of Arthurian materials in *That Hideous Strength* is that Arthur himself remains

---

14. Lewis, *That Hideous Strength*, ch. 1, 27.

in the background. He is suggested at various points, first by the fact that one of the company of St Anne's is named Arthur Denniston, and by Jane's reaction to meeting Ransom. When she sees the golden-bearded Ransom, seated on a couch that is somehow throne-like, she is reminded of "the imagined Arthur of her childhood," an impression that helps to convey "the bright solar blend of king and lover and magician" that causes her, in an intuitive flash, to realize "her world was unmade.... Anything might happen now."[15]

An early feature of the Arthurian legends is the idea that Arthur, though wounded in his final battle, does not die but is rather taken to the Isle of Avalon (*Insula Avallonia*, the Island of Apples), whence he shall one day return. Lewis deftly folds this into his cosmology in making Perelandra, the planet Venus, the site of Avalon. When Merlin appears at St Anne's, he challenges Ransom with three questions, the second of which is "Where is the ring of Arthur the King?" Ransom replies:

> The ring of the King ... is on Arthur's finger where he sits in the House of Kings in the cup-shaped land of Abhalljin, beyond the seas of Lur in Perelandra. For Arthur did not die; but Our Lord took him, to be in the body till the end of time and the shattering of Sulva, with Enoch and Elias and Moses and Melchisedec the King. Melchisedec is he in whose hall the

---

15. Lewis, *That Hideous Strength*, ch. 7, 189.

steep-stoned ring sparkles on the forefinger of the Pendragon.[16]

The placement of Arthur in the Perelandrian Avalon is consistent with the legendarium; what is distinctive is that Lewis de-emphasizes his traditional role as "the once and future king." He will not return to save Britain, but will wait on Perelandra until "the end of time"; his authority has passed to Ransom as the current Pendragon (a point to which we will return later). And so, in *That Hideous Strength* it is not Arthur himself who represents the forces of good, but rather his kingdom of Logres.

LOGRES

In one sense, "Logres" is simply the name for King Arthur's realm, as with the geographical observation that "Edgestow lay in what had been the very heart of ancient Logres."[17] By extension, the name applies to his loyal followers, as with Merlin's exhortation that Ransom and his small company should fight: "I saw the time when Logres was only myself and one man and two boys, and one of those was a churl. Yet we conquered."[18]

Lewis knew the term from Malory: in a 1916 letter he described a mood in which "the quaint, old mystical parts of Malory are exactly suitable: you can read a chapter or two in a sort of dream & find the forests of 'Logres & of

---

16. Lewis, *That Hideous Strength*, ch. 13, 377.

17. Lewis, *That Hideous Strength*, ch. 9, 272.

18. Lewis, That Hideous Strength, ch. 13, 404.

Lyonesse' very agreeable."[19] Here Lewis is also alluding to Milton's *Paradise Regained*, a passage that he later quotes in *The Discarded Image*:

> And Ladies of th'Hesperides, that seem'd
> Fairer than feign'd of old, or fabl'd since
> Of Fairy Damsels met in Forest wide
> By Knights of Logres, or of Lyones—[20]

Lewis was familiar with the literary conceit of Logres as a liminal place, not merely a place-name. He would also have been aware of the way in which, in the medieval literary tradition, Logres has deep associations with a sense of national identity. As Rouse and Rushton put it:

> for medieval writers, the locating of Arthurian geography within the actual landscape of the British Isles was not merely of antiquarian interest: rather, it was often a serious matter of political, cultural and institutional importance. Authors writing in numerous languages and hailing from a variety of courts looked towards Britain for indelible signs of that ancient conqueror who could validate the regimes of their own day, interpreting Arthur's actions through their own contemporary lens: for this was Logres, the

---

19. Lewis, Letter 44, *They Stand Together*, 135.

20. Quoted in C. S. Lewis, *The Discarded Image* (Cambridge: Cambridge University Press, 1964), 123.

legendary Britain of the past over which Arthur had once reigned so gloriously.[21]

Lewis is drawing from an existing body of associations in medieval and early modern literature to develop his imagery of a spiritual tension between "Logres" and "Britain." As he put it in a 1954 letter, "About Logres—I do think there is a 'better England' always getting lost in, but always showing through, the actual one."[22]

Hence, we have Dimble explaining:

> something we may call Britain is always haunted by something we may call Logres. Haven't you noticed that we are two countries? After every Arthur, a Mordred; behind every Milton, a Cromwell: a nation of poets, a nation of shopkeepers; the home of Sidney—and of Cecil Rhodes. Is it any wonder they call us hypocrites? But what they mistake for hypocrisy is really the struggle between Logres and Britain.... There has been a secret Logres in the very heart of Britain all these years; an unbroken succession of Pendragons.... [I]n every age they and the little Logres which gathered round them have been the fingers which gave the tiny shove or the almost imperceptible pull, to prod England out of

---

21. Robert Allen Rouse and Cory James Rushton, "Arthurian Geography," in *A Cambridge Companion to the Arthurian Legend*, ed. Elizabeth Archibald and Ad Putter (New York: Cambridge University Press, 2009), 218.

22. Lewis, *Collected Letters*, 3466.

the drunken sleep or to draw her back from the final outrage into which Britain tempted her.[23]

Recognizing the medieval sources of Lewis's Logres helps us recognize a subtle theme in his use of the imagery by contrasting it with Charles Williams's use of the same term in his Arthurian poetry. Lewis's idea of Logres and Britain is in fact very different from Williams's. For one thing, although for Williams, "Logres is Britain regarded as a province of the Empire with its centre at Byzantium,"[24] Lewis makes Logres and Britain into antagonists on the spiritual level.

More significantly, Lewis also takes a completely different approach with regard to the image of the Empire. Williams's use of the imperial symbolism of Logres emphasizes order, precision, and control; as Karl Heinz Göller points out, "Divine order was for [Williams] a matter of geometrical precision, with complete harmony of all the component parts. Rivalry of the member states of the Empire, or manifestations of national thought, did not fit into his conception."[25] In contrast, in *That Hideous Strength*, when Merlin suggests that Ransom and his company ask the Emperor for help, Ransom replies simply, "There is no Emperor." However, he does not suggest re-forming the Empire, starting with Logres; rather, the

---

23. Lewis, *That Hideous Strength*, ch. 17, 514–15.

24. Charles Williams, *The Arthurian Poems of Charles Williams, Including Taliessin Through Logres and The Region of the Summer Stars With Other Poems* (Hannacroix: Apocryphile, 2022), 84.

25. Karl Heinz Göller, "From Logres to Carbonek: The Arthuriad of Charles Williams," *Arthurian Literature* 1 (1981), 123.

work that they need to do, though ultimately of cosmic significance, is grounded in Britain.

Indeed, Lewis presents Logres not in terms of its contribution to an Empire (as Williams does), but as good in itself precisely because of its unique identity. As Dimble puts it, it is a mistake to envision goodness only "in the abstract … something standardized."[26] To be sure, he explains, there is a "grammar of virtue," "universal rules to which all goodness must conform"—that is, the reality of objective value, the *Tao*, as Lewis articulates it in *The Abolition of Man*. However, Dimble goes on to say that the healing of the world entails nurturing the individual and distinct goodness of each person, and indeed each nation: "When Logres really dominates Britain, when the goddess Reason, the divine clearness, is really enthroned in France, when the order of Heaven is really followed in China—why, then it will be spring."[27]

Lewis's Logres, then, offers a distinct affirmation of goodness expressed in the particular, unrepeatable circumstances of different nations and different individuals. St Anne's is far from having a Williams-like "geometrical precision," with its rambling vegetable gardens, wandering bear, and idiosyncratic assemblage of personalities. This, not an Empire, is Lewis's view of the "better England."

MERLIN

We turn now to the magician alluded to in the novel's preface, namely Merlin. Drawing on the Arthurian ma-

---

26. Lewis, *That Hideous Strength*, ch. 17, 517.

27. Lewis, *That Hideous Strength* ch. 17, 517.

terials, Lewis had many options for Merlin's role; it is curious to note the way in which he hints at each of these but then turns away from them. Merlin is most often seen as a magician, but Ransom explicitly forbids him from attempting any magic. In Geoffrey of Monmouth's *Vita Merlini*, Merlin is a wild man of the woods, as his grief-induced insanity leads him to forget his identity and live as an animal. Lewis gives a nod to this tradition in the scene where Merlin, realizing what Ransom is asking him to do, gives a "yell of primitive Celtic lamentation. It was horrifying to see that withered and bearded face all blubbered with undisguised tears like a child's ... babbling out entreaties."[28] Yet when Ransom tells him to stop, he regains his self-control instantly.

Lewis also hints at Merlin's role as a seer by having him, in a moment of trance, prophesy about Mr. Bultitude, but this is an isolated incident and he has no vision of the larger issues at stake. Another typical role for Merlin is that of the wise advisor, which Lewis gestures toward by his membership in the college of druids and knowledge of the *Oyéresu*. However, this knowledge is immediately shown to be limited compared to Ransom's first-hand acquaintance with the Powers themselves; Merlin's arcane knowledge only allows him to recognize that Ransom's claim to be Pendragon is legitimate. The only advice that he offers is immediately rejected by Ransom.

It would seem that Lewis has defined Merlin in purely negative terms, refusing to place him into any of the roles available to him in the Arthurian tradition. This, I believe, is deliberate, and allows Lewis to use the character

---

28. Lewis, *That Hideous Strength*, ch. 13, 402–3.

in a distinctive way: to take us further into the theme of matrimony.[29]

Lewis had various ways in which he could have brought Merlin into the story; he chooses to awaken him from a centuries-long magical sleep. This method brings into the narrative one of the stranger elements of the Merlin story. In the earliest Arthurian tales, Merlin fades out of the story at a certain point, and we don't know what becomes of him. In the later French developments, his story concludes with his relationship with a mysterious woman, most often called Vivien or Vivian, but also known by names such as Niniane or Nimue. In the Vulgate *Merlin*, Merlin falls in love with her, and she with him—but with a possessive edge. She learns all his magic, and then uses it to imprison him in a tower, so that she can keep him entirely for herself, visiting him regularly for their mutual satisfaction.[30] Another version of the story has a darker end. When Merlin shows her a tomb in which two lovers are magically sealed, she enchants him and seals him in the tomb with the dead lovers, leaving him to die.[31]

Lewis had been interested in the relationship between Merlin and Nimue as far back as 1919, when he attempted a literary treatment of it, relating, as he explained, "the events of a single evening—Merlin coming back & catch-

---

29. This theme is explored in detail in Michael Ward's contribution to this volume.

30. See further, Stephen Knight, *Merlin: Knowledge and Power through the Ages* (Ithaca: Cornell University Press, 2009).

31. Alan Lupack, *Oxford Guide to Arthurian Literature and Legend* (Oxford: Oxford University Press, 2005), 474.

ing Nimue at last."[32] He took "Nimue" seriously enough to attempt its publication (unsuccessfully) in 1922.[33]

In *That Hideous Strength*, the very first mention of Merlin is connected with Nimue, through the (invented) fourteenth-century medieval song that the unnamed narrator quotes as indicating the source of the name "Merlin's Well" in Bragdon Wood:

In Bragdon bricht this ende dai
Herde ich Merlin ther he lai
Singende woo and welawai.[34]

---

32. Lewis, Letter 99, *They Stand Together*, 261. The poem has not survived, except for a stanza that Lewis quotes in a letter. Walter Hooper is, unusually, mistaken, as he misidentifies the quotation as coming from Lewis's abandoned draft poem "Medea."

33. C. S. Lewis, *All My Road Before Me: The Diary of C. S. Lewis 1922–1927* (San Diego: Harvest, 1991), entries for May 4 and May 9, 1922, 29–32. At some point, Lewis came to see an additional level of meaning in the figure of Nimue, whom he associates with the figure of Venus. In his commentary on Williams's poem "The Calling of Taliessin," Lewis remarks on the name of Broceliande, referencing his own notes "either transcribed or abridged from a letter of Williams's" about the nature of that place: It is "both a forest and a sea—a seawood.... A place of making, home of Nimue." Lewis calls Nimue the "sovereign mistress of Broceliande" and "the 'mother of making'," and identifies her with the figure of Venus, explaining that she "is that energy which reproduces on earth a pattern derived from 'the third heaven,' i.e. from the sphere of Venus, the sphere of Divine Love." That this is Lewis's own imaginative extension of Williams' imagery is apparent in his admission that Williams "does not use those words" to describe Nimue in the poem, but rather calls her "the feeling intellect" (*Arthurian Torso*, 99).

34. Lewis, *That Hideous Strength*, ch. 1, 13.

Merlin is singing "woo and welawei," that is, words of lament, because he has been magically imprisoned by his lover Nimue. The Merlin whom we meet later on never refers to Nimue or, indeed, to why he was magically asleep; it is irrelevant to the narrative, and in any case, Lewis does not need an actual Nimue in the story to achieve his effect. He has already deftly woven in the sexual imagery through this allusive reference, enhanced by the way that he locates Merlin's resting-place beneath Bragdon Wood.

Following close on this allusion to Nimue is the first of four references to Merlin's ambiguous parentage. First, the narrator alludes to Merlin being called a "Devil's son," a recurring idea in the legendarium. Dimble refers to this point later, remarking that Layamon, one of the Arthurian poets, "goes out of his way to tell you that the kind of being who fathered Merlin needn't have been bad after all."[35] As it turns out, Merlin himself twice declares that this story of demonic parentage is untrue, but his very denials bring the topic of his conception into the narrative for a third and fourth time. Themes of sexuality and generation are thus closely associated with the figure of Merlin as he appears in *That Hideous Strength*. Indeed, Dimble uses a matrimonial analogy to explain the way that Merlin's use of magic, though licit at the time, had a withering effect on him:

> It's the result of having laid his mind open to something that broadens the environment just a bit too much. Like polygamy. It wasn't wrong

---

35. Lewis, *That Hideous Strength*, ch. 1, 28.

for Abraham, but one can't help feeling that even he lost something by it.[36]

It is Merlin who calls attention to the fact that Jane and Mark are contracepting in their marriage.[37] Encountering Jane at St Anne's, he declares that she is "the falsest lady of any at this time alive."[38] In the Arthurian context, the description of Jane as "false" is suggestive of both Guinevere's adultery and, in some tales, of Arthur's own. In Malory's *Morte*, the text Lewis knew and loved best, Arthur begets Mordred through a union with Morgause, his half-sister. Merlin prophetically declares that this will bring about the fall of the realm: "ye have done a thynge late that God ys displesed with you, for ye have lyene by youre syster and on hir ye have gotyn a childe that shall destroy you and all the knyghtes of youre realme."[39]

In *That Hideous Strength*, Dimble hastens to tell Merlin that he is "mistaken," for "the woman is chaste."[40] But as Merlin makes clear, what he is condemning is not adultery but the fact that "Of their own will they are barren," that the contraceptive use has rendered her marital union

---

36. Lewis, *That Hideous Strength*, ch. 13, 394.

37. Mark's name is possibly another Arthurian allusion, to King Mark in the legend of Tristan and Isolt. He is married to Isolt, but she has magically fallen in love with Tristan and is unfaithful to him.

38. Lewis, *That Hideous Strength*, ch. 13, 384.

39. Quoted in Corinne Saunders, "Religion and Magic," in Archibald and Putter, *A Cambridge Companion to the Arthurian Legend*, 211.

40. Lewis, *That Hideous Strength*, ch. 13, 384.

false.⁴¹ The besetting sin of the modern day, it seems, is not lust but voluntary sterility, the refusal of full self-gift to one's spouse and (as we see it extended at Belbury) the rejection of fertility and organic life itself.

Merlin is more than a commentator on this theme; he is a participant. He is presented as strongly masculine, bearded, and immensely tall and strong, and is likened to a tree, imagery that connects him to the masculine symbolism of the landscape: "his great mass stood as if it had been planted like a tree.... [T]he voice, too, was such as one might imagine to be the voice of a tree, large and slow and patient, drawn up through roots and clay and gravel from the depths of the Earth."⁴² However, his role in the defeat of Belbury is not the active, masculine role that his appearance might suggest. Rather, he is called upon to be receptive: to allow himself to be penetrated by the Powers, the gods descending on St Anne's, so that they can act through him to destroy Belbury. This role is not a confusion or undermining of his masculinity, however, but a reframing of it in spiritual terms. As Ransom points out to Jane in a different context, "What is above and beyond all things is so masculine that we are all feminine in relation to it."⁴³

THE FISHER KING AND THE PENDRAGON

After Ransom's appearance in the previous two volumes of the trilogy as a middle-aged academic, it is surprising to

---

41. Lewis, *That Hideous Strength*, ch. 13, 384.

42. Lewis, *That Hideous Strength*, ch. 13, 374.

43. Lewis, *That Hideous Strength*, ch. 14, 437.

find him in *That Hideous Strength* with a new appearance and new titles. It is curious that Ransom should be called *both* Mr. Fisher-King and Pendragon, for they come from different strands in the Arthurian tradition, and their intersection is entirely Lewis's invention. We will take each in turn.

The Fisher King

The Fisher King is associated with the Grail cycle. He is generally the guardian of the Grail, usually wounded either in the thigh or the genitals; his health, and in some cases also the health of the land, can be restored only if the questing Grail knight asks him a key question. Chrétien de Troyes' *Perceval* (ca. 1180s) is the earliest and most influential of the Fisher King stories; in it, Perceval observes the Grail procession but, as Lewis remarked, "all was lost because Percevale failed to ask 'for what does it serve?' "[44] Chrétien left *Perceval* unfinished, but later authors took up the story; it is in these continuations that the mysterious Grail at the Fisher King's court becomes identified as the cup used by Jesus at the Last Supper and then, in the traditional narrative, used by Joseph of Arimathea to collect some of his blood at the Crucifixion, making it the "Holy" Grail.[45]

---

44. Lupack, *Oxford Guide to Arthurian Literature and Legend*, 215; Lewis, *Collected Letters*, 2:723.

45. As a young man, Lewis read a translation of one of these, the French prose narrative *Perlesvaus* or *The High History of the Holy Grail*. He declared, "It is absolute heaven: it is more mystic & eerie than the 'Morte' & has [a] more connected plot." *The Collected Letters of C. S. Lewis*, vol. 1, *Family Letters 1905–1931*, ed. Walter Hooper (New York: HarperCollins, 2004), 1:249–50.

In the later versions of the Grail story, the Fisher King figure becomes diffuse. Sometimes he is referred to only by the title; sometimes he is named King Pelles.[46] In Malory's version, there is no Fisher King, but there are two "Maimed Kings," one named Pelles and another named Pellam;[47] neither is the keeper of the Grail. Pelles, however, is connected to the Grail quest by being the grandfather of Galahad, the knight who achieves the quest.[48]

This overview, confusing as it is, is only a simplified summary of the multiple, conflicting treatments of the Fisher King in the medieval and early modern Arthurian texts. The point to keep in mind is that Lewis was aware of the many different options that he had when drawing on the legendarium. In *That Hideous Strength*, Lewis apparently extracts the Fisher King from the Grail sequence. There is no equivalent of the Grail or the spear at St Anne's, and no mystery about his wound, nor is there any suggestion that he can be healed if someone asks about it: the members of the Company know how he was wounded, from fighting the Satanic Un-man on Perelandra, and Ransom himself refuses Merlin's offer to ease his pain.

By detaching the Fisher King from adventures of the Arthurian legendarium, Lewis emphasizes his spiritual significance as a Christ-figure. Ransom's diet of bread and wine is a eucharistic allusion, and the wound in his heel,

---

46. Corinne Saunders, "Religion and Magic," 206.

47. Lupack, *Oxford Guide to Arthurian Literature and Legend*, 465.

48. Lupack, *Oxford Guide to Arthurian Literature and Legend*, 38, 107, 140

rather than his thigh or genitals, associates him further with Christ.

Lewis provides a further clue to the significance of Ransom's role as Mr. Fisher-King in the mode by which he acquires the name: "He had a married sister in India, a Mrs. Fisher-King. She has just died and left him a large fortune on condition that he took the name."[49] It is a peculiarly prosaic way to endow Ransom with this mythically resonant title, and some critics have found it puzzling or irrelevant,[50] but we will do well, as always, to assume that Lewis puts in his details on purpose.

The fact that he gets the title from his *married* sister means that it is not inherited; with this title, Lewis introduces a theme of spiritual inheritance alongside that of biological descent: both are of importance for incarnate human beings.[51]

---

49. Lewis, *That Hideous Strength*, ch. 5, 147. Why India? There is no connection to India in the medieval Grail stories. Possibly Lewis is alluding to the tradition that Thomas the Apostle preached the gospel in India, or is making a connection, via the invented "native Christian mystic," the Sura, with the universal values of the *Tao*, as articulated in *The Abolition of Man*.

50. Margaret Hannay calls it "a bit far-fetched" ("Arthurian & Cosmic Myth in *That Hideous Strength*," *Mythlore* 2, no. 2 [1970], 9).

51. The idea of the title of Fisher King being passed on to a spiritually worthy successor, rather than to a son, appears in the cycle begun by Robert de Boron, in which Perceval eventually returns to the Fisher King's castle, asks the requisite questions, and assumes the role of Fisher King himself (Lupack, *Oxford Guide to Arthurian Literature and Legend*, 226).

Pendragon

Ransom's other new title is that of the "Pendragon": as he declares frankly in response to Merlin's challenge-questions: "I am the Pendragon."[52] Once more, Lewis has subtly reworked his source material.

The title of "Pendragon" in the medieval source material has no connection with Arthur himself. Rather, in Geoffrey of Monmouth's *History*, we learn that Arthur's father Uther was given the epithet of Pendragon because of the appearance of a dragon-shaped comet portending the death of his brother and his accession to the kingdom.[53] The name turns up again, much later, only in Tennyson's *Idylls of the King*, in which he uses it as a title for Arthur.

In *That Hideous Strength*, Lewis transforms the epithet into an inheritable role, and therefore a dynasty: the Pendragon is "the successor of Arthur and Uther and Cassibelaun."[54] However, both the Pendragon's authority and his lineage are spiritual, rather than material. Although Ransom declares to Merlin, "In the sphere of Venus I learned war.... I am the Pendragon," this is not the sort of warfare typical of the Arthuriad.[55] On Venus, Ransom's battle with Weston was of one naked middle-aged man fighting another hand-to-hand; insofar as he "learned war," it was the spiritual lesson of being ready to accept

---

52. Lewis, *That Hideous Strength*, ch. 13, 378.

53. Lupack, *Oxford Guide to Arthurian Literature and Legend*, 473. The celestial nature of this portent might perhaps have fed into Lewis's decision to use the Pendragon title in a cosmic setting.

54. Lewis, *That Hideous Strength*, ch. 17, 515.

55. Lewis, *That Hideous Strength*, ch. 13, 378.

the task given to him, even if it meant his own destruction. Ransom emphasizes this when he rejects Merlin's suggestion of overthrowing the apparently useless "Saxon king of yours who sits at Windsor": "In the order of Logres I may be Pendragon, but in the order of Britain I am the King's man."[56]

Lewis underscores the spiritual aspect of the Pendragon title with a curious connection to the figure of Melchisedec, the mysterious priest-king who appears in Genesis 14. Ransom declares that Arthur is on Perelandra "with Enoch and Elias and Moses and Melchisedec the King. Melchisedec is he in whose hall the steep-stoned ring sparkles on the forefinger of the Pendragon."[57] Melchisedec is a precursor to Christ in the Old Testament, referred to in the book of Hebrews as "king of righteousness" and "king of peace" (Heb. 7:2); furthermore, "He is without father or mother or genealogy, and has neither beginning of days nor end of life, but resembling the Son of God he continues a priest for ever" (Heb. 7:3 ESV). This reference adds to the Christ-like imagery associated with Ransom and underscores the manner in which the Pendragon role is martial in a spiritual rather than a material way.

Ransom has also inherited the title in a spiritual manner, not through a biological line: he received "the office and the blessings" from "an old man then dying in Cumberland," who was the seventy-eighth in the line.[58] It was then that the company learned of "a secret Logres in the

---

56. Lewis, *That Hideous Strength*, ch. 13, 404.

57. Lewis, *That Hideous Strength*, ch. 13, 377.

58. Lewis, *That Hideous Strength*, ch. 17, 515.

very heart of Britain ... an unbroken succession of Pendragons." As Ransom received the office from this man, so too the next Pendragon will be in some mysterious way appointed: not Ransom's biological child, but another. Who will it be?

When some of the company of St Anne's go out to find Merlin, Ransom tells Camilla Denniston that Camilla cannot go: "I am afraid you must stay at home. We in this house are all that is left of Logres. You carry its future in your body."[59] Her unborn child seems, then, to be the next Pendragon—but only provisionally.

When Merlin chastises Jane for her voluntary sterility, as we discussed above, he also declares its consequences: "she has done in Logres a thing of which no less sorrow shall come than came of the stroke that Balinus struck.[60] For, Sir, it was the purpose of God that she and her lord should between them have begotten a child by whom the enemies should have been put out of Logres for a thousand years."[61] When Ransom tells him that "The child may yet be born," Merlin pessimistically declares, "be assured that the child will never be born, for the hour of its begetting is passed. Of their own will they are barren."[62]

---

59. Lewis, *That Hideous Strength*, ch. 10, 311.

60. This is a reference to Balin and the Dolorous Stroke, which is in the Arthurian legendarium is connected to the Grail cycle in a manner that is far too convoluted to explain here, but which would have been well known to Lewis.

61. Lewis, *That Hideous* Strength, ch. 13, 384.

62. Lewis, *That Hideous Strength*, ch. 13, 384.

This exchange raises an interesting point. Merlin is not in prophetic mode, as he is on another occasion when he predicts (accurately) the future deed of Mr. Bultitude; he is, rather, drawing a conclusion. Based on the attitudes of Jane and Mark at that moment, he is correct to say that "Of their own will they *are* barren." But this is a fault that can be corrected.

As Michael Ward explains, "In his priestly-kingly capacity, Ransom acts as wounded healer": he guides Jane to her moment of conversion when she encounters Maleldil (God) "with no veil or protection between," and it is at St Anne's where, in the Lodge he has had prepared for them, Mark and Jane reunite in a marital embrace that is no longer sterile but is now fully self-giving.[63] At last, "their act of love will make up for the missed opportunity of which Merlin speaks."[64] It is at this time, with the crisis past and conversions effected, with Ransom on the very cusp of his departure to Venus, that Dimble explains that "tomorrow we shall know, or tonight, who is to be the eightieth" in the line of the Pendragons.[65] Camilla's unborn child might have been the Pendragon, but now that Jane and Mark have embraced their married vocation, we know that it will be their child, conceived that night, who will carry on the spiritual line of the Pendragons.

---

63. Michael Ward, *Planet Narnia: The Seven Heavens in the Imagination of C. S. Lewis* (Oxford: Oxford University Press, 2008), 50.

64. Ward, *Planet Narnia*, 53.

65. Lewis, *That Hideous Strength*, ch. 17, 515.

CONCLUSION

Where has our consideration of Arthurian imagery taken us? We saw in Lewis's use of the imagery of Logres that he envisioned the flourishing of distinctive national characters, within the framework of objective morality: the entire planet and all of humanity is threatened by The Hideous Strength, but it is not saved by some supra-national organization. Rather, Tellus is saved by Logres, the true expression of Britain. Since the NICE settled in Edgestow, it was necessarily the people of that particular place who had to confront and defeat it, however few or weak or oddly assorted: even if they are just "four men, some women, and a bear." Likewise, the destruction of Belbury is achieved by Merlin's willingness to accept the role that only he could fill, to receive the Powers and allow them to work through him.

On the level of the individual characters, this theme highlights the irreducibly incarnational quality of Christianity. It is the NICE who treat human beings in the abstract: one of Mark's weaknesses, which brings him nearly to destruction, is his reluctance to consider people as people: "He preferred to write about 'vocational groups,' 'elements,' 'classes' and 'populations.' "[66] Part of his own conversion involves embracing Christianity's scandalous particularity, accepting that the Holy Spirit deals with us as individuals.

In this context, it is entirely suitable that Lewis would support his theme with imagery from the Arthurian legendarium. It is a story deeply rooted in British culture; even when the legendarium was exported to France, developed,

---

66. Lewis, *That Hideous Strength*, ch. 4, 109.

and then re-imported to England, the essential connection between Arthur and Britain remained unbroken. The story of the Grail added a dimension of spiritual quest to the national story. Lewis's use of the Fisher King element and his adaptation of the role of Pendragon from a warrior's epithet into a spiritual lineage of leadership draws all these elements into *That Hideous Strength*: the individual's spiritual battle against the powers of evil, the search for the Divine, and the recognition of man's fallenness and hope for redemption. We find that these realities can be experienced anywhere: in Edgestow as much as in Camelot.

As we have seen, despite the prominence of the Fisher King role, Lewis does not include either the Grail or an overt quest element in the story, a puzzling choice at first sight. However, he has in fact embedded the theme in the story implicitly. In the medieval sources, Lancelot fails in the Grail quest because of his adultery and sexual incontinence—yet God brings good out of evil, for Galahad, the son Lancelot begets outside of marriage, becomes the perfect knight who achieves the Grail. In the Fisher King segment of the cycle, the self-absorbed Percival fails to ask the right questions and heal the maimed king—but he later grows in self-knowledge, repents, and (at least in some versions) returns to heal the Fisher King. There are no direct Grail, Lancelot, or Perceval analogues in *That Hideous Strength*, but the themes associated with these tales are present below the surface, especially with the characters of Merlin, Jane, and Mark.

Each of these characters faces up to their own weaknesses, sins, and fears, and chooses to accept God's calling. Merlin learns that his role is not to use his magic or his wisdom, but rather to accept that his weakness (in having opened himself to not-quite-lawful forces) makes him the only one who can receive the Powers. Though we are not told it specifically, it is suggested that this breaks him and that we glimpse him near to death. Jane and Mark must each repent, experience conversion, and gain self-knowledge. Lewis emphasizes the ordinary, even prosaic nature of these insights. For Mark it is a major epiphany when, on the way toward St Anne's after the destruction of Belbury, he stops at a little hotel and enjoys a hot bath, a good nap, a cup of tea, and the reading of a children's story that he had long ago abandoned in order to seem more grown-up. These simple pleasures are extremely significant precisely because they are embodied, in contrast to the gnostic, disembodied, sterile evils of the NICE. Both he and Jane experience, in effect, "the triumphant vindication of the body," which allows them at the end of the novel to turn their sterile contracepted marriage into genuine self-gift, thus benefitting not only themselves, but Logres, for the next Pendragon is conceived that night.

Lewis shows us that repentance, conversion, and self-gift are in one sense perfectly ordinary, even prosaic—and yet they participate in the most extraordinary, epic adventure we can imagine. Arthur is King in Avalon, and in Edgestow.

XI

THE PROBLEM OF JANE

Susannah Black-Roberts

When considering Lewis and women, one can take one of two routes: one can postulate a Susan problem, or a Jane problem, but not both. They cancel each other out. And in that cancelling—in finding what it was that was really wrong with Susan Pevensie in the end, and with Jane Studdock in the beginning—we get to the heart of what Lewis wanted to say about something entirely different from what we first imagine.

Explanations (brief ones) are in order. The Problem of Susan refers, of course, to the fact that Susan, the elder Pevensie sister, was apparently barred from Narnia in the final book—permanently or not, we are not told.[1]

---

1. The precise phrase "The Problem of Susan" has probably been cemented in the popular imagination by Neil Gaiman's 2004 short story of the same name. See Neil Gaiman, "The Problem of Susan," *Flights: Extreme Visions of Fantasy*, vol. 2, ed. Al Sarrantonio (New York: Penguin, 2006), 151–64.

It is the Last Battle, the final confrontation. Once a King or Queen in Narnia, always a King or Queen. And where is Queen Susan?

> "My sister Susan," answered Peter shortly and gravely, "is no longer a friend of Narnia."
>
> "Oh Susan!" said Jill. "She's interested in nothing nowadays except nylons and lipstick and invitations. She always was a jolly sight too keen on being grown-up."[2]

The canonical interpretation of this passage is by none other than J. K. Rowling. "There comes a point," she wrote, "where Susan, who was the older girl, is lost to Narnia because she becomes interested in lipstick. She's become irreligious basically because she found sex. I have a big problem with that."[3] Philip Pullman reads it the same way:

> I just don't like the conclusions Lewis comes to, after all that analysis, the way he shuts children out from heaven, or whatever it is, on the grounds that the one girl is interested in boys. She's a teenager! Ah, it's terrible: "Sex—can't have that."[4]

---

2. C. S. Lewis, *The Last Battle* (London: HarperCollins, 2023), 168.

3. Quoted in Lev Grossman, "J. K. Rowling Hogwarts and All," *TIME*, July 17, 2005, https://web.archive.org/web/20050719235224/http://www.time.com/time/magazine/article/0,9171,1083935,00.html. Accessed July 24, 2024.

4. "A Conversation with Philip Pullman," *Slate*, November 5, 2015

The Problem of Jane

All this, we are told, is down to Lewis himself having a problem with women's sexuality.

But this is not in fact what happened: this is neither an accurate reading of Lewis, nor of Susan. And we can see this because the other problem that some have had regarding Lewis and women is the Problem of Jane.

Jane Studdock, 23, married for six months to Mark at the beginning of *That Hideous Strength*, is introduced to us procrastinating. What she is procrastinating on, that morning, when her husband has gone away to his fellowship at Edgestow, is her doctoral dissertation. It was meant to be on Donne.

> She had always meant to continue her own career as a scholar after she was married: that was one of the reasons why they were to have no children, at any rate not for a long time yet. Jane was not perhaps a very original thinker and her plan had been to lay great stress on Donne's "triumphant vindication of the body." She still believed that if she got out all her notebooks and editions and really sat down to the job, she could force herself back into her lost enthusiasm for the subject.[5]

But the enthusiasm isn't there, and what we are told is that her and Mark's other form of procrastination has been that which may cost Logres—the true Britain, the deep Britain, Arthur's Britain—dearly. We learn this by the mantic

---

5. C. S. Lewis, *That Hideous Strength* (London: HarperCollins, 2003), ch. 1, 2.

insight of Merlin, when, later on, he joins the company at St. Anne's-on-the-Hill, where she has taken refuge.

"Sir, you have in your house the falsest lady of any at this time alive," says Merlin to Ransom in his Latin that is halfway to being any number of other Romance languages. Ransom answers:

> "Sir, you are mistaken. She is doubtless like all of us a sinner; but the woman is chaste."
>
> "Sir," said Merlin, "know well that she has done in Logres a thing of which no less sorrow shall come than came of the stroke that Balinus struck. For, Sir, it was the purpose of God that she and her lord should between them have begotten a child by whom the enemies should have been put out of Logres for a thousand years."
>
> "She is but lately married," said Ransom. "The child may yet be born."
>
> "Sir," said Merlin, "be assured that the child will never be born, for the hour of its begetting is passed. Of their own will they are barren: I did not know till now that the usages of Sulva were so common among you. For a hundred generations in two lines the begetting of this child was prepared; and unless God should rip up the work of time, such seed, and such an hour, in such a land, shall never be again."[6]

Sulva is the Moon, in her fallen aspect: not the virgin huntress, chaste and fair, but the contracepting woman

---

6. Lewis, *That Hideous Strength*, ch. 13, 384.

who refuses to be either virgin or wife. The "uses of Sulva" are the various ways of having unfruitful sex, or of manufacturing children rather than begetting them.

What does this mean? Lewis is so very careful here. He thinks of everything. Mrs. Dimble is the wife of Jane's old tutor; she and Dr. Dimble have been turfed out of their house by the NICE, which has seized the property. She and Jane had at one time been close:

> A liking for the female pupils of one's husband is not, perhaps, so common as might be wished among dons' wives; but Mrs. Dimble appeared to like all Dr. Dimble's pupils of both sexes and the Dimbles' house, away on the far side of the river, was a kind of noisy salon all the term.[7]

But Jane has rather neglected Mrs. Dimble since her marriage, perhaps because, as the wife of an academic who is not herself an academic, she represents to Jane her own dread: that of being "just a wife." Mrs. and Dr. Dimble have never had any children—yet it is not she, but Jane, whom Merlin calls barren. Why?

Though the Dimbles have never conceived a child, neither have they contracepted: they have been faithful in their submission to the possibility of fruitfulness, and this fidelity of love has itself borne fruit in their lives. Though Mrs. Dimble has no children of her own, she is, profoundly, a mother; "One tended to call her Mother Dimble,"

---

7. Lewis, *That Hideous Strength*, ch. 1, 24.

we are told parenthetically when Jane first runs into her.⁸ And when her archetypal self is unveiled, she is revealed to be something like an avatar of the maternal Venus. It is that feminine being that Jane confronts as she prepares the bridal bed for Ivy and her husband, for their first night since his release from prison.

> A flame-coloured robe, in which her hands were hidden, covered this person from the feet to where it rose behind her neck in a kind of high ruff-like collar, but in front it was so low or open that it exposed her large breasts. Her skin was darkish and Southern and glowing, almost the color of honey. Some such dress Jane had seen worn by a Minoan priestess on a vase from old Cnossus. The head, poised motionless on the muscular pillar of her neck, stared straight at Jane. It was a redcheeked, wet-lipped face, with black eyes—almost the eyes of a cow— and an enigmatic expression. It was not by ordinary standards at all like the face of Mother Dimble; but Jane recognized it at once. It was, to speak like the musicians, the full statement of that theme which had elusively haunted Mother Dimble's face for the last few hours.⁹

Venus, the earthly Perelandra, is the fullest statement of fruitful eroticism. She is attended by laughter and by the

---

8. Lewis, *That Hideous Strength*, ch. 1, 24.

9. Lewis, *That Hideous Strength*, ch. 14, 420–21.

fructification of the very earth itself, and by the creatures that make up the St. Anne's household and its neighborhood.

After Jane perceives Venus's presence, others do as well. The first thing that happens is that a bear shows up in the kitchen of the house, an escapee from Belbury's experimental animal lab. Another bear, that is—the household already had one bear: Mr. Bultitude, whose history and destiny are only hinted at. Ivy comes running in to tell Ransom about the interloper, who has found the pantry and is eating her way through it.

> "And what line is Mr. Bultitude taking about all this, Ivy?" asked Ransom.
> "Well, that's what I want someone to come and see. He's carrying on something dreadful, Sir. I never seen anything like it. First of all he just stood lifting up his legs in a funny way as if he thought he could dance, which we all know he can't. But now he's got up on the dresser on his hind legs and there he's kind of bobbing up and down, making the awfullest noise—squeaking like—and he's put one foot into the plum pudding already and he's got his head all mixed up in the string of onions and I can't do nothing with him, really I can't."
> "This is very odd behaviour for Mr. Bultitude. You don't think, my dear, that the stranger might be a she bear?"
> "Oh, don't say that, Sir!" exclaimed Ivy with extreme dismay.

"I think that's the truth, Ivy. I strongly suspect that this is the future Mrs. Bultitude."

"It'll be the present Mrs. Bultitude if we sit here talking about it much longer," said MacPhee, rising to his feet.

"Oh, dear, what shall we do?" said Ivy.

"I am sure Mr. Bultitude is quite equal to the situation," replied the Director. "At present, the lady is refreshing herself. *Sine Cerere et Baccho*, Dimble. We can trust them to manage their own affairs."

"No doubt, no doubt," said MacPhee. "But not in our kitchen."[10]

And it's not just Mr. Bultitude either.

"What's the matter with that jackdaw?" said Dr. Dimble.

"I think it's trying to get out," said Denniston.

"Shall I open the window?"

"It's warm enough to have the window open anyway," said the Director. And as the window was opened Baron Corvo hopped out and there was a scuffle and a chattering just outside.

"Another love affair," said Mrs. Dimble. "It sounds as if Jack had found a Jill … What a delicious night!" she added. For as the curtain swelled and lifted over the open window all the freshness of a midsummer night seemed to be blowing into the room....

---

10. Lewis, *That Hideous Strength*, ch. 17, 523–24.

> "This," said MacPhee with great emphasis, "is becoming indecent."
>
> "On the contrary," said Ransom, "decent, in the old sense, *decens*, fitting, is just what it is. Venus herself is over St. Anne's."[11]

And it has been this that Jane has been avoiding in herself. She has been avoiding stepping into that aspect of herself. And it is in stepping into that aspect of herself that her full conversion happens.

It is something so delicate that Lewis does here that in anyone else's hands it would not have been brought off. "I suppose," says Jane to Ransom—she is treating him, the community, as though he were a kind of therapist; that is what she had thought St. Anne's was, a place to fix her nightmares and her marriage to Mark in a psychoanalytic way—"I suppose our marriage was just a mistake."

> The Director said nothing.
>
> "What would you—what would the people you are talking of—say about a case like that?"
>
> "I will tell you if you really want to know," said the Director.
>
> "Please," said Jane reluctantly.
>
> "They would say," he answered, "that you do not fail in obedience through lack of love, but have lost love because you never attempted obedience."
>
> Something in Jane that would normally have reacted to such a remark with anger or laughter

---

11. Lewis, *That Hideous Strength*, ch. 17, 524–25.

was banished to a remote distance (where she could still, but only just, hear its voice) by the fact that the word Obedience—but certainly not obedience to Mark—came over her, in that room and in that presence, like a strange oriental perfume, perilous, seductive and ambiguous …

"Stop it!" said the Director, sharply.

Jane stared at him, open mouthed. There were a few moments of silence during which the exotic fragrance faded away.

"You were saying, my dear?" resumed the Director.

"I thought love meant equality," she said, "and free companionship."

"Ah, equality!" said the Director. "We must talk of that some other time. Yes, we must all be guarded by equal rights from one another's greed, because we are fallen. Just as we must all wear clothes for the same reason. But the naked body should be there underneath the clothes, ripening for the day when we shall need them no longer. Equality is not the deepest thing, you know."

"I always thought that was just what it was. I thought it was in their souls that people were equal."

"You were mistaken," said he gravely. "That is the last place where they are equal. Equality before the law, equality of incomes—that is very well. Equality guards life; it doesn't make it. It is medicine, not food. You might as well try to warm yourself with a bluebook."

The Problem of Jane

"But surely in marriage … ?"

"Worse and worse," said the Director. "Courtship knows nothing of it; nor does fruition. What has free companionship to do with that? Those who are enjoying something, or suffering something together, are companions. Those who enjoy or suffer one another, are not. Do you not know how bashful friendship is? Friends—comrades—do not look at each other. Friendship would be ashamed …"

"I thought," said Jane and stopped.

"I see," said the Director. "It is not your fault. They never warned you. No one has ever told you that obedience—humility—is an erotic necessity. You are putting equality just where it ought not to be. As to your coming here, that may admit of some doubt. For the present, I must send you back. You can come out and see us. In the meantime, talk to your husband and I will talk to my authorities."[12]

It is through falling under Ransom's charisma that Jane is converted. She is, after this conversation,

> taken utterly off her guard, shaken out of the modest little outfit of contemporary ideas which had hitherto made her portion of wisdom, and swept away on the flood tide of an experience which she did not understand and could not control.… And she found [it] intolerable. To have

---

12. Lewis, *That Hideous Strength*, ch. 7, 195–97.

surrendered without terms at the mere voice and look of this stranger, to have abandoned (without noticing it) that prim little grasp on her own destiny, that perpetual reservation, which she thought essential to her status as a grown-up, integrated, intelligent person ... the thing was utterly degrading, vulgar, uncivilized.[13]

Her response to Ransom is a channel for her submission to God Himself, to that other invasive and demanding "masculine" power; and only in submitting to this can she then be in the fullest sense a wife to Mark, her proper husband.

It is a shocking conversion. But one cannot have it both ways. One cannot have both a Lewis of the Susan Problem, afraid of feminine sexuality, and a Lewis of the Jane Problem, insisting on the ferocious primacy of feminine sexuality in the ongoing creation of the world. What, then, precisely is going on here?[14]

As it turns out, what was wrong with Susan is what was wrong with Jane, and it was the same thing that was wrong with Mark as well, and it turns out not to have anything to do with sex at all.

"She always was a jolly sight too keen on being grown-up," says Jill of Susan.[15] The first thing to go in Jane's con-

---

13. Lewis, *That Hideous Strength*, ch. 7, 200.

14. It could be objected here that Jane is proof of Lewis's low view of female sexuality because her sexuality is imagined only with reference to childbearing, rather than for its own sake. Such a view of female sexuality, however, is precisely what Lewis is objecting to—it is neither feminine enough, nor sexual enough, as we will see.

15. Lewis, *The Last Battle*, 168.

The Problem of Jane

version is "that perpetual reservation, which she thought essential to her status as a grown-up, integrated, intelligent person." And Mark—it is there in Mark's conversion, too:

> There were no moral considerations at this moment in Mark's mind. He looked back on his life not with shame, but with a kind of disgust at its dreariness.... He saw himself making believe that he enjoyed those Sunday afternoons with the athletic heroes of Grip while all the time (as he now saw) he was almost homesick for one of the old walks with Pearson—Pearson whom he had taken such pains to leave behind. He saw himself in his teens laboriously reading rubbishy grown-up novels and drinking beer when he really enjoyed John Buchan and stone ginger. The hours that he had spent learning the very slang of each new circle that attracted him, the perpetual assumption of interest in things he found dull and of knowledge he did not possess, the almost heroic sacrifice of nearly every person and thing he actually enjoyed, the miserable attempt to pretend that one could enjoy Grip, or the Progressive Element, or the N.I.C.E.—all this came over him with a kind of heart-break.[16]

Here is the commonality, and it shows what Lewis's problem with Susan actually was—not a problem with girls growing up into women or female sexuality or anything of the sort, but rather, the problem of false maturity. Jane,

---

16. Lewis, *That Hideous Strength*, ch. 11, 337–38.

after all, shows that the same false maturity can take you away from adult womanhood and sexuality. By contracepting she's holding her own sexuality at a distance, and her own real adulthood.

Academia, in other words, was for Jane what boyfriends and lipstick were for Susan—fake adulthood, the desire to be taken seriously. Ironically it is this that, in Lewis's view, is precisely what provides an escape from one's actual progress to maturity and one's real calling.

Lewis makes this clear in a letter he writes to Daphne and Cecil Harwood:

> Re: Jane, she wasn't meant to illustrate the problem of the married woman and her own career in general: rather the problem of everyone who follows an *imagined* vocation at the expense of a real one. Perhaps I shd. have emphasised more the fact that her thesis on Donne was all derivative bilge. If I'd been tackling the problem wh. Cecil thinks I had in mind, of course I'd have taken a woman capable of making a real contribution to literature.[17]

This is very closely linked in Lewis's mind with the problem of false adulthood. "Critics who treat adult as a term of approval," he writes in his 1953 essay "On Three Ways of Writing for Children,"

---

17. C. S. Lewis, To Cecil and Daphne Harwood, in *The Collected Letters of C. S. Lewis*, vol. 2, *Books, Broadcasts and War 1931–1949* (London: HarperCollins, 2004), 669–70.

instead of as a merely descriptive term, cannot be adult themselves. To be concerned about being grown up, to admire the grown up because it is grown up, to blush at the suspicion of being childish; these things are the marks of childhood and adolescence. And in childhood and adolescence they are, in moderation, healthy symptoms. Young things ought to want to grow. But to carry on into middle life or even into early manhood this concern about being adult is a mark of really arrested development. When I was ten, I read fairy tales in secret and would have been ashamed if I had been found doing so. Now that I am fifty I read them openly. When I became a man I put away childish things, including the fear of childishness and the desire to be very grown up.[18]

This is what, famously, Lewis forewarns his goddaughter, Lucy Barfield, about in the dedication of *The Lion, the Witch, and the Wardrobe*—that though she may have outgrown them by the time he had finished writing the book, one day she "will be old enough to start reading fairy tales again."[19]

We can see this most clearly perhaps in Mark's besetting sin. Mark's problem is not, particularly, the Flesh. Nor is it—he is not a diabolist, though others of Belbury

---

18. C. S. Lewis, "On Three Ways of Writing for Children," in *Of Other Worlds: Essays and Stories* (London: HarperOne, 2017), 38.

19. C. S. Lewis, *The Lion, the Witch and the Wardrobe* (London: HarperCollins, 2023), 5.

certainly are—the Devil. It is instead the World. Lewis describes Mark's passion, his addiction, the thing he must kick like heroin if he is to be saved, in a 1944 lecture at King's College, London, that is titled "The Inner Ring." Of this group, he says,

> There are no formal admissions or expulsions. People think they are in it after they have in fact been pushed out of it, or before they have been allowed in: this provides great amusement for those who are really inside. It has no fixed name.... From inside it may be designated, in simple cases, by mere enumeration: it may be called "You and Tony and me." ... When it has to be expanded to meet a particular emergency it calls itself "all the sensible people at this place." From outside, if you have despaired of getting into it, you call it "That gang" or "they" or "So-and-so and his set" or "The Caucus" or "The Inner Ring." If you are a candidate for admission you probably don't call it anything. To discuss it with the other outsiders would make you feel outside yourself. And to mention talking to the man who is inside, and who may help you if this present conversation goes well, would be madness.... I believe that in all men's lives at certain periods, and in many men's lives at all periods between infancy and extreme old age, one of the most dominant elements is the

desire to be inside the local Ring and the terror of being left outside.[20]

And it is this desire, this terror, that is how "the World" ensnares. It is worth noting that Christians can very easily fall into these snares: theological schools, in-groups of various kinds, can just as easily have Inner Ring dynamics as secular ones. Lewis goes on:

> To nine out of ten of you the choice which could lead to scoundrelism will come, when it does come, in no very dramatic colours. Obviously bad men, obviously threatening or bribing, will almost certainly not appear. Over a drink, or a cup of coffee, disguised as triviality and sandwiched between two jokes, from the lips of a man, or woman, whom you have recently been getting to know rather better and whom you hope to know better still—just at the moment when you are most anxious not to appear crude, or naïf or a prig—the hint will come. It will be the hint of something which the public, the ignorant, romantic public, would never understand: something which even the outsiders in your own profession are apt to make a fuss about: but something, says your new friend, which "we"—and at the word "we" you try not to blush for mere pleasure—something "we always do." And you will be drawn in, if you are

---

20. C. S. Lewis, "The Inner Ring," in *The Weight of Glory and Other Addresses* (New York: Macmillan, 1949), 57–58.

drawn in, not by desire for gain or ease, but simply because at that moment, when the cup was so near your lips, you cannot bear to be thrust back again into the cold outer world. It would be so terrible to see the other man's face—that genial, confidential, delightfully sophisticated face—turn suddenly cold and contemptuous, to know that you had been tried for the Inner Ring and rejected. And then, if you are drawn in, next week it will be something a little further from the rules, and next year something further still, but all in the jolliest, friendliest spirit. It may end in a crash, a scandal, and penal servitude; it may end in millions, a peerage and giving the prizes at your old school. But you will be a scoundrel.[21]

But, adds Lewis, there is a thing of which the Inner Ring is a corruption. The contrast between these two kinds of societies is very precisely that between St. Anne's and Belbury. Those at St. Anne's do indeed look, from some angles, like an Inner Ring: they are a small group, doing important work (though a surprising portion of that work is, to McPhee's perpetual frustration, apparently the growing of winter vegetables—hardly the most effective form of supernatural realpolitik.) But it is in fact something infinitely better than an inner ring: it is a fellowship. Its principle is not exclusion but obedience to a calling, not enmity with those outside but friendship with each other. And it is precisely in such a society that both Mark and Jane can become themselves. It is here that the problems

---

21. Lewis, "The Inner Ring," 62–63.

of Jane, Mark, Susan, and goodness know how many others can be solved.

To truly grow up, into one's purpose, into one's *telos* as a man or a woman: *that* is the Problem, the challenge. And the first thing one must do is reject the false adulthood, the false sense of importance, presented by all the various inner rings of taste and society and ethics, the friendships of utility, the marriages that refuse to be fruitful, the politics that shun the common good as a fool's dream.

This "becoming oneself" aspect of the book, this honesty, has a strange quality to it. Mark, in his passion for the Inner Ring, Jane, in her passion to be taken seriously, have done something very specific: they have refused to embrace their archetypes. In the other inhabitants of St. Anne's, we see people who have become themselves precisely by stepping into their archetypal roles. Camilla and Arthur Denniston are Husband and Wife, the young married couple. Ransom himself is, of course, Jove. And Mother Dimble, again.

It is at the time of the Descent of the Gods, of the angelic intelligences connected with the planets, on St. Anne's, that we see this most clearly. Ivy, Jane, Camilla, and Mrs. Dimble have been directed to an upstairs room—it is called, in a playful Lewisian self-reference, the Wardrobe—to choose their clothes for the ceremonial visit. They've picked out ones for Ivy, Camilla, and Jane. And then:

> "Put it on, Mother Dimble," said Ivy. "You know you got to." It was of that almost tyrannous flame color which Jane had seen in her vision down in the lodge, but differently cut, with

fur about the great copper brooch that clasped the throat, with long sleeves and hangings from them. And there went with it a many-cornered cap. And they had no sooner clasped the robe than all were astonished, none more than Jane, though indeed she had had best reason to foresee the result. For now this provincial wife of a rather obscure scholar, this respectable and barren woman with gray hair and double chin, stood before her, not to be mistaken, as a kind of priestess or sybil, the servant of some prehistoric goddess of fertility—an old tribal matriarch, mother of mothers, grave, formidable and august. A long staff, curiously carved as if a snake twined up it, was apparently part of the costume: they put it in her hand.

"Am I awful?" said Mother Dimble, looking in turn at the three silent faces.

"You look lovely," said Ivy.

"It is exactly right," said Camilla.

Jane took up the old lady's hand and kissed it. "Darling," she said, "*aweful*, in the old sense, is just what you *do* look."[22]

It is perhaps the one moment when Jane's literary scholarship serves her well.

There is an exchange at the ending of the book that those who are deeply exercised about the Problem of Jane find particularly objectionable. All has come to pass that the fellowship has been warned about by Jane's prophetic

---

22. Lewis, *That Hideous Strength*, ch. 17, 506–7.

dreams; the attempt at the suborning of the human represented by Belbury and the NICE has been thwarted, and Jane and Mark are well on their way to becoming the people they ought to be. Venus herself is over St. Anne's. And Ransom sends Jane away.

> "You are waited for."
>
> "Me, Sir?"
>
> "Yes. Your husband is waiting for you in the Lodge. It was your own marriage chamber that you prepared. Should you not go to him?"
>
> "Must I go now?"
>
> "If you leave the decision with me, it is now that I would send you."
>
> "Then I will go, Sir. But—but—am I a bear or a hedgehog?"
>
> "More. But not less. Go in obedience and you will find love. You will have no more dreams. Have children instead. *Urendi Maleldil.*"[23]

Give up her dreams! Is that what is meant? No, of course not. It is a reference to her unsettling prophetic dreams from earlier in the novel, to cure which she had originally come to St. Anne's-on-the-Hill, on the theory that the dreams were signs of psychological disturbance and that she might find some kind of therapist in the red-brick house surrounded by vegetable gardens. These dreams are precisely what pulled her into the battle with the NICE, which Merlin tells us is ultimately a battle for Jane and Mark to conceive a child who will be the new Arthurian

---

23. Lewis, *That Hideous Strength*, ch. 17, 530.

Pendragon—"a child by whom the enemies should have been put out of Logres for a thousand years," whose begetting was prepared for over "a hundred generations in two lines." It is too late for that original plan, it seems, but then again Providence may have something else up its sleeve. In any case, their child, as well as their obedience, is crucial. With all of this now at hand, reconciled both to herself and to Mark, Jane's ominous dreaming is now at an end.

Jane and Mark have both found that their vocations have been false. Jane was not a good Donne scholar. Mark was not a good sociologist. Mark's true work is still to be found; I think it will be some form of journalism, because he is very skilled at the corrupt version of journalism he has been doing for the NICE, and often vocations are found, after conversion, in the good version of whatever one had been doing a bad version of. But their primary vocation, that first night, is to each other.

XII

BUREAUCRATIC SPEECH IN *THAT HIDEOUS STRENGTH*

Jake Meador

The first words recorded in Scripture are spoken by God as he commands the universe into existence. By the end of the creation account, only one other creature has been endowed with speech: man. And like God, man doesn't just speak—he names. Viewed this way, language itself is one of the greatest gifts God has given to humanity. And, as with all of God's gifts, a large part of learning to live well in the world is learning to use the gifts he has given well. It is for this reason, and many others besides, that the state of our language should be of concern not only to writers or the small number of people who read a lot of books and essays, but should be a matter of concern to all people. As George Orwell wrote in "Politics and the English Language,"

> A man may take to drink because he feels himself to be a failure, and then fail all the more completely because he drinks. It is rather the same thing that is happening to the English language. It becomes ugly and inaccurate because our thoughts are foolish, but the slovenliness of our language makes it easier for us to have foolish thoughts.[1]

A key part of wisdom, then, is a competent tongue. We can recognize only the things that we have language to name. If we lack a word for something, it is easier to misunderstand what that something is. And so the state of a people's collective wisdom is wrapped up in that people's relationship to language.

This is not to make a point about elitism, to be clear. The idea is not that someone who spends years studying obscure poetry will automatically be more wise than a working class person without a high school diploma. Indeed, one of the key tropes that runs through C. S. Lewis's fiction is that common people often have a firmer grasp on reality than the educated. The first king of Narnia is an ordinary London cabbie named Frank, for example.. Or, indeed, we could think of Ivy Maggs in *That Hideous Strength*—an ordinary maid who is actually far wiser than her more respectable employer, Jane Studdock. What makes for linguistic competence for Lewis is not accumulating academic degrees, power, or the ability to speak codified language in the pursuit of such things. Rather,

---

1. George Orwell, "Politics and the English Language" in *All Art is Propaganda: Critical Essays* (Boston: Mariner Books, 2009), 149.

linguistic competence for Lewis is about one's ability to name reality, and on this point commoners are generally far shrewder and more capable than the credentialed.

That Hideous Strength foregrounds the issue of language in a way that seldom occurs in Lewis's wider body of work. Because Lewis had such a concern with being understood by ordinary readers, his "linguistic philosophies," as you might call them, are often buried in the background. Or, to use a quite different image, you might say that Lewis's linguistic philosophy does for his work what the poet Ted Kooser describes poetic forms as doing for a poet. Kooser likens the forms to a kind of plastic wrap a butcher stretches tightly over meat displayed to customers, so tightly in fact that the wrap itself becomes unnoticeable. The wrap insures that everything is kept in its rightful place and remains fresh, all while remaining relatively invisible to the viewer.[2] This isn't the most pleasant comparison, but it does the job.

Yet it is not so in *That Hideous Strength*. The only other book to foreground language as much is *The Screwtape Letters*—and it is not a coincidence that both books involve depictions of heavily bureaucratic institutions.

WHAT IS BUREAUCRATIC SPEECH?

So what marks speech as bureaucratic? For that matter, what do we mean here by "bureaucratic"? Theologian Myles Werntz argues that "bureaucracy—which literally means 'rule by desk'—is a kind of social body in which members are broken down into their smallest component

---

2. Ted Kooser, *The Poetry Home Repair Manual* (Lincoln: University of Nebraska Press, 2005), 47.

parts with each part sundered from the others and isolated.³ Returning to Lewis, you might say that bureaucracy is one of the chief tools that modern man uses, as Lewis writes in *The Abolition of Man*, to "subdue reality to the wishes of men."⁴ Bureaucracy, you might say, is an organizational tool for tracking and directing men without chests.

If that is bureaucracy, then what is bureaucratic speech? That is a bit more complicated. Bureaucratic speech actually operates on two distinct levels, both of which Lewis well understood.

Paperwork Speech

Werntz, following David Graeber, argues that paperwork is at the heart of bureaucracy because paperwork is what actually makes such an inhuman and synthetic form of "community" possible.⁵ Bureaucracy is a kind of impersonal social machine in which the engine is a precisionistic regime of documentation made possible only first by modern printing and later by digital surveillance technology. There is, then, an echo in bureaucracy of a species of what the Reformed jurist Johannes Althusius called *collegia*.⁶ In his work on politics, Althusius distinguished

---

3. Myles Werntz. "The One in Whom All Things Hang Together: Bureaucracy and the Christian Life," https://myleswerntz.substack.com/p/the-one-in-whom-all-things-hang-together, accessed June 29, 2024.

4. C. S. Lewis, *The Abolition of Man* (New York: Harper Collins, 2001), 77.

5. Werntz, "The One in Whom."

6. Johannes Althusius, *Politica*, trans. Frederick S. Carney (Indianapolis: Liberty Fund, 1995), https://oll.libertyfund.org/titles/althusius-politica.

between naturally reproducing human communities, the natural family above all, and communities that must be contrived and created anew every so often through an act of human volition, usually accomplished through a contract or covenant. Bureaucracy, you might say, is a *collegia* that has been unplugged from the moral law because, by its very nature, it treats human persons in synthetic, artificial ways that can exist only on paper. Lewis covers this side of bureaucratic speech with the character of Fairy Hardcastle, to whom we will return later. The key point to keep in mind for now is that "paperwork speech," as we might call it, is relentlessly precise and always closely tied to coercive threat. The point of paperwork, after all, is documentation—documentation that can be reproduced to coerce desired behaviors when softer means fail. It is only natural that Lewis depicts this sort of speech through a butch lesbian-coded police officer like Miss Hardcastle.

"Informal" Speech

Yet there is another way in which speech works within a bureaucracy. That is the (seemingly) informal level of actual spoken language used between members of the bureaucracy as they go about their work days. Whereas written bureaucratic speech is lawyerly and relentlessly, exhaustingly precise, spoken bureaucratic speech is quite the opposite: it is airy, imprecise, abstract, and meandering. Its function is to maintain appearances of busyness and ordinary communal life, while actually doing nothing of the sort. It is a parody of human conversation. It must be so, in fact: because bureaucracies are made through dismembering and then reinventing human life in contrived, unnatural ways, the only way they can be ultimately held together is the hard threat of coercion, which is secured through paperwork. Yet human beings still live in space and encounter one another in bodies with voices and so we have to speak informally (although this part of working life is increasingly mediated remotely by screens and video calls). But this sort of speech, when happening in bureaucracies, can never actually mean anything; it is simply a space filler, a compromise with the inherently (and regrettably) embodied members of the bureaucracy. All the *real* communication is happening elsewhere.

Anyone who has sat in a large, low-level corporate work meeting or attended a professional conference has likely experienced such speech first hand. A sign that you've partaken of it is when you walk out of a meeting or a paper and find yourself utterly unable to explain what was actually said to someone who was not present. "What was your meeting about?" a coworker asks. You find yourself unable to answer. In its most extreme form, you might even find yourself thinking "What on earth am I talking about?" *during the conversation*.

WITHER AND "INFORMAL" SPEECH

Here we turn to Wither, Director of the National Institute for Co-ordinated Experiments and Lewis's model for spoken bureaucratic speech. The names of *That Hideous Strength* are all quite Dickensian. Phonetically speaking, "Wither" has an airy, indefinable quality—it sounds breathy even as you say it. It is also a verb meaning "to lose vitality," or, brilliantly, "to render speechless."

When we first meet Wither, the sociologist Mark Studdock, one of the novel's two protagonists, has been brought before him for what Studdock thinks is a job interview. But it is an interview unlike anything Studdock has ever experienced. Wither is described as having "watery" eyes and as being "very large," with a face that is "vague and chaotic."[7] The man himself resembles his manner of speaking. His language is stretched, elongated, lacking definition or direction, flowing wherever (or, whither!) it will with little guiding thought or purpose. When Mark asks Wither what his actual job description would be were he to come work for the institute, Wither replies,

> I assure you, Mr. Studdock, that you needn't anticipate the slightest—er—the slightest difficulty on that point. There was never any idea of circumscribing your activities and your general influence on policy, much less your relations with your colleagues and what I might call in general the terms of reference under which you would be collaborating with us, without the fullest possible consideration of your own views and, indeed, your own advice. You will find us, Mr. Studdock, if I might express myself in that way, a very happy family.[8]

Note first the tortured construction of the sentences—tortured, at least, if the goal of the sentence is to communicate anything concrete. The second sentence is stacked with needlessly long verbs, clauses upon clauses. Orwell considers how such linguistic choices render a language

---

7. C. S. Lewis, *That Hideous Strength*. (London: HarperCollins, 2003), ch. 3, 58.

8. Lewis, *That Hideous Strength*, ch. 3, 59.

less lively and humane, and thus bureaucratic language does to language what bureaucracies do to human persons. In a particularly memorable passage, Orwell translates a passage of Scripture into "modern" English. Thus this memorable passage in Ecclesiastes 9:11 in the King James Version,

> I returned and saw under the sun, that the race is not to the swift, nor the battle to the strong, neither yet bread to the wise, nor yet riches to men of understanding, nor yet favour to men of skill; but time and chance happeneth to them all

is transformed into the following by Orwell's sharp wit:

> Objective consideration of contemporary phenomena compels the conclusion that success or failure in competitive activities exhibits no tendency to be commensurate with innate capacity, but that a considerable element of the unpredictable must invariably be taken into account.[9]

The first example is active, full of strong verbs and vivid imagery. The latter is scientific, needlessly complex, and confuses a lifeless precision (which ends up meaning nothing) for felicity of speech.

Suppose instead that Mark had asked Wither about his job and Wither said the following, "We will not restrict your work within the institute in any way, nor will we force you to do work you do not wish to do." The diffi-

---

9. Orwell, "Politics and the English Language," 152.

culty, of course, is that if Wither had simply said that it would have been both quite confusing and quite false. But this is the point: it is precisely the vagaries of the speech that allow it to function at all; were it to be made more concrete it would quickly become apparent that it is either meaningless, false, or both.

Note also how long the response is: 89 words, yet only three sentences. Read it aloud, and you'll find that it has a breathless quality to it, too many words stuffed into too small a container. To read the second sentence in particular is to exhaust yourself. But, again, that is precisely the point: bureaucracies are founded on unreality. They maintain their hold on reality only by preventing their subjects from ever becoming aware of this. And so bureaucratic speech tends to drone on and on by design. The sheer exhaustion of trying to follow it will itself distract the listener from the realities being set before him.

In a scathing review of hedge fund founder Ray Dalio's book *Principles*, Catholic writer Matthew Walther excoriated the book for many reasons, one of which is closely related to this point:

> It's still not entirely clear to me what *Principles* is. Part of the reason for this, no doubt, is that its author is not entirely sure what principles are. I underlined the word more than 150 times in my copy. An exhaustive search of dictionaries turned up no definition that would meet even a handful of the wide-ranging denotations that Dalio seemed to be imparting to this noun, much less satisfy them all. A principle, for Dalio, is not what the New Oxford American Dictionary de-

fines as "a fundamental truth or proposition that serves as the foundation for a system of belief or behavior or for a chain of reasoning." Nor, rather emphatically, is it "a natural law forming the basis for the construction or working of a machine" or "a general scientific theorem or law that has numerous special applications across a wide field." Least of all are principles "morally correct behavior and attitudes."[10]

It is no coincidence that the rising pervasiveness of bureaucratic speech has paralleled the American economy becoming ever more financialized and digitized, such that "business speech" and "bureaucratic speech" can almost be regarded as synonyms. This needn't be the case. If you pick up older business writing, something like Peter Drucker perhaps, it doesn't have the vague and inhuman qualities we now associate with the genre. But as America's businesses become increasingly bound up in abstractions (and as the American people become increasingly divorced from given markers of identity, such as family or place) it is no surprise that their speech becomes unreal and bureaucratic. Bureaucratic speech, in its relationship to *reality*, tends to hover above the waters, as it were, never landing, never saying anything definite. That is how Wither speaks throughout *That Hideous Strength* and it is, likewise, how a hedge fund founder can write a 600 page book on "prin-

---

10. Matthew Walther, "Principles for Dummies," *American Affairs* 2, no. 4 (Winter 2018), https://americanaffairsjournal.org/2018/11/principles-for-dummies/.

ciples" without bothering to come to a clear, easily communicated definition of the term.

HARDCASTLE AND PAPERWORK SPEECH

There is a flip side to this, however, which we have already mentioned. Bureaucracy doesn't function *purely* through evasion, distraction, and loquaciousness. As Werntz notes, there is a hard power that undergirds it that is symbolized by paperwork. While spoken communication tends toward Mr. Wither, the written communication of bureaucracy tends toward the hard power and policing style of Fairy Hardcastle, the head of the NICE police.

There are two occasions on which we see the previously unperceived hard power of bureaucracy at work in *That Hideous Strength*. The first occurs when Mark has been at Belbury for a few days and receives a bill for the food, alcohol, and other goods consumed during his short stay. He realizes he has already worked through much of his salary from the university, placing him in a financially precarious position as he realizes that his Belbury lifestyle can really be supported only by a Belbury salary. So he finds himself locked into the institute without ever having resolved internally to commit himself to it. The imperceptible hard power of capital and the figures on the paperwork presented to him have made the "choice" for him as it were.[11]

Later we come to the second instance. It is far more alarming. Despite himself, Mark has resolved to leave the institute. However, because they need him (for reasons that Mark himself does not comprehend), the Fairy along

---

11. Lewis, *That Hideous Strength*, ch. 5, 130, 137.

with Director Wither have developed another strategy dependent on hard power and paperwork to ensnare him: they accuse him of murder. Through a chain of events, Miss Hardcastle has constructed a set of circumstantial evidences and a plausible narrative by which Mark could credibly be accused of the murder of his old colleague, the chemist Bill Hingest—who, ironically, was himself murdered for leaving the NICE because it had nothing to do with science but was more "like a political conspiracy."[12]

This, then, is the double reality of bureaucratic speech: an iron fist in a velvet glove. The initial presentation is vague and unthreatening, perhaps even soothing. Yet should you ever begin to poke or prod at the wrong thing, the glove comes off, swiftly.

LIVING AMONG A PEOPLE OF BUREACRATIC LIPS

What is to be done about this problem? We should first begin by recognizing that it *is* a problem. Bureaucratic speech is not simply an irritant, a kind of vapid ritual one participates in as an employee or citizen. Bureaucratic speech erodes our capacity to recognize, name, and even *know* reality. And when we are unable to know reality, we are unable to act meaningfully in the world. Among other things, the mass incapacitation of a people through bureaucratic linguistic stupor allows the Hardcastles and

---

12. Lewis, *That Hideous Strength*, ch. 3, 85. It seems noteworthy that Hingest is said to be from an aristocratic family "of almost mythical antiquity," and that he values his lineage far more than his own revolutionary work in chemistry (Lewis, *That Hideous Strength*, ch. 3, 65). Coming from such "old world" stock, it's no surprise that Hingest has little time for the distinctly modern NICE bureaucracy.

Withers of the world to engage in horrific abuses without anyone so much as noticing.

Consider the recent example of Claudine Gay, now former President of Harvard University, who resigned in January 2024 after severe criticism over how she responded to questioning by the United States congress regarding anti-Semitic protests and speech on Harvard's campus. At one point in the hearing, Rep. Elise Stefanik asked President Gay, "Dr. Gay, a Harvard student calling for the mass murder of African Americans is not protected free speech at Harvard, correct?"[13] Gay immediately sought to dodge the question with obfuscation and misdirection. Rather than answering it plainly, she began to respond by saying, "Our commitment to free speech," before Stefanik cut her off and asked for a yes or no answer. Gay continued the same dance, talking about the university's commitment to free speech while also maintaining that she found speech of the sort described by Stefanik to be "personally abhorrent."

Stefanik and Gay continued to go back and forth for several minutes:

> "At Harvard, does calling for the genocide of Jews violate Harvard's rules of bullying and harassment?" Stefanik asked.
>
> "It can be, depending on the context," Gay responded.
>
> But Stefanik pressed Gay to give a yes or no answer to the question about whether calls for

---

13. https://www.thecrimson.com/article/2023/12/8/gay-apology-congressional-remarks/.

the genocide of Jews constitute a violation of Harvard's policies.

"Antisemitic speech when it crosses into conduct that amounts to bullying, harassment, intimidation—that is actionable conduct and we do take action," Gay said.

Stefanik tried again.

"So the answer is yes, that calling for the genocide of Jews violates Harvard code of conduct, correct?" Stefanik asked.

"Again, it depends on the context," Gay said.

"It does not depend on the context. The answer is yes and this is why you should resign," Stefanik shot back. "These are unacceptable answers across the board."

Stefanik then continued to press Gay before finally ending her questioning by saying, "Your testimony today, not being able to answer with moral clarity, speaks volumes."[14]

It is worth attending carefully to the linguistic games played by Gay during the hearing: She sought to redefine the question so as to avoid taking a firm position—something Wither does *constantly* in *That Hideous Strength*. She sought to shift a question of moral principle to one of personal conviction, another common move amongst Lewis's NICE apparatchiks. And lest we become distracted ourselves, return to the point: Gay used these linguistic methods of distraction and misdirection in a context of being asked to plainly condemn racist and anti-Semitic

---

14. https://rollcall.com/2023/12/13/transcript-what-harvard-mit-and-penn-presidents-said-at-antisemitism-hearing/.

speech. So the specifically bureaucratic language games Gay was playing were being used to distract from injustices being visited upon Jewish students at Harvard. Man is a linguistic being; abuses of language will nearly always lead to abuse of people. This is why contending for reality in our language matters: plain speech elevates and dignifies; it names what is real and true. And human beings are made for truth.

In the aftermath of the hearing, Gay faced immense pressure to resign. Eventually she offered an apology, but one that seemed drafted by the NICE. Another feature of bureaucratic speech, as noted above with Wither, is its tendency toward the passive, the abstract, and toward multi-syllabic, needlessly complex vocabulary. With that in mind, consider Gay's "apology" offered in an interview to the Harvard student newspaper:

> What I should have had the presence of mind to do in that moment was return to my guiding truth, which is that calls for violence against our Jewish community—threats to our Jewish students—have no place at Harvard, and will never go unchallenged. Substantively, I failed to convey what is my truth.

Two aspects of the apology leap off the page: first, the anchoring of moral claims not in universal moral principle, but in personal "truth;" second, the remarkably tortured phrase that concludes the apology: "I failed to convey what is my truth." It is a disarming way of speaking, if only because of how bewildering it is as a piece of language. What are the appropriate consequences, after all, for "failing to convey what is my truth"? The lifeless nature of Gay's language drains the life from the controversy.

    The whole affair calls to mind a key scene in the 2015 film *Spotlight*, which tells the story of the Boston *Globe*'s investigation into clerical sexual abuse in the Boston diocese of the Roman Catholic Church. Early in the investigation, one of the paper's reporters, Sacha Pfeiffer, played by Rachel McAdams, is meeting with a victim, who shares the story of his abuse, telling the reporter that a priest coerced him, while he was still a child, into playing strip poker with him. Then he says, "and things went on from there." The reporter presses him for detail. The victim says the priest "molested" him. The reporter, gently, presses again saying, "I think the language here is going to be very important. We can't sanitize this. Just saying 'molest' isn't enough. People need to know what actually happened."

    What happened in that congressional hearing was not a simple failure to convey one person's personal judgments. It was a failure to condemn evil. "The language is very important," indeed.

    This point, of course, also arises most forcefully in the context of so-called gender reassignment surgery. What has been rendered by the left as "a surgical procedure that affirms a person in their felt gender identity" is something much more violent and horrifying: healthy parts of the body are mutilated or chopped off not for any medical reason, but purely because of the internal sense of the "patient," an internal sense often strongly encouraged by parents, school staff, celebrities, and social media. Still another example, of course, concerns the issue of abortion: The intentional, surgical, and quite brutal killing of otherwise healthy unborn children is masked under the language of "reproductive choice" or even, in an especially galling Orwellian turn, "healthcare." These grave moral offenses are obviously not limited to the domains of the spoken and written word. And yet our failure to attend to the language on these matters certainly plays a role in the ongoing mainstreaming and acceptance of grievous moral offenses against both God and human dignity.

Yet it is not only the progressive left that engages in linguistic games of the sort attacked by Lewis. One of the interesting aspects of our moment is that some anti-liberal traditionalist scolds have latched onto *That Hideous Strength* as a text for their movement. And so, as they fantasize about violent revolution, they appeal to Lewis's text as a searing indictment of their great enemy. Yet there is actually something almost quietistic about *That Hideous Strength*. This, indeed, is precisely why Orwell came to a negative opinion of Lewis's book, which he actually reviewed for a British magazine in 1948 not long before his death.[15] What so vexed and frustrated Orwell was the supernaturalism of the story. Orwell wanted a revolution against the NICE. And what Lewis offered was something altogether different.

For Lewis, the "solution" to the problem (though even here I expect he would object to such language) is not the cultivation of a power that can rip and tear the NICE just as the NICE ripped and tore Bragdon Wood. Lewis's heroes are, actually, rather ordinary Christians (and one skeptic) who live a quiet life in the English countryside, caring for the things put in front of them that need care

---

15. George Orwell, "Review of *That Hideous Strength*," *Manchester Evening News*, August 16, 1945.

and seeking to live together under the law of love. This is all they do. Indeed, the resident skeptic, a Scotsman named MacPhee, who is obviously modeled after Lewis's boyhood teacher Professor Kirkpatrick, complains about their lack of activity, asking what exactly anyone at St Anne's has done aside from growing vegetables and fraternizing with unusually friendly bears. But this is precisely Lewis's answer: remain human while you wait and hope for God to act. In its imagination of Christian resistance to tyranny, *That Hideous Strength* actually shares far more with Rod Dreher's *Benedict Option* than it does with the revolutionary vision of the supposedly Christian hard right. Consider Dreher's vision of a thriving and faithful Christian community in a post-Christian nation:

> We live liturgically, telling our sacred Story in worship and song. We fast and we feast. We marry and give our children in marriage, and though in exile, we work for the peace of the city. We welcome our newborns and bury our dead. We read the Bible, and we tell our children about the saints. And we also tell them in the orchard and by the fireside about Odysseus, Achilles, and Aeneas, of Dante and Don Quixote, and Frodo and Gandalf, and all the tales that bear what it means to be men and women of the West.
>
> We work, we pray, we confess our sins, we show mercy, we welcome the stranger, and we keep the commandments. When we suffer, especially for Christ's sake, we give thanks, because that is what Christians do. Who knows what

God, in turn, will do with our faithfulness? It is not for us to say. Our command is, in the words of the Christian poet W. H. Auden, to "stagger onward rejoicing."[16]

It is hard to imagine a better description of St. Anne's-on-the-Hill. Yes, there are times when Christians need to contend with the devil over the body of Merlin, so to speak. But this is not what principally characterizes us. Rather, what characterizes Christians for Lewis is a sort of plainspoken, ordinary faith that does not seek revolution or political upheaval, but simply seeks to be faithful to the life Christians are called to live, whatever the consequences of that fidelity might be. That doesn't, of course, preclude Christians from gaining or wielding political power. But it *does* limit the means they can use to pursue power. It is better to walk in the truth without power, for Lewis, than to gain power by compromising the truth. When one considers the nature of Lewis's community at St. Anne's, it is quite plain that the machinations of many of the new Christian right would, in his eyes, be an eminent example of such an unhappy and foolish compromise.

Why does Lewis adopt this approach rather than the strategy of finding a bigger bully who can beat the NICE, as both Orwell and the new Christian right de-

---

16. Rod Dreher, *The Benedict Option: A Strategy for Christians in a Post-Christian Nation* (New York: Sentinel, 2017), 241

sire?¹⁷ Even here, I think the language itself helps to answer that question.

Lewis recognized how language knits us to reality and how the attempt to displace language from the real can actually over time displace the speaker, cutting him or her off from the real as much as their words have been cut off. Crucially, this happens in an automated way; you simply *can't* adopt Wither's posture toward language without becoming like Wither. And what becomes of Wither it is a sober warning to us all.

As the judgment falls on Belbury, Wither escapes the room of the banquet where the curse of Babel has fallen. Lewis describes him as knowing that his side had lost, knowing that there could be no escape for him, even if he has absconded from the banquet room. Yet this knowledge has no effect on him. He regards it the way one might regard a banal statement of fact that has no bearing on oneself. The way Lewis draws this out is worth quoting at length:

> It is incredible how little [the knowledge of his imminent death] moved him. It could not, because he had long ceased to believe in knowledge itself. What had been in his far-off youth a merely aesthetic repugnance to realities that were crude or vulgar, had deepened and darkened, year after year, into a fixed refusal of every-

---

17. One might retort that "a bigger bully" is precisely what Merlin is. But St. Anne's does not initiate the quest to dig the ancient druid up from the earth; it only becomes incumbent on them to do so in order to prevent the NICE from getting their hands on him.

thing that was in any degree other than himself. He had passed from Hegel into Hume, thence through Pragmatism, and then through Logical Positivism, and out at last into the complete void. The indicative mood now corresponded to no thought that his mind could entertain. He had willed with his whole heart that there should be no reality and no truth, and now even the imminence of his own ruin could not wake him. The last scene of *Dr Faustus* where the man raves and implores on the edge of Hell is, perhaps, stage fire. The last moments before damnation are not often so dramatic. Often the man knows with perfect clarity that some still possible action of his own will could yet save him. But he cannot make this knowledge real to himself. Some tiny habitual sensuality, some resentment too trivial to waste on a blue-bottle, the indulgence of some fatal lethargy, seems to him at that moment more important than the choice between total joy and total destruction. With eyes wide open, seeing that the endless terror is just about to begin and yet (for the moment) unable to feel terrified, he watches passively, not moving a finger for his own rescue, while the last links with joy and reason are severed, and drowsily sees the trap close upon his soul. So full of sleep are they at the time when they leave the right way.[18]

---

18. Lewis, *That Hideous Strength*, ch. 16, 490–91.

The techniques and powers the NICE had acquired, the very things that had made them so formidable, were also the things that unmade them. It had to be so, for they belonged together: the NICE had built itself up through a forced dismembering of reality and now at its end the members of the NICE themselves were dismembered, their souls severed from the last links connecting them to reason and joy. This is what we see in those who lose themselves in the empty speech of bureaucracy in our great institutions, and increasingly in everyday life as those modes of speech trickle down into the wider culture: they become empty, self-sundered, withered.

We also see the same happen in some conservative critics who come out fighting against the vagaries of bureaucratic newspeak. In response, they deploy crass and incendiary language under the guise of "straight talk." In one particular case, a new Christian right activist described a publishing company that publishes pornographic material as "a successful business." When we lose the capacity to name evil plainly, choosing instead, like Wither, to sanitize it with misdirection and euphemism, we lose our connection to reality as surely as Wither himself did.

Indeed, before long such professing Christians become lost in their rhetoric, unable to open their mouths without trying to smash some sacred cow. And all too often, such people become sorely tempted by the promise of Merlin's pagan powers. Usually, they cover up their embrace of it in winks and irony—an obfuscation no different, in the end, to the inanities of the NICE. Whether you slowly disappear into shibboleths, or set yourself ablaze with your own verbal fireworks, you end up withered in the end.

TELLING IT LIKE IT IS

What is to be done? Near the end of his life the comedian George Carlin gave an address to the National Press Club in Washington, DC. Near the end Carlin remarked on the ways in which euphemism and misdirection had come to dominate the spoken word even in his own lifetime, saying,

> It used to be that when an old person died the undertaker put him in a coffin. We sent flowers to the funeral home, where they held a wake. Then after the funeral they drove the dead person in a hearse to the cemetery and his body was buried in a grave. Now though when a senior citizen passes away, the mortician places him in a burial container. We send floral tributes to the slumber room where the grief coordinator supervises the viewing. After the memorial service the funeral coach transports the departed to the garden of remembrance where his remains are interred.[19]

Carlin's advice to us is to reject such euphemistic language for the inherently dehumanizing and demeaning thing that it is. Rather, speak plainly. What does that mean? Some of it can be distilled down to basic rules:

---

19. George Carlin, "George Carlin – National Press Club [complete]," YouTube, Feb 6, 2013, 24:11–24:42, https://www.youtube.com/watch?v=Pc0ZHsoHAlE.

1. Use active verbs
2. Mostly avoid the passive voice
3. Don't use a clinical, multisyllabic word when a simple, monosyllabic word will do
4. Do not speak of creatures as if they are machines
5. Do not use clinical language or business speak to mask moral evil

How should this be done in practice? Carlin himself is not a good guide here, for the man took a delight in provoking people, and Scripture commands the people of God to not be given to quarrelling. God commands his people to live quiet, peaceable lives insofar as it depends on them. The person who counters bureaucratic speech by transforming language into a tool to acquire power is doing no less violence to the gift of language than are the bureaucrats.

Rather, begin here, as you consider how to apply such rules of humane language and speech in your own life and context: language is a gift given to you by God and to no other sort of creature. It is a thing to be stewarded for the glory of God and the good of your neighbor. The words you choose to speak, the way you seek to name reality faithfully, this in itself is an occasion to love God and love your neighbor. And so, as you go about your life, when you encounter unreality in language, do not indulge it. Rather, with a spirit of love and gentleness, speak in ways that dignify God's creation (and God's creatures!) by naming that creation with truthfulness and integrity.

In the final pages of *The Last Battle*, Lewis describes the experience of his beloved Narniad heroes when they arrive in Aslan's country. They pluck some unnamed fruit from a nearby tree and taste it. Lewis writes,

> What was the fruit like? Unfortunately, no one can describe a taste. All I can say is that, compared with those fruits, the freshest grapefruit you've ever eaten was dull, and the juiciest orange was dry, and the most melting pear was hard and woody, and the sweetest wild strawberry was sour. And there were no seeds or stones, and no wasps. If you had once eaten that fruit, all the nicest things in this world would taste like medicines after it. But I can't describe it. You can't find out what it is like unless you can get to that country and taste for yourself.[20]

We shouldn't pass over this too quickly: True, there is a clear difference between the fruit of Aslan's country and what the children knew in Narnia or England. But even here they seem to know by analogy: they recognize the superiority of the fruit in that country through a comparison of it with what they have previously known.

Something similar can apply to our world even now: plain, fitting, beautiful speech can crash against a person anesthetized by bureaucratic speech with a similar disruptive and shocking power as the fruit of Aslan's country. One of the greatest gifts we can give a world under the dominion of our own modern-day Hardcastles and Withers is to speak with the ordinary, lovely candor of Ivy Maggs or, indeed, of Ransom himself. For just as Ransom descended to earth as a man whose citizenship now belonged elsewhere, so our language itself can mark us as citizens of

---

20. C. S. Lewis, *The Last Battle* (New York: HarperCollins, 2005), 169.

another country, where no one seeks to deceive, where no one seeks to dominate neighbor, but where all are united in bonds of fellowship and love, devoted to the good.

SCRIPTURE INDEX

Genesis
2:19	136
6	194
14	265
38:8–10	157n25

Exodus
16	141n35

Job
1:21	143

Psalms
19:1	20
45	176n80
45:10	176n80

Proverbs
31	61n20

Ecclesiastes
9:11	300
12:13	47

Song of Solomon
4:12	164

Isaiah
45:8   149

Matthew
7:12   70
22:23–33   126
22:29–30   127

Mark
10:45   71

John
14:15–17   97
15:13   70

Romans
1:20   20
12:2   18

1 Corinthians
7   127
15:35   125–26
16:13   65–66, 235

Galatians
6:2   89

Ephesians
2:2   173
5:11   174

5:25	71
5:29	70
6:12	120

Colossians

3:10	20

1 Timothy

4:3	140

Titus

2:5	61n20

Hebrews

7:2	265
7:3	265
11:25	140

James

1:14	138
1:17	140

1 John

4:18	66

Revelation 187n1

AUTHOR AND SUBJECT INDEX

A

abortion, 181, 308–9

activism, xi–xiii

Adey, Lionel, 158n28

adult, as term of approval, 284

algorithmic governance, 197–98

Althusius, Johannes, 296–97

androgyny, 50–52

angels, 126

animal death, 112

antisemitism, 200

apocalyptic literature, 185–86, 190–91

apologetics, i, iii–iv, xi, xiii

appreciation, 136, 139

Aquinas, Thomas, 7

archetypes, embracing, 289

Aristotle, 232, 236, 237

Arthuriana, ix, xxii, 154, 242–70, 273, 291–92

artificial intelligence, 113, 203

atmosphere, x, 2, 56, 62, 66, 81–82

audience, educated, 197

Augustine, 126
authority, 11, 14, 85–86, 230, 237, 238, 250, 264
awe, 21, 28–32, 223

B

Balthasar, Hans Urs von, ix
Barach, John, vn4
Barfield, Owen, 3, 23, 150n3, 246
Bebbington, David W., xi
becoming oneself, 289
Bede, 247
Belbury. *See* NICE
Benedict Option, 310–11
Berry, Wendell, ix
biblicism, xi–xii
birth control. *See* contraception
Blake, William, 19
blood, shed, 236, 238–39
Bloom, Alan, 218–21, 223, 227–29
Boethius, 6
Bragdon Wood, 161–68, 172, 184, 256–57, 309
Britain, Matter of. *See* Arthuriana
Budziszewski, J., 68n30
Bultitude, Mr., 154, 165n47, 176n80, 255, 267, 277–78
Bultitude, Mrs., 154, 277–78
bureaucracy, 187, 295–98, 303, 304n12, 314

bureaucratic speech, xxii, 296–309, 314–17
    and abuses, 305–7
    antidote to, 315–18
    and distraction, 303, 306–7
    euphemism, 13, 314, 315
    evasion, 303
    "informal" speech, 297–303
    and linguistic stupor, 304
    and misdirection, 306, 314, 315
    and new Christian right, 309–12, 314
    paperwork speech, 297, 303–4
    and reality, 301, 302, 304
Burroughs, Edgar Rice, 49

C

Calvin, John, 75–76
Cassidy, Michael, 99–101
cave, allegory of (Socrates), 43n43
chastity, 152n6, 157, 163n39, 181, 259, 274
Chaucer, Geoffrey, 6, 53
chest, chests, 45–46, 156, 160, 163n39, 232–33, 237
Mark's restored, 237
men without, ii, v, xviii, xxi–xxii, 231, 296
Ransom's restored, 46
Chesterton, G. K., 57n16
childishness, fear of. *See* false maturity

Chrétien de Troyes, 244, 247, 261

Christ, ii, xii, 9, 71, 101, 126, 175, 239, 261, 262–63, 265. *See also* Maleldil

Christian Reconstructionism, 189–90

Christmas, 176

Coffin, Patrick, 160n34

Collins, William, 163n39

Confucius, 227n21

contemplation, xxi, 77–81, 82, 83–91, 95–97. *See also* self–examination

contraception, xxi, 156n20, 157–58, 160, 167, 169, 171n60, 172–75, 177–82, 259–60, 270, 274–75, 284

    and emotional disharmony, 158

    fruit of, 169

    Lambeth Conference (1930) on, 178–80

    Lewis's Aunt Lilly on, 179n90

    Pope Pius II on, 180–81

    as "usages of Sulva," 172–75, 274–75

conversion, xii, 128, 195–96, 207, 267, 268, 270, 279, 282, 283, 292

conversionism, xi–xiii

cosmos, cosmology

    egocentric, 14, 21

    medieval model, ii, xx, 1–8, 14, 15–17, 24, 31, 50, 81

    modern model, 15–17

Author and Subject Index

    theological significance of, 17–22

courage, xx, 10–11, 18, 24, 36–41, 45, 52, 54, 62–67, 69–72, 234–39

    bent, 37–40

"covenant of works," Perelandrian, 140

Cowper, William, 141

crucicentrism, xi–xii

crucifixion of Jesus, 239

"cultural Marxism," 189–90

culture wars, xxi, 187, 188, 196, 204

D

Dante, x, 6, 7, 23, 118, 143, 310

de Boron, Robert, 263n51

Denniston, Arthur, 249, 289

Denniston, Camilla, 246, 266, 267, 289–90

desire, desires, 11, 18, 19, 21, 33, 34, 40, 57n16, 127, 135, 138, 139, 140, 141, 156n20, 172, 216, 227, 229, 232, 284, 285, 287–88. *See also* passions

    for glory, 39

Devine, Dick (Lord Feverstone), 9, 12, 18, 19, 25, 26, 32, 33, 40, 41, 54, 55, 64, 66, 69, 102, 155n19, 198

Dickerson, Matthew, 164

Dickieson, Brenton, vin5, xivn23

Digby, Kenelm, 162n39

Dimble, Cecil, 160n36, 161, 163n39, 201, 203, 209, 243n3, 247–48, 252–53, 254, 258, 259, 267, 275, 289

Dimble, Margaret, 163n39, 166n51, 209, 275–76, 289–90
    barren, 163n39, 275
    as "Mother Dimble," 275–76, 289–90
dispensationalism, 187, 188–89, 190, 191
"Donegality," x, 2
Donne, John, 6, 273, 284, 292
Dostoyevsky, Fyodor, 106n17
Downing, David, 151n4
Dreher, Rod, 211–12
dystopian novels, 185, 190

E

education, 226
eldila, ii, 33, 39–40, 44, 47, 137, 143, 238
emotions, 18, 24, 45–46, 101, 151, 158, 192. *See also* desire, desires; passions
"Encore," 34, 138n33, 141–42
enjoyment, xxi, 77–81, 82, 83, 84, 87, 94–96, 137, 144, 270, 281, 283
    as spiritual warfare, 144
Enlightenment, 3, 5, 14, 17–18, 217
epithalamium, 150, 166, 176
equality, 16, 196, 202, 229, 280–81
    and hierarchy, 7
    between sexes, 51, 153
    in marriage, 60, 153

euphemism, 13, 314, 315

evangelical, evangelicalism, i, ii, v, xi–xiii, xv, xviii, xxi, 185–191, 204, 205

F

false maturity, 282–85, 289

fatherhood, xx, 62, 67–68, 72

fear, 24–29, 35, 36–38, 40, 41–42, 45, 46, 55, 62, 64, 66, 237, 269

femininity, xxii, 49, 52, 58–59, 61, 149, 153, 161, 164, 165, 167, 174, 207, 209n50, 229–30, 260, 273, 276, 282–84

    of creation vis-à-vis God, 174, 260

    inwardness of, 61

    and melody, 59, 209

    and Perelandra, 58–59, 61, 149, 161, 207, 209n50

    and receptivity/responsiveness, 59, 61, 230, 260

    and shedding of blood, 236

    and submission, 230, 282

    and water, 164–65

feminism, xvii, xxii

fertility, 152n6, 155, 156n21, 157–58, 163n39, 168, 171, 174, 231, 234, 236, 239, 240, 260, 290. *See also* fruit, fruitfulness; procreation

fiction, and pastoral ministry, v

Fisher King, 241, 261–63, 269

    Ransom as, 241, 261–63

Fox, Nathaniel, 163n39

Freud, Sigmund, 221n13

Frost, Augustus, 154n15, 195–96, 231, 236–37

fruit, fruitfulness, 59, 68, 82, 150, 153, 155–56, 159, 161, 169, 174, 176, 231, 275, 276, 281, 289. *See also* fertility; procreation

Fukuyama, Francis, ix

G

Gaiman, Neil, 271n1

Gay, Claudine, 305–8

gender, xv, xvi–xviii, xxi, 207–8, 209n50, 210–11, 229–39. *See also* femininity; masculinity; sex, sexes, sexuality

    and choice, 211

    interdependence, 211

    oriented to the other, 211

    as vocation, 211

"gender reassignment surgery," 308

geocentrism, 3–4, 14, 15, 16

Geoffrey of Monmouth, 243, 247, 255, 264

George II, 163n39

Giddens, Anthony, 190

Gildas, 247

goeteia, 167, 241n2

Goetz, Stewart, xin19, 128

Göller, Karl Heinz, 253

Gore, Charles, 178–80

Grail, 261–62, 263n49, 269

Great Chain of Being, 7, 14

Green Lady (Tinadril), xiv, 82–87, 90–96

Green, Roger Lancelyn, 245

grown–up, desire to seem. *See* false maturity

H

Hale, Christiana, 24n1

Hamm, Victor M., 124nn2–3

Hannay, Margaret, 263n50

Harari, Yuval Noah, 109–10

Hardcastle, Fairy, 156n22, 199–200, 203, 297, 303–4, 317

hatred, 99, 100–101, 115, 116, 119, 120
    of man, 105–6

hearts, 160n36

Heaven, heavens, 5, 9, 10, 16, 20, 21, 24, 31, 32, 38, 155n19, 174, 254, 257n33

Hegel, Georg Wilhelm Friedrich, 107n25, 313

Heiser, Michael, 194

heliocentrism, 4n5, 14, 16

Henrietta Maria, 181–82

Herodotus, 235n36

hierarchy, 7, 8, 9, 11, 14, 15–16, 18, 43

Hingest, Bill, 172, 304

Hitler, Adolf, 115–16

hnau, 8, 11, 12, 14, 16, 19, 21–22, 33, 35, 38, 39, 46, 57, 63, 121

homoeroticism, homosexuality, 181, 231

Hooper, Walter, 245

Hopkins, Gerard Manley, 135–36

Houellebecq, Michel, 195n14

hrossa, 8, 10–12, 14, 28, 33–36, 38, 40, 41, 42, 43, 44, 46, 57, 59, 62–64, 67

Hume, David, 313

humility, xxi, 32–33, 46–47, 92, 95, 140, 239, 281

Hummel, Daniel, 187n1

Huxley, Aldous, 135, 185

I

Illich, Ivan, xviin26

incarnation, incarnational, 124n3, 268

India, 263n49

influence, 46, 81

    divine, 6

    of heavenly bodies, 2, 6–7, 8, 15, 32, 38

    martial (of Malacandra), 11, 13, 38, 53–54

    of Perelandra, 174n73

individual, individuals, 15, 103, 254, 268

Inner Ring, 159, 192–93, 196, 206, 220, 286–89

    vs. fellowship, 288

Ironwood, Grace, 155, 163n39

J

Jacobs, Alan, ix
Jesus. *See* Christ
Johnson, Bryan, 110–11
Jones, Timothy Willem, 178n86
Jove/Jupiter, 5, 6, 50, 52, 81, 154, 166n51, 289
    ancestor of Jane, 154
    Ransom as, 289
Joy, 127–29

K

Kass, Leon, ix
King Arthur. *See* Arthuriana
Knight, Stephen, 256n30
Kooser, Ted, 295
Kort, Wesley A., 128n11, 129n12

L

LaHaye, Tim, 185–86
language. *See also* bureaucratic speech
    competence in, 294–95
    crass, 314
    games, 308–9
    as gift, 293, 316
    humane, 315–18
    and reality, 312, 316
    state of, 293–94

stewardship of, 316
as tool to gain power, 316

Larkin, Philip, xvii

Laverty, Rhys, 214n2

leadership, 57, 59, 269

Lewis, C. S.
as apologist, i, iii–iv, xi, xiii, 3, 169
as children's author, i, iii–iv, xi
as hedonist, 128
influenced by Charles Williams?, 245–46, 253, 257n33
"Lewis" the narrator, 161–62
as literary scholar, i, iv, 242–43, 245
as prophet, ii–iii, iv, viii
and women, 271

Works:
The Abolition of Man, iii, vi, viii–ix, xn17, xi, xiii, xviii–xix, 17, 45, 138n33, 155–57, 176, 179, 182–83, 196, 210n52, 214–15, 218n7, 223–24, 231, 232, 237n41, 240, 254, 263n49, 296
The Allegory of Love, 165–66, 244
Arthurian Torso, 245, 257n33
Chronicles of Narnia, i, iii, v x, xii, xiii, xv, 1–2
"Dear Mr Marshall, Thank You," 170–71
The Discarded Image, 3–8, 15–16, 50, 53–54, 81nn4–5, 251

English Literature in the Sixteenth Century, 166n51, 244

The Four Loves, 128, 136

"The Funeral of a Great Myth," 32n174

"The Future of Forestry," 171n62

The Great Divorce, ii, x, xin17, xii, 114, 118

A Grief Observed, ii, xii

The Horse and His Boy, ii

"The Inner Ring," 286–88

"Is Theology Poetry," 32n17

"Lancelot," 244

The Last Battle, 272

Letters to Malcolm, ii, xii, 141n37

The Lion, the Witch and the Wardrobe, 1, 285

The Magician's Nephew, 103, 165n47

"Meditation in a Toolshed," xx, 76–77, 87

Mere Christianity, i, xii, 59–61, 65, 169–70

Miracles, xii, 16, 210n54

Narnia. *See* Chronicles of Narnia.

"The Necessity of Chivalry," 65n26

"On Science Fiction," vin7

"On Three Ways of Writing for Children," 284–85

Out of the Silent Planet, vi–vii, xix, xx, 2, 3, 8–15, 16–22, 25–47, 49, 52, 54–57, 59, 62–64, 66–71, 102–5, 152, 174

Perelandra, v, vii, xiv, xx–xxi, xxiii, 2, 24n1, 40n34, 58–59, 63n24, 81–86, 90–97, 100–102, 104n8,

105–7, 111–15, 117–18, 119–21, 123, 124, 127, 129–43, 144n41, 145, 152, 165, 170–71, 173n66, 209n50, 238

The Pilgrim's Regress, xn17, 51, 135n26, 177n81, 180n92

"The Planets," 53, 71, 174n71

A Preface to Paradise Lost, 21n31

"Priestesses in the Church," 51, 175n75, 183n101, 214n2

The Problem of Pain, ii, xii, 174n69

"The Quest of Bleheris," 244

Ransom Trilogy, iii, v–xv, xviii, xx–xxiii, 1–2, 24, 31, 46, 49, 52, 81, 101, 124, 149, 165n46, 170, 241

Reflections on the Psalms, 176n80

The Screwtape Letters, ii, xii, xiv, 86, 88–90, 92, 95, 96, 152, 191–92, 201, 206, 208, 235, 295

"The Small Man Orders His Wedding," 166n51

"Sometimes Fairy Stories May Say Best What's to Be Said," xiiin22

Spenser's Images of Life, xn15, 2n2

Studies in Medieval and Renaissance Literature, 166n51, 244n8

Studies in Words, 219n9

Surprised by Joy, ii, vin6, 88n13, 127nn6–7, 128n8

That Hideous Strength, vii, xn17, xx, xxi–xxii, 2, 24, 102, 130, 136, 149–150, 152–55, 157–77, 181–84, 185–86, 188, 192–209, 214, 215, 219, 220, 222n16, 229–32, 236–38, 241–42, 243n3, 245–46,

247–50, 252–61, 262–70, 273–84, 285–86, 288–92, 294–95, 297, 298–304, 309–10, 311–14

Till We Have Faces, iiin2, 78n3

"Transposition," 131nn18–19

"The Weight of Glory," 127

"Why I Am Not a Pacifist," 120n48

Lewis, W. H., 115–16

linguistic competence. *See* language: competence in

Logres, 154, 181n95, 250–54, 265, 266, 268, 270, 273, 274, 292

love, 33, 35, 66, 70, 90, 93, 97, 104, 116, 139, 140–41, 157, 160n36, 177, 257n33, 267, 275, 278, 279–80, 291, 310, 316

    of cosmos, 5, 24

of enemies, xxi, 115–17, 119

    of humanity, bent, 12–13, 17–19, 21, 68, 70n33, 102–5, 106

    of neighbor, 70, 139, 316

    Oyarsa's, for creatures he rules, 12

    of self, 70

    and self–sacrifice, 71–72

Lucas, John, ix

Lupack, Alan, 256n31, 261n44, 262nn47–48, 263n51, 264n53

Lydgate, John, 166

M

MacDonald, George, 246

Machiavelli, Niccolò, 13

MacPhee, Andrew, 130, 155, 163n39, 201, 278–79, 288

Maggs, Ivy, 154, 176n80, 202, 294, 317

magia, 167, 241n2

magic, magician, 167, 193, 241, 243n3, 249, 254–256, 258, 259n37, 269

    materialist, 191–92

Malacandra (Mars)

    martial influence of, 11, 13, 38, 53–54

    martial inhabitants of, 57

    and masculinity, 52–72, 149, 161, 207, 209n50

    pathos of, 52–54

    perpendicularity of, 56

    and Roman mythology, 52–53

    social order of, 42–44, 45–46, 59

    terrain of, 55–56, 164

Maleldil, xiii, xix, 8, 9, 13, 18, 35–36, 37, 40, 43–44, 47, 68, 69, 71, 86, 90–92, 105, 112, 120, 121, 136, 140–41, 143n40, 175, 267, 291

Malory, Thomas, 242–43, 244, 250–51, 259, 262

man taking charge of man, 198

Manu, 227n21

Markos, Louis, 1n1

Marlowe, Christopher, 113, 313

marriage, 49, 52, 149–61, 169, 176, 177, 181, 182, 229, 258–59
- and Bragdon Wood. *See* Bragdon Wood
- as "matrimony," 150, 169, 176, 177, 181, 182, 229, 256
- as "fountain of history," 151
- male headship in, 60–61
- and procreation, 150–25
- purposes of, 151–52
- sentimentalism about, 151–52

"martial sex," 72

martial spirit, 6, 11, 13, 38, 44, 53, 54, 57, 62, 67, 68, 70, 72

martial virtues, 54

masculinity, xx, 49, 52–72, 149, 153, 161, 165, 167, 174, 204, 207, 209n50, 229, 230–40, 260, 282
- difficult to define, 57–58, 59
- externality of, 56
- and Malacandra, 52–72, 149, 161, 207, 209n50
- and martial spirit, 52–72
- outwardly directed, 59–61
- without potency, 230–31
- and prominence, 59, 61
- and rhythm, 59, 209
- and shedding of blood, 236
- as "sturdy hardiness," 53, 54, 55, 57, 61, 63
- and trees, 164–65

virtues of, 54, 62–72

materialism, iv, 80, 110, 120n48, 191–92, 193, 201

matrimony. *See* marriage

McCarthy, Cormac, 185, 233–34

McClatchey, Joe, 150n1

McPhee. *See* MacPhee, Andrew

McVicar, Michael J., 189n3

Meilaender, Gilbert, 129n13, 150n2, 239n43

Merlin, 154n15, 156n22, 163n39, 167, 168, 173, 200, 238, 241, 243, 244, 248, 253, 254–60, 262, 264–65, 266–67, 269, 274, 275, 291, 311, 312n17, 314

as advisor, 255

"Devil's son"?, 258

as magician, 167, 241, 243n3, 254–56, 258, 269

as masculine 260

and Nature, 167

and Nimue, 244, 256–58

as prophet/seer, 176n80, 255, 259, 266–67

receiving the Powers, 260, 268

Merlin's Well, 167–68

Midgley, Mary, ix

Milton, John, 6, 19–20, 23, 31, 113, 174, 251, 252

Minich, Joseph, iiin3, xvi, xviii, 144, 210n53

modern, modernity, iii, xvi–xix, xxi, 9, 11, 12, 15–16, 30, 57n16, 79, 80, 139, 155n20, 157, 167, 186, 190, 201, 210, 211–12, 215, 216, 216, 222–226, 228, 232, 260, 296, 304n12 moral formation, 226

morality, morals, 18, 70n33, 155n20, 193, 203, 215, 221, 226, 230, 268. *See also* natural law; *Tao*; values

motherhood, 82–83, 92, 150, 176, 229, 275, 276, 290

Murdoch, Iris, 183

music of spheres, 5, 14, 173

N

naming, 136–37, 314

naming evil, 314

Narnia Code, ii, x, 1, 50

narrator, 161–62

natural and unnatural, xv, 60, 61n20, 158, 163n39, 169, 179, 297

natural law, 209, 215, 234, 238, 239, 302

Naturalists, 16

nature, 68, 155n19, 156n21, 157n25, 167, 179, 196, 216, 222n15, 223, 224, 239, 241n2

    human, 49, 156, 160, 207, 215, 223, 224, 227, 239, 240

    man's power over, 196

    of things, 183

Network (dir. Sidney Lumet), 200–201

neutrality, 201–2, 243n3

new Christian right, 309–12, 314

NICE, xxii, 155n19, 170, 193, 194–96, 197, 199–202, 204, 205, 219, 231, 236, 238, 260, 268, 270, 275,

277, 285–86, 288, 291, 292, 303, 304, 306, 307, 309, 311, 312n17, 314

contrasted with St. Anne's, 201–2, 288

destruction of, 260, 268, 270, 312

dispensing with others, 201

and equality, 201–2

and Inner Ring, 159

and magic, 241n2

Mark locked into, 303

and masculinity, 204, 250

and neutrality, 201–2

nonpolitical, 199

propaganda of, 200

rejection of fertility, 195, 230, 260

and state, 199

theoretical progressivism of, 202

treating humans in abstract, 268

Nietzsche, Friedrich, 13, 217–18, 221–22, 223, 224, 226–29

Noll, Mark, xiin20

nonpolitical power, 199

Nuttall, Tony, ix

O

obedience, xxi, 10, 38, 40, 47, 90–93, 95–97, 152n6, 209, 279–81, 288, 291, 292

O'Hara, David, 164

ordo timoris, 237

Ortlund, Gavin, xiiin21

Orwell, George, 185, 293–94, 299–300, 309, 311

Oyarsa, Oyéresu, 8–9, 11, 12, 21, 25, 28, 33, 35, 36, 37–41, 44, 46, 47, 58, 61, 64, 66, 68, 69, 70, 104, 105, 153, 209n50, 255

    Bent, xix, xxi, 8–9, 12–13, 18–19, 22, 36, 47, 63n24, 68, 104, 105, 112, 114, 118, 121, 172. *See also* Satan

P

pacifism, 120n48

Paglia, Camille, 51n2

paperwork, 297. *See also* bureaucratic speech: paperwork speech

paradise, 124, 125, 127, 130

passions, xx, 18, 19, 28, 45, 78, 89, 156, 160, 286, 289. *See also* desire, desires

pathos, of Malacandra, 52–54

Patterson, Nancy–Lou, 164

Pendragon, 24, 46, 125n3, 154n15, 181n95, 204, 250, 252, 255, 264–67, 269, 270, 292

    and Melchizedec, 265

    on Perelandra, 249–50

    Ransom as, 24, 46, 125n3, 250, 255, 261, 264–67

    and Studdocks, 154n15, 181n95, 266–67, 204, 270, 292

Perelandra (Venus)

as Avalon, 249–50
   and eroticism, 277–79, 291
   and femininity, 58–59, 61, 149, 161
   and motherhood, 82–83
   as "Paradise Retained," 124n3
Peretti, Frank E., 185
Perpetua, 236n37
pfifltriggi, 8, 12, 14, 36, 43, 57, 59
Pieper, Joseph, 237
pietism, xi–xii
piety, xi–xiv, xv
Planet Narnia. See Narnia Code.
Plato, ix, 13, 23, 42–44, 45, 232
pleasure, xxi, 33, 34, 36, 44, 64, 67, 83, 84, 88, 101n2, 115, 124, 127–45, 150, 158n27, 176, 206, 270
   and appreciation, 136, 139
   ecstatic, 132, 134, 135, 137
   embrace of, 132, 140–45
   vs. Joy, 127–29
   life-giving, 133, 134
   naming of, 136–37
   nourishing, 132, 134, 138
   qualitative and quantitative, 135, 138
   quenching, 133, 134
   refreshing, 132, 134
   repeated, 34, 138n33, 141–42

restraint of, 132, 137–39, 141–42

sexual, 67, 150, 176

simple, 206, 270

spoiled, 88

taxonomy of, 131–37

potency, 158, 214, 229, 230, 231, 232, 234, 238, 239

procrastination, 273

procreation, 33, 150–51, 158, 178. *See also* fertility; fruit, fruitfulness

propaganda, 199–200

Pullman, Philip, 272

Q

quietism, 309

R

Ransom, Elwin, xiv, 3, 9–12, 13, 14, 17, 18, 19, 21, 24–47, 52, 54–58, 62, 66–72, 83–87, 90, 92–95, 97, 100–103, 105, 111–15, 117, 119–21, 124, 129–38, 141–43, 153–55, 163n39, 165, 173, 174, 194, 200, 201, 202, 203, 209, 230, 238, 241, 249–50, 253, 255, 260–67, 274, 277, 279–82, 289, 291, 317

Adamic, 136

arranging marriages, 153

battle with Un–man, 82, 92, 95, 100–102, 112–15, 119–20, 262

becoming martial, 54–55, 62, 66–67

bent courage of, 37–40

as bridge, 155
as Christ–figure, 71, 262–63, 265
conversation with Green Lady, 83–87, 90
and cosmos, 20, 29–31, 125n3
diet of bread and wine, 262
distaste for hierarchy, 11–12
editor of *The Screwtape Letters*, xivn23
and fear. *See* fear
growth in courage, 62–63, 66–67
heel wound of, 262–63
as *hnakra*–slayer, 38–40, 63
humility of. *See* humility
and Jane Studdock, 153–54, 159, 176n80, 249, 267, 279–282
as Jove, 289
as king, 153, 230
as knight, 11, 13, 119
learning to master himself, 24
like Arthur, 249
and marital relationships, 153–55
as Mr. Fisher–King, 241, 261–63
as Pendragon, 250, 255, 261, 264–67
as Pedestrian, 25, 45
as pilgrim, 24, 45
and pleasure. *See* pleasure
as priest, 153

reborn on Perelandra, 82–83

restored chest, 46

and self-sacrifice, 68–72

as wounded healer, 267

Ratzinger, Joseph, ix

reality, 2, 18, 21, 32, 33, 37, 46, 52, 75, 90, 94, 135, 138, 157, 174, 203, 205–6, 209, 221, 223, 225, 226, 239–40, 254, 294, 301, 302, 304, 307, 312, 313, 314

and bureaucratic speech, 301, 302, 304

conforming to, 157

embracing of, 239–40

humility before, 32, 46

instruction by, 32–33, 46

and language, 301, 302, 304, 307, 312

Mark's discovery of, 205–6

naming, 135, 295, 304, 316

of sexual differences, xvi

subduing, 157, 296

submitting to, 183

Red Pill movement, 208

reenchantment, xiv

relativism, 220, 222, 226

"reproductive choice," 309

resurrection life, 125–26

Rigney, Joe, 24n1, 88, 89n16

Roberts, Alastair, xviin26
Romanticism, 18–19
Rouse, Robert Allen, 252n21
Rowling, J. K., 272
Rushdoony, R. J., 189
Rushton, Cory James, 252n21

S

Satan, 8, 63n24, 86, 100, 101, 104, 112, 113, 173, 174. *See also Oyarsa, Oyéresu*: Bent
    Marlowe's Mephisopheles, 113
    Milton's, 19–21, 113
    statue of, 99, 101
Saunders, Corinne, 259n39, 262n46
Sayer, George, viii
Scarface (1983), 213–14
Schwartz, Sanford, 24n1
science fiction, vi–vii, 27, 107–8, 214, 216
scientism, scientific outlook, 10, 24, 31, 32–33, 68
screens, xv, 298
"seeing through," 182–83, 220, 240
self–control, 137–39, 141–42
self–examination, 87, 89–90, 92. *See also* contemplation
self–gift, 260, 270
self–preservation, 70
self–sacrifice, xx, 62, 69–72, 231

"Seventh Law," 155

sex, sexes, sexuality, xv, xvi, xxii, 33, 50–52, 61, 155, 174, 175, 183, 192, 195, 211, 215, 230, 236n37, 239, 258, 273, 282, 283, 284. *See also* femininity; masculinity

    conflict between, 208–9

    and custom, 210

    distinction of, 50–52

    equality between, 51

    givenness of, xv, xvi,

    healing of conflict, 208–9

    interchangeableness of, 51

    and natural law, 209–10

    nature of, 61

    oriented to the other, 211

    reality of, 52

    and reproduction, 61

    and tradition, 210

sexual intercourse, xvii, 33–34, 61, 67, 158–59, 166, 167, 175, 178, 192, 195, 221n13, 267, 272, 275, 282

    au naturel, 160

    and fruitfulness, 156n21

    as Fun, 156n21

    as modern grown-up fairy tale ending, 160

    natural consequences of, 157

    pleasure of, 67

promiscuous, 67
symbolism, 175
sexuality, women's. *See* femininity
Shakespeare, William, 6, 23, 176n80
Shelley, Percy Bysshe, 19
Shippey, T. A., 219n9
Smothers, Colin J., 51n3
Social Darwinism, 103
social order, Malacandrian, 43–44
sociology, 198
sorns, 8, 11–12, 26–28, 36, 37, 42, 43, 57, 59, 62
Souder, Mark, ix
Space, 9, 10, 30–31, 103
Spenser, Edmund, 166
Spirit, 106–7
spiritual warfare, 9, 13, 120, 144, 172, 269
spirituality, xii, 106, 156
Spotlight (2015), 308
St. Anne's, 309–11, 312n17, 249, 254, 266, 267, 270, 277, 279, 309–11, 312n17
and Benedict Option, 309–11
community of love, 309–11
contrasted to Belbury, 201–2, 288
equality in, 201
fellowship, not inner ring, 288
lack of activity, 310

    limited by morality, 203

    and neutrality, 201

    openness to others, 201

    traditionalism of, 230

state and science, 197–98

Stefanik, Elise, 305–6

sterility, voluntary. *See* contraception

Strauss, Leo, 218n7

Studdock, Jane Tudor, xvii, 159, 161, 166n51, 168, 175, 177, 201, 202, 204, 206, 207, 243n3, 260, 269, 277, 282, 289–91, 294

    based (partly) on Mary Neylan, 151

    conversion of, 202, 208–10, 267, 279–82

    as democrat, 202

    descended from Jupiter, 154

    "drawn in," 206–7

    encountering Maleldil, 175–76

    and equality, 202,

    "eugenically interesting," 154n15

    as "false," 259–60, 266, 274

    false maturity of, 282–84

    following imagined vocation, 284

    holding sexuality at distance, 279, 284

    learning to be a woman, 230

    literary scholarship of, 273, 284, 290, 292

    and Mrs. Dimble, 275–76

mother of Pendragon, 181n95, 291–92

no more dreams, 291–92

problem of, xxii, 271, 273, 282, 290

procrastination, 273–74

and purposes of matrimony, 152

and Ransom, 153–54, 159, 176n80, 249, 267, 279–282

and submission, 230, 282

not "taken in," 206–7, 211

as Tudor, 154

use of contraception, 273–75

Studdock, Mark Gainsby, 161, 168, 176, 204, 238, 269

becoming man with a chest, 237

body wiser than mind, 203

chest, 156n22, 237

conversion of, 195, 208–10, 270, 283

and crucifix, 175, 236–37

discovery of reality, 205–6

"eugenically interesting," 154n15

as Fabian, 229

false maturity of, 282–83

growing a pair, 235, 237

and Inner Ring, 159, 196, 206, 220, 230, 285–86, 289

interview with Wither, 298–300

lineage, 154n15

logical outworking of views, 195–96

lured by male energy, 230

as "man of straw," 158

meaning of names, 158, 259n37

rediscovering reality, 205–6

and self-preservation, 220

and simple pleasures, 270, 283

stubborn humanity of, 206, 229

studying humans in abstract, 202–3, 268

trapped by Belbury, 303–4

writing propaganda, 199–200

Studdocks, Mark & Jane

becoming themselves, 288–89, 291

conception of Pendragon heir, 160n35, 267, 291–92

embracing marital vocation, 267

false vocations of, 292

hearts, 160n36

independent conversions, 208–10, 270

"laboratory outlook upon love," 157

marriage, 149, 154, 158–59, 175

remaining modern, 209

use of contraceptives, 157–58, 160, 174–75, 239, 267, 273–74

subjectivism, 155–56, 182–83, 236, 240

Sulva (Moon), 172–75, 274–75

Supernaturalists, 16

Susan, problem of, 271–73, 282, 283–84, 289

Sylvestris, Bernardus, 165

T

Tao, xviii–xix, xxii, 17, 138n33, 179, 210n52, 225, 254, 263n49

"taste for the other," 174

technique, technicians, 157, 241n2

technocracy, xv, xviii, 17, 192

technology, xv–xvii, xxi, 10, 14, 16, 17, 31, 108, 139, 144, 157n25, 191, 204, 296

telos, growing into, 289

Tennyson, Alfred Lord, 242, 264

testicles, xxii, 214, 232–34, 237

Thulcandra, xix, 9, 25, 36, 39, 46, 47, 63n24, 120, 161

thymos, 231–32, 233

Tinadril. *See* Green Lady

Tolkien, J. R. R., vii, 3, 181, 245–46

Tolstoy, Leo, 123

traditionalism, traditionalists, 170–71, 230, 309

transgenderism, xv, 181

transhumanism, xv, 69, 109–10, 192, 195n14, 203–4

Traxler, Janina P., 242n3

trees. *See* wood

U

Un–Man, v, 86, 90–95, 100–102, 112–15, 117, 118, 119–20, 171

    and nature of evil, 100, 102, 113–14

    Ransom's battle with, 82, 92, 95, 100–102, 112–15, 119–20, 262

    tempting Green Lady, 86, 90–95, 113, 115, 143n40

V

values, 216–21, 224–25, 227–28, 236, 238, 240

van Boxel, Lisa, 222n17

Vaughan, Geoffrey M., 218n7

Venus. *See* Perelandra (Venus)

violence, 63n24, 120, 213, 214, 238, 309. *See also* war

vocation, imagined, 284

W

Walther, Matthew, 301–2

war, 24, 26, 52, 57, 63n24, 65n26, 71, 120n48, 192, 215, 216, 220, 236, 264. *See also* culture wars; spiritual warfare; violence

    between sexes, 207, 209

Ward, Michael, ii, viii, ix, x, xxi, 1–2, 50, 53n7, 54, 70–71, 83n7, 178n85, 267

water, 164–66

"war of the worldviews," vi

Weber, Max, 217, 219

Wells, H. G., vi–vii, ix, 24, 26, 27, 32, 42, 43, 44, 49

"Wellsianity," 32

Werntz, Myles, 295–96, 303

Weston, Edward Rolles, 3, 9, 12–14, 17–19, 20–21, 25–26, 32, 33, 38, 40, 41, 54–55, 64, 66, 68, 69–70, 86, 102–15, 117–18, 119, 121, 155n19, 264

    as egoist, 21

    as "humanist," 12–13, 17–19, 21, 68, 70n33, 102–5, 106

    and masculine vice, 54

    as Un–man. *See* Un–man

Williams, Charles, 165n47, 245–46, 253–54, 257n33

Williams, William Carlos, 223

Wilson, A. N., ix

wisdom, 6, 17, 33, 34, 36, 45, 46, 68, 76, 84–85, 87, 157, 225–26, 234, 269, 294

    in creation, 4, 22

Wither, John, 188, 194, 231, 298–307, 312–13 ,314, 317

wonder, 21, 28–32, 46, 144

Woke movement, 204, 208

wood, 164–66

Z

Zogby, Edward J., 153n8

MORE FROM
DAVENANT PRESS

INTRODUCTION TO PROTESTANT THEOLOGY

Reformation Theology:
A Reader of Primary Sources with Introductions

Grace Worth Fighting For: Recapturing the Vision of God's Grace in the Canons of Dordt

Synopsis of a Purer Theology

On the Death of Christ and Other Atonement Writings

PETER MARTYR VERMIGLI LIBRARY

Dialogue on the Two Natures in Christ

Philosophical Works:
On the Relation of Philosophy to Theology

The Oxford Treatise and Disputation on the Eucharist, 1549

Predestination and Justification: Two Theological Loci

VERMIGLI'S COMMON PLACES

On Original Sin (Vol. 1)

On Free Will and the Law (Vol. 2)

On Providence and the Cause of Sin (Vol. 3)

LIBRARY OF EARLY ENGLISH PROTESTANTISM

James Ussher and a Reformed Episcopal Church: Sermons and Treatises on Ecclesiology

The Apology of the Church of England

Jurisdiction Regal, Episcopal, Papal

Radicalism: When Reform Becomes Revolution

Divine Law and Human Nature

The Word of God and the Words of Man

In Defense of Reformed Catholic Worship

The Word Made Flesh for Us

A Learned Discourse on Justification

The Laws of Ecclesiastical Polity: In Modern English, Vol. 1 (Preface–Book IV)

Christian Ethics Vol. 1: The Shining Human Creature

Christian Ethics Vol. 2: Made Like the Maker

A Treatise on Christian Moderation

Richard Hooker on Natural Theology and Scriptural Authority

AMERICAN THEOLOGY SERIES

Communicating God's Trinitarian Fullness

Religion & Republic: Christian America from the Founding to the Civil War

DAVENANT GUIDES

Jesus and Pacifism:
An Exegetical and Historical Investigation

The Two Kingdoms: A Guide for the Perplexed

Natural Law: A Brief Introduction and Biblical Defense

Natural Theology:
A Biblical and Historical Introduction and Defense

DAVENANT RETRIEVALS

A Protestant Christendom?
The World the Reformation Made

People of the Promise: A Mere Protestant Ecclesiology

Philosophy and the Christian:
The Quest for Wisdom in the Light of Christ

The Lord Is One: Reclaiming Divine Simplicity

CONVIVIUM PROCEEDINGS

For the Healing of the Nations:
Essays on Creation, Redemption, and Neo-Calvinism

For Law and for Liberty:
Essays on the Legacy of Protestant Political Thought

Beyond Calvin:
Essays on the Diversity of the Reformed Tradition

God of Our Fathers:
Classical Theism for the Contemporary Church

Reforming the Catholic Tradition:
The Whole Word for the Whole Church

Reforming Classical Education: Toward A New Paradigm

OTHER PUBLICATIONS

Enduring Divine Absence:
The Challenge of Modern Atheism

Without Excuse:
Scripture, Reason, and Presuppositional Apologetics

Being A Pastor: Pastoral Treatises of John Wycliffe

Serious Comedy: The Philosophical and Theological Significance of Tragic and Comic Writing in the Western Tradition

Protestant Social Teaching: An Introduction

Begotten or Made?

Why Do Protestants Convert?

Made in United States
Troutdale, OR
11/25/2024